China's Changing Role
in the World Economy

edited by
**Bryant G. Garth
and the Editors of the**
*Stanford Journal of
International Studies*

Published in cooperation with the
National Council on U. S. -China Trade

The Praeger Special Studies program—
utilizing the most modern and efficient book
production techniques and a selective
worldwide distribution network—makes
available to the academic, government, and
business communities significant, timely
research in U.S. and international economic, social, and political development.

China's Changing Role in the World Economy

PRAEGER SPECIAL STUDIES IN INTERNATIONAL ECONOMICS AND DEVELOPMENT

Praeger Publishers   New York   Washington   London

Library of Congress Cataloging in Publication Data
Main entry under title:

China's changing role in the world economy.

    (Praeger special studies in international economics
and development)
    Papers originally presented at a conference held at
Stanford University in the spring of 1974.
    1. China—Economic conditions—1949- Congresses.
2. China—Commerce—Congresses.
I. Garth, Bryant, G.   II. Stanford journal of
international studies.
HC427.9.C56538   338.91'52   75-22250
ISBN 0-275-01280-8

PRAEGER PUBLISHERS
111 Fourth Avenue, New York, N.Y. 10003, U.S.A.

Published in the United States of America in 1975
by Praeger Publishers, Inc.

Second printing, 1976

Printed in the United States of America

CONTENTS

i

77-03347

LIST OF TABLES AND FIGURES (BY AUTHOR)

Foreword

FOR COMPANIES AND AGENCIES that think in the long run, China is more of an enigma than any other large country, if only because the People's Republic publishes no national accounts or trade figures. If with other Asian countries the question is of reliability and consistency of economic data, the problem with respect to China is making do with practically no figures at all.

Thus, economic analysis of China is not easy. There are no readily available economic indicators registering the pulse of economic health of the People's Republic. All industrial production and G.N.P. figures must be estimated using whatever data are available. The picture formed is crude and unverifiable.

We at the National Council for U.S.-China Trade are particularly concerned with the practical, trade-oriented aspect of this problem: What can the foreign corporate planner do to form a picture of China's past and future economic development? Beyond foreign trade figures, which must be gathered from all China's major trading partners in a rather time-consuming exercise, the planner must rely on the estimates of the experts in the field. He may come to his own conclusions, but he will find that obtaining the data he needs to formulate those conclusions is a considerable task—if only because of the period during which, as Secretary of State Henry Kissinger remarked to a gathering of National Council members in June 1974, China and the U.S. were so long "unproductively estranged."

A corporate planner, when regarding the economic future of any nation, considers many more aspects of a nation's life than the raw statistics. He wants to know how the country is administered, about its political future, its attitude toward trade and economic development, its potential for given projects, its place in the world economy, and potential development problems that it may have. He wants to see a nation from all sides, from the social and political angles as well as the economic. How has a nation been handling its currency and trade transactions? What are its priorities in trade and economic development? What is its international posture on economic matters?

A company trying to work out a nation's future course, and its own potential role (if any) in that course, must consider these things; yet as of January, 1975, U.S. companies' usable knowledge about China remains very limited. The picture many companies have of China has tended to be rather one-dimensional, sketched only in terms of figures such as total trade statistics, estimates of present oil production, or latest grain imports. Very good material has been researched on the growth of certain Chinese industries and on the experiences of other companies in doing business with China. But as to digging below the surface and forming a more rounded image of China's economy and China's relationship to the economies of the rest of the world, little has been done. Such analysis will surely be of growing importance to U.S. firms. In every area, from seabed rights to technology transfer and impact on world commodity markets, China is playing an increasingly significant role. Its international presence seems ever more confident and far-reaching.

If, as one U.S. government estimate has it, China's Gross National Product in 1973 was $170 billion, the People's Republic is already among the world's top ten economies. (Even if one estimates China's G.N.P. at a lower figure, such as $120 billion, China's economy is still among the top dozen.) Almost certainly, if China's economy continues to grow at the same speed, its G.N.P. will be among the world's top five within ten years. This is a prospect for China, for China's impact on Asia, and for China's impact on the rest of the world that few companies will be willing to dismiss. As for the impact of the rest of the world on China during the next two decades, that is an interesting question too.

The National Council hopes that the chapters of this book will add substance and new dimensions to the picture of China's economy we have to date. Perhaps the most important task of this book is to ask questions and in some cases to suggest answers. The U.S. firm interested in selling to or buying from China must inevitably be concerned with such questions as those pursued in this volume. Is China's role in championing the cause of the Third World one likely to have devastating effects on world commodity markets, or is China more of a cheerleader? To what extent is China capable of absorbing foreign technology and what is China's attitude toward that technology? Is its attitude likely to change? How far do development and "self-reliance" go hand in hand?

The National Council hopes that for U.S. firms these chapters will be of interest, enlightenment, and help in answering these complex questions and in gathering knowledge of China and its future economic attitudes. The more information about China's domestic and foreign economic policies, the better, for it is essential to have China's future role in the world as closely defined as possible.

In cosponsoring the publication of this book, the National Council wishes to stress that it does not necessarily agree or disagree with the views or terminology found in this book. The volume is presented to Council members as a contribution to knowledge and interest in the economic affairs of the P.R.C., in the expectation that

China's economic development will have an increasingly significant impact on the world in the years to come.

Nicholas H. Ludlow
National Council for U.S.-China Trade

Preface

HAVING PREVIOUSLY FOCUSED on such topics as international arms control and world environmental problems, the *Stanford Journal of International Studies* last year turned its attention to the People's Republic of China. Virtually all China scholars were unprepared for the huge increase in trade between China and the United States in 1973 and 1974; this confusion suggested the importance of a fresh and comprehensive look at China's changing role in the world economy. The *Journal* sought to provide such a study, recognizing that an understanding of China's trade requires a thorough knowledge of the unique economy of China.

With the invaluable guidance of Professor Victor Li of the Stanford Law School, we selected the authors of this volume. This group came together for a conference to discuss the first drafts of the papers in the spring of 1974. A wide range of scholars participated in the conference, which was made possible with the help of the Stanford University Center for East Asian Studies and the Stanford Law School. The conference discussions served their proper function, showing in some detail the strengths and weaknesses in the first drafts of the papers.

It has taken some time, but the final papers show the extensive revision, reorganization, and updating that have taken place since the time of the conference. The authors and the student-staff of the *Stanford Journal of International Studies* have worked very hard, and the results, as Professor Li notes in his introduction, should be a special contribution to understanding China and the world economy.

For putting together this volume and helping with the work of the *Journal*, the entire staff merits listing. For the sake of space, however, only those with primary responsibility will be named. Primary responsibility for editing went to Laurence Sullivan, Managing Editor, and David Clark, David Kimport, David Luther, and Edward Schneider, Articles Editors. Of these individuals, Edward Schneider's extraordinary effort deserves special mention and credit for the successes of the volume. In addition, valuable contributions to the *Journal* were made through the endeavors of the Book Review Editor, Peter Osinoff; the Business Manager, James Overman; the Conference Planner, Janet Embry; and the Topics Development Editors, Harvey Harrison and Andrew Willard. Finally, the *Journal* owes special thanks to Robert Naon, former Editor-in-chief and the initiator of this project; Professor Li, who has advised us throughout this endeavor; and Dean Joseph Leininger of the Stanford Law School, who has struggled with us to maintain the vitality of our *Journal.*

Bryant G. Garth
Editor-in-chief
Stanford Journal of International Studies

China and the World Economy: An Introduction

VICTOR H. LI*

The improvement of material life is a primary goal of all societies. However, adopting a particular strategy for economic development produces political and social consequences beyond a simple rise in the living standard. Rapid development may conflict with other goals, such as redistribution of political power, elimination of social and economic inequalities, development of military strength, and fostering of certain philosophical or spiritual values. These goals may have to be traded or delayed for the achievement of economic growth. For example, selective concentration of industrial plants may be most effective in generating large leaps in industrial production, but in many cases, such concentration may lead to uneven development across the various sections of the developing country. It is necessary to balance the desirability of economic growth with the consequences of a particular strategy for growth.

The need for economic growth is particularly acute for the poor developing countries. Lacking their own resources, they must look to the outside for capital, technology, and even personnel to bring about industrialization and modernization. In doing so, however, they have suffered from the adverse effects of foreign dependency. Foreign help through trade, aid, and assistance simply has not produced acceptable results in the eyes of many of the recipients. The President of Algeria, H.E. Houari Boumedienne, commented: "All the initiatives taken with a view to providing a solution to the problem of development have met with universally recognized failure, since, at best, they are rather palliatives than concrete solutions."[1] He pointed out that while substantial foreign-aid grants were given to developing countries during the 1960-70 "decade of development," the amount of profits taken out of these countries by foreign corporations was one and one half times the amount of aid given to them. Moreover, the developing countries are now indebted by approximately $80 billion to the industrialized nations, with the annual cost of debt service approaching $9 billion.

During the past quarter of a century, China has been one of the few developing countries that has in fact achieved substantial growth,

*Professor of Law, Stanford Law School, and Director, Center for East Asian Studies, Stanford University.

though not at the pace of such countries as South Korea and Taiwan. In reviewing China's economic performance, Alexander Eckstein recently concluded that the average rate of growth for China has been 4 to 4.5 percent per year since 1952.

> The growth performance by China... seems modest in comparison with that of the Soviet Union and a number of Eastern and Western European Countries since the Second Wrold War, not to mention post-war Japan. ... On the other hand, by long-term historical standards of currently industrialized countries, Chinese growth rates may be considered high. Thus they fall within the range of, or even exceed, the long-term rates for the most rapidly growing economies such as the United States, Sweden and Japan. ...
>
> ... [such] growth rates as 4 to 4.5 per cent, which appear moderate by contemporary standards, were characteristic historically of the most rapidly expanding and dynamic economies. This is the rate which transformed Japan into a major industrial country between 1870 and 1940 . . . .[2]

China appears to be on the verge of becoming a major industrial power.

In fact, China's path to development has been quite different from that attempted by most Third World countries. There was a massive technological transfer from the Soviet Union in the 1950's (which China had to pay for). The pattern was reversed in the 1960's, however, as the Sino-Soviet dispute worsened. Relations with the West had not yet substantially improved, precluding massive assistance from other industrialized nations. China's strategy shifted toward an autarkic model stressing self-reliance, self-sufficiency, and development of domestic resources and personnel. One of the indicators of this shift is that total foreign trade for the period 1957-1970 remained at about $4 billion per year, despite China's growing economy and world inflation. In the past several years, another change appears to be taking place. China's international position has been strengthened a great deal, with admission to the United Nations, establishment of diplomatic relations with Japan and others, and the growing Sino-United States detente. Accompanying this more active role in world affairs, foreign trade voluem has doubled to about $9 billion.

The articles in this volume represent a beginning effort to understand the complex interplay of politics and economics in China's present strategy for development. Since industrialization is a key to economic growth, the articles generally deal with the issues concerning the acquisition and use of technology.

The first three articles discuss the very important yet very elastic concept of self-reliance. Edward Friedman urges that greater emphasis be placed on how the actions of foreign powers shaped the nature of China's choices. Thus, while the policy of self-reliance may have reflected in part domestic practices and preferences, it also was a response imposed by outside forces. As far back as the 1940's China had wanted greater foreign and international exchange. The Western embargo and later the Sino-Soviet dispute, however, forced China to adopt a go-it-alone approach. Presumably, as relations between China and the West (and Japan) improve, trade and other exchanges should increase substantially.

Hans Heymann, Jr., agrees that China will rely even more heavily on foreign trade and technology in the future, but reaches this conclusion in a different manner. He examines domestic Chinese factors and finds that foreign technology has played and will play a crucial role in enabling China to industrialize rapidly. The principal problem in the future is more likely to concern China's capacity to pay for foreign technology and goods, rather than China's desire to become a part of the international economic and technological system.

Domestic Chinese factors are examined further by Dennis Ray, who comes to the conclusion that the policy of self-reliance will be continued. Reliance on things foreign may lead to disadvantageous dependency relationships in political, military, and economic matters. More subtly but no less important, the dependent country begins to adopt the values of the foreign power, values which may conflict with other important domestic concerns. For example, emphasis on productivity and high technology may conflict with the effort to distribute goods and benefits as equally as possible.

Each of the authors in this volume has his or her own view on the elasticity of the limits of self-reliance and on the extent to which China will continue to adhere to this policy. Assessing the extent of that adherence, and thus China's future involvement in the international economy, also requires an understanding of the topics detailed in the more specific articles.

A basic factor in China's economic and political considerations is that of population. In a series of calculations, Judith Banister estimates that the population of China may be greater than the figure of 800 million that is usually cited, by a factor of 100 million or more. This raises major questions concerning our view of China's aggregate production and consumption (if our per capita figures are correct) and about its per capita figures as well (if our aggregate figures are correct). She also explains China's efforts to slow population growth through a program that goes well beyond simply providing the necessary birth control technology and devices.

Kim Woodard points out that while China's per capita energy use is relatively modest, its aggregate energy use places China third in the world, and is equivalent to the aggregate energy use of all of the rest of East Asia, including Japan. Moreover, China has the potential to be a large producer of energy. A portion of this excess production can be exported to pay for the purchase of foreign technology and goods.

The assessment of China's energy capabilities may be significantly affected by the prospect of oil resources on the continental shelf. In addition to the technical problems of locating and extracting these resources, attempts to exploit the continental shelf and the ocean bottom present new political and legal problems, which I examine in my article. These questions will grow in importance in the years to come as more attention is directed toward off-shore resources.

To the extent that China's imports cannot be paid for through exports of petroleum and other goods, China may rely heavily on foreign credits. David Denny describes the longer term financial effects of using foreign credits. Noting that China is quite familiar with the workings of the international banking system, he shows that China should have little trouble in becoming a much more active participant in this field.

The attitude of China toward foreign trade may have substantial regional political and economic effects, particularly on Japan. The contribution by P. Edward Haley and Harold W. Rood looks at China from the Japanese point of view—one which must consider that nation's dependency on foreign sources of raw materials. In the future Japan must look to China and the Soviet Union as new sources of raw materials; at the same time, Japan possesses considerable economic power and technological knowledge. While this establishes a certain complementarity between Japan and China and between Japan and the Soviet Union, deep differences between China and the Soviet Union severely constrain Japan's capacity to act.

The rapid growth in trade between the United States and China has been one of the most striking aspects of the recent detente. Yet, there are difficulties which must be overcome before trading relations are normalized. Three years after Henry Kissinger's initial visit to China, the questions of compensation for the assets of American citizens confiscated by China and the release of Chinese bank accounts frozen by the United States remain unresolved. David Luther analyzes the domestic legal implications of a lump-sum settlement of these claims.

These articles as a whole examine the complex economic and political issues concerning development. There are disagreements in the articles, particularly as to the meaning of self-reliance and the extent to which China will continue to adhere to that policy in the future. The disagreements are partly due to different beliefs and approaches of the authors, but they also reflect the uncertainty present in China itself. On the one hand, the volume of foreign trade has doubled in the past several years. On the other hand, there appears go be a certain ambivalence about the ultimate desirability of increasing foreign trade and therefore increasing dependence on foreign goods and technology. For example, a recent article praised the growth of foreign trade as a means of "mutual economic development" based on the "principles of equality and mutual benefit in supplying each other's needs." At the same time, the article also stressed "building the country independently, through self-reliance," and "relying on [the Chinese people's] own strength and wisdom and using their domestic accumulation of funds and their own natural resources.[3]   Even with the recent National People's Congress and the promulgation of the new constitution, it may be some time before China decides at what point participation in the world economy becomes inconsistent with the principle of self-reliance.

NOTES

[1] *Speech Delivered by H.E. Houari Boumediene*, PETROLEUM, RAW MATERIALS, AND DEVELOPMENT vii (Memorandum submitted by Algeria to the United Nations General Assembly, Apr. 1974).

[2] Eckstein, *Economic Growth and Change in China: A Twenty Year Perspective.* THE CHINA QUARTERLY 211, 236 (No. 54, 1973).

[3] Wang Yao-ting, *China's Foreign Trade,* 17 PEKING REV., Oct. 11, 1974, at 18. *See also Taking the Road of Self-Reliance,* 17 PEKING REV., Oct. 18, 1974, at 5.

The International Political Economy and Chinese Politics

EDWARD FRIEDMAN*

WHAT IS THE MOST USEFUL WAY to comprehend the relationship between Chinese international economic policy and Chinese politics? If "useful" refers to accuracy in predicting or foreseeing future trends and possibilities, it seems clear that the traditional approach to comprehending this relationship has failed. That U.S.A.-P.R.C. trade had expanded so rapidly and unexpectedly is only the most recent of a long list of occurrences incorrectly predicted by Western analysts. To be honest, one must admit that focusing on Chinese politics, as is generally done, fails even to explain past trends very well. The real world seems far richer than the poor models of mainstream social science.

I. THE NEED TO FOCUS
ON THE INTERNATIONAL POLITICAL ECONOMY

Some recent events call our attention to a very different and more fruitful way of addressing the problem. Instead of looking for the root cause inside China, it is first necessary to focus on how the changing and conflictful international political economy relates to, and shapes possibilities for, China. All nations have been deeply affected by the powerful international events of the late 1960's and 1970's, including the decline of the dollar—indeed, of paper currency in general; cooperation and collusion of raw material and primary producing countries (including the U.S.A.); international inflation; shortages, real and artificial; international economic warfare; and the rise in the value of gold. In fact, the shrewdest students of peasant rebellions occurring from the seventeenth century on, such as Roland Mousnier and Barrington Moore, Jr., have long insisted on the centrality of just such politico-economic factors even to supposedly embedded events such as rural rebellions. To illustrate, the question of cotton prices for rural Chinese was tied to disruption in the cotton-producing Southern states during the American Civil War. Similarly, as China became ever more involved in the world market, the amount of silver available for stable currency and imports related to a complex of Japanese, Portuguese, Dutch, British, French, and Mexican relations. The acts of the powers have even influenced the

*Associate professor of Political Science, University of Wisconsin-Madison.

struggle with nature. While climate could over a semi-global region affect crops, surpluses or scarcities, even epidemics, international power has helped to determine who got what; the general international situation could encourage larger armies and heavier taxes. In sum, domestic political choices, especially of rural nations with more or less tradition technologies, have been tightly constrained and channelled by tremendous international pressures.

American analysts serving the expansionist interests of ruling groups in the U.S. have long slighted such factors, particularly the influence of the industrial powers on the choices available to the countries of the so-called Third World. As expressed in works such as W.W. Rostow's *The Stages of Economic Growth*, the traditional society striving for independence is blamed for its weakness and for its supposed reactive nationalism—a combination of power vacuum and hostility which "compels" the industrialized nations to intervene in order to check each other and limit alleged Third World aggressive tendencies. By contrast, Rostow asserts, a "rational" society in transition supposedly gets on with the task of domestic development, preferably through openness to foreign investment. Most mainstream social science interest therefore is focused on the domestic forces and factions in the Third World countries which prevent or facilitate such "rational" emergences. Little concern is given problems of economic independence, initiative, and equality. Little analysis is devoted to the far-reaching consequences of politics in the industrial world which have the power to alter the course of the weaker nations. In short, mainstream social science in America has largely served to obscure the power impact of the "free world"—America, Europe, and Japan—as well as the U.S.S.R., on the possibilities and prospects of the Third World, including China. This inverted approach helps explain why even today there is little dissent from the dangerously misleading line that only a sudden threat from the U.S.S.R. in 1968-1969 forced China to turn to the U.S.A. We are even told that had Lin Piao been successful in the internal Chinese power struggle at that time, everything would now be different. The power levers in the hands of U.S. ruling groups, according to most western specialists, are virtually irrelevant to U.S.-P.R.C. relations.

A more serious, thorough, and balanced attempt to comprehend China's international economic policies must place those policies within the larger changing context which so shaped their dynamic development. The decline of America's international economic position, as evidenced by revaluation of the dollar and a new U.S. emphasis on export promotion, created a new international situation. Competition with Japan for the China market, for example, became more important to the U.S. than alliance with Japan against Chinese politics. In 1973 U.S. exports to China accounted for almost 40 percent of the total world U.S. trade surplus, with a possibility that the contribution to the U.S. balance of payments would be even greater in 1974.[1] The new U.S. position explains China's greater participation in the international economy.

The recent changes in America's international position permit mainstream social scientists to look at crucial features of reality about which they once blinded themselves. That is, while America seemed to have an unchallenged international hegemony which its ruling groups tried to manage by political means, all seemed politics and strategy. With that hegemonic position undermined, the need to grant economic challenges a higher priority is generally conceded. For a weak, poor, and ambitious China, the priority given to economic challenges from the outset has had to be considerably greater than for the U.S. The continuities and imperatives of this priority within Chinese politics and that imposing and conflictful international political economy are my focus.

II. AMERICAN POLITICS AS A LIMIT ON CHINESE CHOICES

A. *The Post-War Era*

As World War II drew toward a close, the Mao Tse-tung group in the Chinese Communist Party well understood the primary changes that had occurred in the international world. Germany and Japan were defeated; the United States was emerging as the dominant imperialist power spreading into the Asian areas once divided up among the other imperialist nations. Mao sought to align his survival with the politics of progressive American capitalists such as Franklin Roosevelt, hoping to insure that the new hegemonic power did not side with Mao's opponent, Chiang Kai-shek, to destroy the revolutionary base areas as had occurred in the early 1930's.

The attempt to align with progressive American capitalists led to the well-known participation by State Department officials in friendly negotiations with Chou En-lai and Mao in the 1940's. During the same period, in Chungking, Chou also wooed Harry Dexter White of the U.S. Treasury Department, which was much more influential than the State Department under the Roosevelt administration. White reported back to his superiors:

Of course, the Yenan Government favored international cooperation in the financial field as well as the political. He [Chou En-lai] concluded by extending the invitation of his Government to the Treasury representative in Chungking to come to Yenan for personal investigation of the situation there . . . .

With regard to the economic and financial situation, Chou stressed the need in the Northwest for foreign technical assistance, capital and machinery . . . .

With regard to China's post-war position, her greatest need would be foreign capital. In this connection, he said that the Communists were prepared to permit foreign ownership of Chinese industries, etc. . . . He said that they recognized the need for peace and security to attract foreign capital and that this would be achieved by the democratic reform of China

which would end the fear of civil war . . . . Moreover, China had to participate in international economic and financial organizations if she was to overcome her present backward state. He ended . . . stressing . . . that China's industrialization would take place within the framework of a capitalist economy.[2]

A U.S. Treasury Department representative was dispatched to Yenan. He spoke to Mao and found Chou's words more than verified.

Mao asked whether there was any chance for American support of the Chinese Communists . . . . The Communists wished to risk no conflict with the United States . . . . *The Communists do not expect Russian help* . . . . Mao thus indicated that the Chinese Communists *would prefer* to have an American rather than a Russian orientation. Cooperation between America and the Chinese Communists would be beneficial and satisfactory to all concerned. Mao said that . . . they support the industrialization of China by free enterprise with the aid of foreign capital. The United States would find the Communists more cooperative than the Kuomintang . . . . [3]

Whatever was politically inspired in such statements, whatever was imposed by the question of security and survival, the Mao group then and after linked its profound commitment to improving the material life conditions of China's people to access to the most advanced technologies in the world, whether capitalist or socialist. Mao did not foresee the resilience of the American economy and its swift remilitarization; as a Leninist, he expected American capitalists to have no choice but to welcome a Chinese outlet for America's heavy industrial products. This Leninist insight kept Mao open to the inevitable: American business would seek to sell goods such as planes, oil equipment, and computers even to an anti-capitalist society. Thus, given Mao's receptiveness to such sources of technology from the 1940's on, what must be explained is why American sales to China surged in the 1970's and not earlier.

The explanation lies in American goals and politics of the period. President Truman understood that Mao's China could serve as a counter to the Soviet Union. Nonetheless, Truman intended to reshape as much of the world as possible in a liberal internationalist form. He found that the content of American politics forced him to present anti-communism as a moral crusade against an international monolith, not as a matter of balancing Soviet Russian power. This stance required him to back Chiang, whom he hated, and to ignore Mao's continuing overtures. Thus, the international consequences of American politics and American power and goals at the end of World War II left Mao no alternative but to seek economic aid and security from the Soviet Union. The only other remaining possible international balance for China was Great Britain, whose billions in investments in China were not immediately nationalized, and with whom Mao soon initiated closer relations.

Thus maneuvers within American ruling groups with access to the greatest concentration of industrial, financial, and military power in the world imposed on Mao and his colleagues narrow options under which alliance with the U.S.S.R. and Great Britain came to seem the lesser of evils. How else might China get the wherewithal needed to build a secure, just, and prosperous new China?

B. *Korea and Beyond*

Douglas MacArthur's analysis of this period as one where Mao's China allied with Communism and Imperialism against Freedom, that is, with the Soviet Union and the United Kingdom against the U.S.A., exaggerates the realities it encapsulates. Mao and his colleagues sought in the continued international strength of the pound sterling, the British Commonwealth, and the remnants of the British empire, a lever which would limit, if not preclude, Soviet hegemony imposed by the American decision to treat liberated China as an enemy.

American leaders, of course, attempted to impede for formation of this alliance, and many Americans at that time considered British trade with Communist nations to be the height of treason. But only for a moment, at the height of the Korean War, could MacArthur, Senator Joseph McCarthy, and their allies muster sufficient force to threaten the London-Peking alliance. Under American pressure, trade through the British colony of Hong Kong swiftly declined, causing a serious depression there. Similarly, rubber from the British-controlled Malayan peninsula was embargoed. Smuggling, however, continued in both cases. Ceylon continued the trade with China legally, and also experienced American pressure. Nevertheless, as British Commonwealth countries led the world outside the Soviet bloc in recognizing China, so these countries continued in the forefront of the non-Soviet world in maintaining economic ties to China.

China benefitted in several important ways from its alliance with London. It gained access to sterling, the major international currency. It was able to work out the Baltic exchange in London, to contract for shipping—and ranked for long periods as the world's largest charterer of commercial tonnage. British intermediaries also served as invaluable role with their extensive contacts in commodity market centers and insurance headquarters around the world. China's bond to Great Britain thus grew because the British empire was rooted in certain elements of free trade imperialism and from strengths of having been the first successfully industralized imperial state. Confronting the closed door policies of the U.S.A., and having a life and death interest in free access to sterling deposits, insurance headquarters, commodity market centers and the like, China from necessity allowed the perpetuation of certain colonial ties with Britain. The semi-colonial link to Britain (and China's subsequent economic ties to Europe) cannot be dismissed as mere politics, an attempt to worry rulers in the Kremlin. The alternative was complete subservience to the international economic whims of ruling groups in Moscow. China, an agrarian nation dedicated to rapid industrialization and in need of secure access to modern technologies, was forced toward semi-colonial relations with at least one sector of the industrialized world as a result. For Mao, however, freer play in political areas enhanced China's independent room for maneuver in both the political and economic spheres.

This approach carried across to China's relations with Japan; the Mao group almost invariably sought an opportunity to keep dependence on the U.S.S.R. to a minimum, while maintaining access to essential industrial technology. As soon as Japan was granted its political independence from the U.S. occupation and the Korean War became stalemated, Mao made overtures to Japan's conservative ruling groups to normalize political and economic relations. As close students of Japanese factional politics, the Mao group seems to have believed that Prime Ministers Hatoyama and Ishibashi, who opposed the narrowly pro-American, reactionary Kishi group and who succeeded in restoring relations with Moscow, would have accommodated the Chinese, too.[4]

Lending his personal prestige to the overtures to Japan, Mao, along with most other top Chinese officials, as well as a million other Chinese, visited a Japanese trade fair in Peking in October 1956. Mao reportedly invited the Japanese Prime Minister to visit China so that he could see "what we are doing and what we are planning for the future . . . ."[5] "We all believe," Mao said, "we have to go hand and hand with Japan."[6] Never placing his political bets on the occurrence of a socialist revolution in a successfully imperialistic capitalist country, Mao looked for friends among the imperialist ruling groups in Japan as he had with the United States. In hopes of enhancing Chinese (and Japanese) independence of what he would eventually call the superpowers, Mao seems to have favored a broad united front in which "the left group of the Liberal Democratic Party is an indirectly allied army of the Chinese Communist Party."[7] ("Left" here means little more than being open to normal relations with China.)

The choice of Japan's Liberal Democratic Party to reject Mao's offers was not decided simply by personalities and factional politics. The peculiar imbalances of international politico-economic forces seem to have had much more to do with it. The conservative capitalist rulership under Prime Minister Kishi felt it could not out-compete the U.S.A. (a similar attempt helped cause World War II). It saw a resurgent Western Europe beginning to form a Common Market and moving competitively into Asian areas which still remembered and resented Japan's military invaders. Kishi believed he had no choice but to throw himself on the mercies of the still-dominant American economy in order to compete with Western Europe. To be sure, Eisenhower and Dulles, as well as Britain's Eden, would have preferred to see Japan move economically into the vastness of China, rather than undercutting the profitable Anglo-American position in the broad Pacific basin. But Chiang Kai-shek's supporters in the U.S. Congress would not permit an opening to China; the liberal internationalist commitment to containment, couched as an anti-Communist Crusade, gave veto power to proponents of rollback in Asia. The international consequences of post-World War II American power left the fate of Chinese overtures to Japan in the hands of the extreme right wing in the U.S. Senate and their militant anti-Chinese associates in Asia.

Even the renewed Chinese overtures to Japan's Prime Minister Ikeda in 1973 and 1974 were reversed not so much by the succession of Kishi's brother Sato as Prime Minister but by the Japanese decision that, given America's renewed commitment to stay in Asia—the Vietnam War—and to open Taiwan and Korea to Japanese capital as part of that commitment, it would be foolhardy to antagonize the U.S.A. for potential gains with China.

Nothing less than the combination of the continued economic rise of Western Europe and Japan, the frustration of American military power in Indochina, and the end of America's international economic hegemony could change the balance of forces among ruling groups in the U.S. and thus open up possibilities which Mao's group had long sought. Faced with inflation, a dollar crisis, a balance of payments deficit, and a costly war in Indochina with an infinitely long dark tunnel, the U.S. could no longer afford rigid anticommunism. Instead, aspects of the "balance of power" outlook again came to the fore. U.S. leaders began using China against Russia, and, in addition, began trading with China to compete with Japan and Europe to reassert the economic power of the U.S.A.

The transformation of American policy came in a peculiar way, from a series of defeats and disillusionments. Only grudgingly would liberal internationalists concede the new realities. American economists related to the leading groups in the executive branch, as well as the individuals within these groups, had long ignored the meaning of facts such as the dollar outflow and the surging competitiveness of West Germany and Japan. They insisted that their allies who needed American overseas expenditures to stop "Communism" would bail the U.S.A. out of its temporary difficulties, and when what was supposedly right and natural did not eventuate, they searched for scapegoats: De Gaulle's "treason," Brandt's opening to the East, Japan's unfair competition, an undisciplined and impatient American citizenry. Such an approach continues to aim at international hegemony as the object of U.S. foreign policy. The opponents of the balance of power approach still claim to see limitless possibilities for that hegemony and, in a continuing illusion of American predominance, have recently condemned Nixon's harshness to capitalist allies for American problems. Acceptance of this line of thinking may yet wipe out many positive achievements that Nixon accomplished with China. But whatever Nixon's successors do, it is safe to predict that political forces in mammoth international economies such as that of the U.S.A. (and Japan) will continue to have much to do with shaping Chinese options.

III. SOVIET POLITICS AS A LIMIT ON CHINESE CHOICES

As American internal politics continue to delimit Chinese possibilities, so do the politics of the U.S.S.R. Mao did not expect China to become economically dependent on the U.S.S.R.; but the war in Korea dragged on as Stalin and Trumal refused to negotiate a peace swiftly and Stalin began charging China for military equipment, with interest payments. These factors unexpectedly tied much of China's exports to repayments to the Soviet economy, thereby making it more difficult for the Chinese to break into other markets.

By the middle and late fifties, Soviet politics began to look outward for Third World, non-Chinese allies. The military stalemate in Europe, symbolized by American passivity before Russian tanks in Hungary, and the U.S.S.R.'s ICBM breakthrough, which reduced the threat of a U.S. attack and decreased the need for a Chinese buffer, both enabled Khrushchev to bid for popular support at home by increasing investment in consumer goods and to bid for anti-imperialist support abroad. Stalin's "fortress Russia" policies were abandoned for economic and political competition with the West in the Third World, starting with India.

China was vital in this new context only to the extent that it did not conflict with Soviet interests in Europe and the Third World. Soviet leaders determined that China should remain non-nuclear to serve Moscow's anti-Germany interests; the Soviet reasoning was that a non-nuclear China could then be used in bargaining for a non-nuclear West Germany. In addition, favoring a strong France in an anti-American Europe, Soviet leaders expected China to remain neutral in the clash between the Algerian rebels and imperialist France. Finally, China was not supposed to hinder Eastern Europe's dependency on the U.S.S.R. by offering an alternative, self-reliant economic model outside of the Russian-dominated Committee for Mutual Economic Assistance (C.M.E.A.). To retain the advantages of Soviet aid, in short, the Chinese leadership would have been forced to remain in a position assigned to them by the Soviets.

Decisions by the Mao group in 1958 on all these restricted choices have done much to determine the subsequent course of Chinese-Soviet relations. Mao refused Khrushchev a finger on the Chinese trigger and opted for a nuclear deterrent; supported the Algerian national independence movement; refused to enter C.M.E.A.; and put forth his own agricultural path to socialist countries as superior to the agricultural failures of the Soviet model. (All this occurred before the 1958 Quemoy crisis, which is often claimed to be the turning point in P.R.C.-U.S.S.R. relations.) Khrushchev retaliated by adding to the American embargo a break in Soviet aid, imposing a petroleum embargo, and warning others that China was a bad credit risk.

Without help from Japan or aid from the U.S.S.R., and with a worsening capital shortage, the Mao group pushed policies of self-reliance, seeking to substitute labor for capital in order to increase output of wheat and steel, to expand purchases in Western Europe, and to stop all leakages of foreign exchange such as those flowing from Tibet to India. As the Chinese in the early 1960's of necessity carried out a national energy conservation program, Mao's policies of self-reliance seemed wisdom and security incarnate—and opposition to Russia became an integral, emotional part of China's search for independence and progress. These policies have enabled

China to survive the difficulties of economic war imposed by America and its allies and then by the Soviet Union.

Instead of focusing on Mao's continuing quest for Chinese independence, however, Western analysts accepted the Khrushchev-Tito line of the early 1960's that China was a war-monger. What actually happened was that Chinese leaders felt that China could not continue to advance if it followed the policies of dependence insisted upon by the Soviet Union. They analyzed the choice involved and found that they could and should break with the Khrushchev group. It was not just that the Soviet joint stock companies in China were as exploitative as American oil companies in the Middle East, or that the Soviets manipulated exchange ratios and prices to the disadvantage of China and other poor nations. A general analysis of imperialism necessarily equated *ta kuo-chui* with *ti kuo chu-i*—big and powerful nations with imperialist nations—thereby placing the U.S.S.R. in the same category as other continental and industrialized "efficient" nations. Knowledge of Soviet policies in Eastern Europe as well as in China proved to Mao that Moscow was imperialist.

The second aspect of the Chinese analysis of the choices posed by the U.S.S.R. policies was based on strict Leninist categories. Mao presented his analysis as a continuing response to critics who insisted that if the Soviet alliance was abandoned, whatever its inequities, dependencies, and humiliations, China would subsequently be overwhelmed by a joint Moscow-Washington front. He merely repeated Lenin's rejoinder to Kautsky on imperialism with one small addition. Like Lenin, Mao argued that what divided the imperialist powers—their roles as international rivals for the biggest possible piece of the take—was more important than what united them. Hence they could not and would not long unite against China. Mao's addition to Lenin's analysis was simply that he put the successors to Lenin in the imperialist camp.

IV. CHINESE UNDERSTANDING
OF THE WORLD POLITICAL ECONOMY

This Leninist analysis of imperialism, which developed out of the events of 1958, and the concomitant quest for independence and development through self-reliance, do not mean that the Chinese leaders ever desired to isolate China from trade with the industrial powers. That "choice" was imposed on them. The Chinese have consistently sought large-scale commercial transactions as a normal part of developing their country. This aim has been apparent from the time of the overtures to the United States in the 1940's, through

1950-1959 when in alliance with the U.S.S.R. their trade grew at an extremely rapid rate, to the present era of huge growth in trade with the U.S. Not only have American analysts continually underestimated China's desire for trade or credits, but because these analysts misinterpreted the past they also cannot understand the dynamic of the present moment. Forgetting, for example, that pressure by the United States and Chiang Kai-shek on Japan in 1964-1965 kept China from getting the credits it requested, they wrongly contend that China has chosen a new course.

The course today is new only because the international powers welcome what they previously rejected from China. The P.R.C.'s gold situation is better than predicted, and as a continental nation with diverse resources its trade base should grow as its primary products earn more money. The Chinese can now purchase the plants and technology needed to strengthen the lifelines of its economy, including the inputs which help to feed its population. Of course, as with all other nations, China cannot avoid the repercussions of a world depression or such other far-reaching economic occurrences, and China's leaders are anxious and conservative in the face of grave international economic uncertainties far beyond their control. Nonetheless, increasingly secure in a self-reliance strengthened by necessity, China has the independent basis to grow through expansive international economic efforts.

How the Chinese will react to their new position of security necessarily depends primarily on how the world economic situation develops and determines Chinese choices. And while the Chinese analysis of the choices afforded them has thus far served them well, there is a potential problem for China if its analysis is not sufficiently flexible. The political crisis and consequences of 1958 may have frozen into Chinese elite politics some images of the actors on the international politico-economic scene which will not swiftly thaw even as world currents flow into new channels. The insistence on the U.S.S.R. as unmitigated evil, for example, obscures how Soviet aid has facilitated greater economic maneuverability for such nations as India and Cuba. While the Mao group has taken China far using Leninist categories as applied to conflict among America, the Soviet Union, Japan, and Western Europe, these categories may be misleading if applied mechanically to a new era.

Naturally the Chinese have begun to explore the meaning of a new world in which the relation of finished products and primary products begins to change to the benefit of both Third World primary producers and continental industrial nations (Australia, Canada, the U.S.A., and U.S.S.R.) and to the detriment of more constricted industrial and agrarian nations. But China's division of the globe into a first world (the two superpowers), a Third World (developing nations), and a second world (the other industrialized nations) is too simple. It obscures the vital differences in the new era between continental industrial nations with potential agriculture surpluses and diverse raw materials and the constricted industrialized nations without such resources. Again, although the Chinese see great potential for more organized economic cooperation among the Third World countries, Mao's long run economic picture may overly slight the extraordinarily explosive political factors which do not facilitate economic cooperation between certain countries such as Pakistan and India, Iran and Iraq, and Thailand and Vietnam. And the Chinese still have said nothing about how the emerging situation benefits the U.S.S.R. and hurts many poor Third World countries, except to denounce the Soviet Union as a scavenger of the crises of oil and the Middle East.

The Mao-Chou leadership proclaims its identity with the struggles of the developing Third World for independence, equality, and industrialization. Indeed, they contend that these ever more conscious, united, and powerful Third World nations are the main force opposing and weakening superpower hegemony. The Chinese see great potential in more organized cooperation of such nations not only in production and prices, but also in shipping and finance. Whatever problems there may be in this approach (which the Chinese began working out in the 1970's), the contrast with the American tendency to slight the long-run impact of such organization is striking. Based on the past record of economic predictions of the two parties, it might be instructive to pay closer attention to the developing Chinese analysis.

V. CONCLUSION

Some may protest that focusing primarily on the consequences of the international political-economic whole for China, as this article has done, puts the cart before the horse, and that an understanding of China's domestic national and sub-national power politics must come first. Ruling groups admittedly must concern themselves first with maintaining power in their home territory; but that observation does not dictate a narrow focus on domestic politics. In fact, as has been pointed out, the "domestic is primary" argument has had a virtually unblemished record of error in predicting China's international economic performance to date.

An examination of two future possibilities, one concerning the international whole, the other limited to the nature of the post-Mao ruling group, can clarify some of the factors involved in deciding which feature is of primary importance. Imagine major international contradictions and complications continuing for another few years such that, in the U.S.A., the voices of liberal internationalists again shout the marching orders in Washington. They oppose "unprincipled" policies which supposedly confuse enemy and ally. They contend that all-out economic war must be avoided at any price. Quickly Japan is wooed on the basis of a shared hegemony in Asia, with the U.S.A. as the junior partner. Despite the fact that there is no intention of antagonizing ruling groups in Peking, the Chinese find themselves virtually shut out of Asian nations. People in Peking then expect that Washington would side with Japan against China in any clash. China consequently looks for other ruling groups also anxious over the Japan-America duopoly, and finds them seated in Delhi and Moscow. The line-up of the first half of the 1950's is replicated but with more equality on the two sides, more tension and danger of an explosion. In this context, the assumption that Maoist politics require hostility to the U.S.S.R. may be just as wrong as the opposite was two decades ago, when endless Moscow-Peking alliance was predicted without regard to the U.S. role in the international political economy.

As a second possibility, imagine the passing of the gerontocracy of those who grew up while China was enslaved. Younger people, born after the revolution and unwilling (perhaps unable) to see limited gains as real gains, insist on true international equality with other continental powers. They refuse to sit back while state capitalists in Asia rally their own people through racist slogans against local merchants of Chinese descent. The Chinese insist on their sovereign claims to the continental shelf, distant islands, oil, shipping lines, Hong Kong, Macao, and Taiwan. They punish the source of Kuomintang and other military acts in Burma, the Hsi-sha islands, and elsewhere. In sum, the powerful nativist passions which in the Cultural Revolution made a scapegoat of alleged traitors in the Overseas Chinese Commission and a hero and political force of Yao Teng-shan, a symbol of Chinese resistance to pogroms in Indonesia, are institutionalized.

Clearly these Chinese domestic political forces of nationalism would have a powerful impact on the course of world events, especially given China's increasing economic independence. However, as the first possibility sketched above suggests, the most explosive outcomes of these second model "choices" would be determined by an American, Japanese, or other decision to repeat the policies of cold war hostility or hegemony against China. As with the fundamental reversals made possible by the success of the Chinese revolution, so with the new options determined by an international politico-economic reversal: the whole has priority. China's choices are still shaped by the ever-changing international political economy, one where the political and economic actions of industrialized nations, especially of American wealth and power, still strongly structure many of China's choices—though to a significantly lesser extent than in China's formative years.

NOTES

[1]THE NATIONAL COUNCIL FOR U.S.-CHINA TRADE, U.S. TARIFFS AND TRADE POLICY TOWARD CHINA at 35 (Special Report No. 8, April 1974).
[2]SENATE SUBCOMMITTEE ON THE JUDICIARY, 85TH CONG., 1ST SESS., INTERNAL SECURITY ANNUAL REPORT FOR 1956 at 77-82 (Comm. Print 1957).
[3]*Id.* (emphasis in original).
[4]"But his [Ishibashi's] hopes weren't realized because he became sick and died while serving as Prime Minister." JEN-MIN JIH PAO, October 7, 1972, at 4. Since Ishibashi had to accept Kishi as Deputy Prime Minister and Foreign Minister, the Chinese analysis may be somewhat optimistic.
[5]*Id.*
[6]Shozo Musata, *Outlook of Japanese-Communist China Economic Interchange*, SEKAI (February 1957) in SUMMARY OF SELECTED JAPANESE MAGAZINES at 10 (U.S. Embassy, Tokyo).
[7]CS, *The Background and Purpose of Maoists' Unscrupulous Abuse on Hirohito*, 7 ISSUES AND STUDIES 22 (Taiwan, July 1971).

'Self-Reliance' Revisited: China's Technology Dilemma

HANS HEYMANN, JR.*

AS THE CULTURAL REVOLUTION drew to a close in 1969, the leadership of the People's Republic of China (P.R.C.) began once again to turn outward for the acquisition of technology on a significant scale. By the spring of 1974, what had begun as a modest trickle of Chinese orders for machinery and equipment had turned into something of a torrent. Contracts for complete production plants and huge plant complexes, some valued as high as a quarter billion dollars, were being concluded at an unprecedented rate, with the aim of raising output and productivity in a half-dozen basic Chinese industries—petrochemical, steel, fertilizer, power, petroleum, and mining. A wide range of sophisticated machine tools, instrumentation, and production and process equipment was being imported from more than a dozen countries, six of which had held elaborate industrial technology exhibitions in Shanghai or Peking during 1973 alone. China's longstanding insistence on balancing trade bilaterally and on paying for its current imports with current exports had fallen by the wayside and "deferred payment purchases"—a euphemism for buying on credit—had become the rule rather than the exception. Most significantly, for the first time in more than a dozen years, the P.R.C. was permitting small numbers of foreign technicians to accompany the new plants and remain on site long enough to monitor proper installation and start-up. Although these technicians are carefully designated as "assistants" rather than "advisors," their admittance represents a substantial easing of past "self-reliance" strictures.

What should we make of this renewed Chinese pursuit of foreign technology? Is it merely a short-lived shopping spree that will quickly run its course? Or does it portend a new long-term trend away from China's basically autarkic, inner-directed philosophy, and toward a more open, world economy-oriented development path?

I. TECHNOLOGY IMPORTATION AND THE 'TWO LINES'

Historically, China's behavior in the sphere of technology acquisition provides little support for any "long-term trend" hypothesis. The Chinese developmental evolution over the past ten

*Member, Senior Research Staff, The Rand Corporation.

15

China's Changing Role in the World Economy

years was marked by sharp oscillations between acceptance and rejection of foreign technology and expertise. These oscillations reflect the shifting fortunes in the "struggle between the two lines," between the conservative Liuist pragmatists and the radical Maoist ideologists. That struggle involves contention over the most fundamental questions of political philosophy and socioeconomic goals, and it affects every aspect of policy and program.

The effect of that struggle on China's development and on its technology acquisition policy has already been vividly described by others.[1] I can therefore confine myself here to only the briefest summary, in the form of a table showing the successive phases of China's economic development and their reflection in its technology acquisition policy (see Table I). While a table cannot hope to mirror the scope and subtleties of the issues, it does display the linkage between technology and development policies in the abrupt changes that have occurred. Periods of receptivity to foreign technology have alternated with periods of xenophobic rejection, in close consonance with reversals on larger policy issues.

TABLE I. PHASES IN CHINA'S DEVELOPMENT AND THEIR REFLECTIONS IN TECHNOLOGY ACQUISITION, 1949-1974

PERIOD	DEVELOPMENT PHASE	TECHNOLOGY ACQUISI- TION POLICY
1949-1952 Reconstruction	Rehabilitation of war-torn economy U.S.S.R. the main source of industrial equipment	Seventy percent of trade with Soviet Bloc Heavy influx of Soviet military technology and training (Korean War)
1953-1957 First Five-Year Plan: "Leaning to One Side"	Maximum rate of fixed capital formation Priority for development of basic industry Forced draft industrialization, large-scale centrally planned integrated plants, Soviet style Acceptance of principle of developing local industry to serve local needs and using local resources, but mostly lip service in practice	Massive Soviet aid in the form of complete plants and industrial systems Soviet support targeted on heavy industry sector

TABLE I. *(Continued)*

PERIOD	DEVELOPMENT PHASE	TECHNOLOGY ACQUISITION POLICY
1958-1960 *Great Leap Forward: "Walking on Two Legs"*	Rejection of Stalinist model of industrialization in favor of Maoist all-out mass mobilization and mass participation Proliferation of small-scale inefficient local enterprises with "backyard" technologies Nurturing of local initiative and regional self-sufficiency	Soviet turn-key projects begin to phase down in the face of mounting Sino-Soviet tension and Chinese resistance to foreign expertise Sudden withdrawl of Soviet assistance in Summer 1960 wreaks havoc
1961-1965 *Great Crisis and Readjustment*	Economic crisis forces a shift of priority to agriculture Return to Liuist approach: centralized planning and administration by professionals at national and provincial levels and return to economic rationality (many Great Leap plants closed) Rural industrialization pushed vigorously	Technology import resumes on a small scale; few package plants; stress on self-reliance; technology source shifted to Western Europe and to Japan
1966-1969 *Cultural Revolution*	Reversion to Maoist principles, pitting masses against technical and managerial elites Worship of nativism and renewed pitting of "red" against "expert" Destruction of party bureaucracy, sporadic economic disruption and some absolute decline in industrial output	Imports of foreign technology drastically curtailed, some plant purchases cancelled, foreign contacts ruptured
1970-1974 *Post-Cultural Revolution*	Return to economic rationality; new wave of expansion Shift in planning and decision-making to regional and provincial levels, and further development of decentralized industrial plants in outlying regions Use of more advanced industrial centers to spread industrial systems into the hinterland	Return to more vigorous technology import policy: emphasis on complete plants, diversification of sources, more liberal interpretation of self-reliance

A. *The Significance of Soviet Tutelage*

The Chinese ambivalence on foreign technology can also be illustrated in a more quantitative way by charting the ebb and flow of China's imports of machinery and complete plants over this same period (Figure 1). As the figure shows, these imports peaked during the era of Soviet tutelage in the latter half of the fifties. It was largely that experience which shaped Chinese attitudes on foreign technology. During that seven-year period, China was the recipient of what was undoubtedly the most comprehensive technology transfer in modern industrial history. The scope and significance of that transfer has not been generally appreciated in the West. At a time when China was weak and isolated, the Soviet Union, hoping to gain hegemony over its new Communist neighbor, provided China with the foundations of a basic industry. The Soviet contribution encompassed much more than production technology. It ran the gamut from scientific and technical education to project design, and from production engineering to the creation of a modern industrial organization, complete with planning, budgeting, and management systems.

Interestingly, in such areas as aircraft manufacture, the style of the Soviet technology transfer was, in some respects, comparable to the United States-to-Japan transfer of the late 1950's and early 1960's.[2] Both cases involved what might be called interim co-production arrangements under license on a succession of increasingly complex products. In the aircraft industry, for example, the transfer progressed from trainers to simple jet fighters to more sophisticated aircraft and helicopters. A gradual phase-in procedure was followed in both cases, beginning with the simple assembly of "knockdown" airframes, advancing then to component manufacture, and finally to complete indigenous production of the entire aircraft. Although the Chinese were far less advanced technologically than the Japanese of the 1950's, and therefore were far less prepared to absorb the new skills and techniques, they nevertheless made dramatic progress during the seven years of the Sino-Soviet association.

Both the Russians and the Chinese worked hard at the transfer task and it proved highly effective. The massive infusion of Soviet capital and know-how proved invaluable in China's subsequent development. It would have taken the Chinese decades to evolve such a comprehensive industrial system on their own.[3]

But the Soviet beneficence was a mixed blessing. It required the Chinese to accept the U.S.S.R. blindly as a prototype for their industrial development, and it engendered a stultifying dependency on Soviet tutelage. Moreover, the Soviet style of assistance was

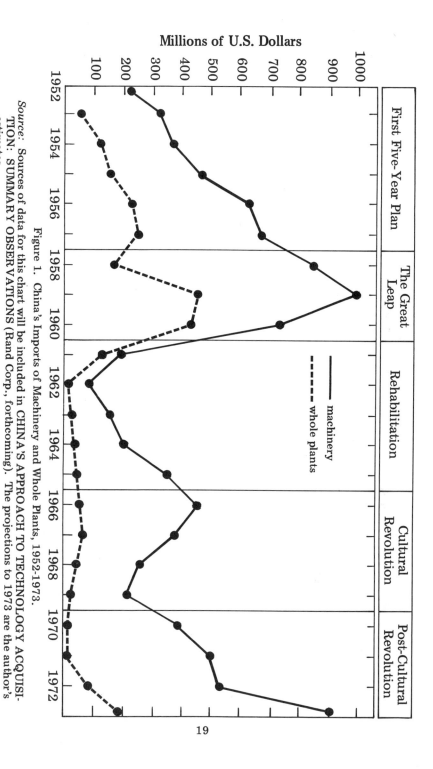

Figure 1. China's Imports of Machinery and Whole Plants, 1952-1973.

Source: Sources of data for this chart will be included in CHINA'S APPROACH TO TECHNOLOGY ACQUISI-TION: SUMMARY OBSERVATIONS (Rand Corp., forthcoming). The projections to 1973 are the author's estimates.

patronizing and paternalistic. Inevitably, it evoked a sharp reaction; to save their independence and self-confidence, the Chinese felt compelled to reject that kind of foreign domination. The Great Leap Forward marked the break with dependency and the reaffirmation of a more traditional Chinese nativism and self-assertion. It spurred a great outpouring of sentiment against foreign technology, a pitting of "red" against "expert," and an effort to inspire peasant initiative and stimulate worker innovation. Its long-run goal was to mobilize the vast human and material resources that lay fallow in the countryside. It signalled the total rejection not only of Soviet technological guidance, but of the entire Soviet forced-industrialization model, in favor of an "agriculture first" model of China's own invention.

B. *The Shift to Dependency Avoidance*

The cataclysmic short-term consequences of the Great Leap are well known. Inept policies and gross mismanagement combined with two successive crop failures and the precipitous Soviet withdrawal in 1960, to bring the Chinese economy, in Eckstein's words, "to a state of prostration similar to that produced by war devastation."[4] In the long run, however, the new inner-directed, go-it-alone, bootstrap approach to modernization that was followed after 1960 has enabled China to achieve a degree of technical and economic independence of the outside world. Quantitatively, its reliance on foreign trade is marginal. China's total imports in 1973 are estimated at roughly $4.5 billion,[5] which represents, perhaps, 2 percent of its gross national product.[6] Moreover, those of its imports most relevant to "technology" are an equally modest fraction of its own domestic "technology" production. Imports of machinery and equipment (including complete plants) in 1973 probably amounted to something less than $1 billion. This probably represents 6 to 8 percent of China's own machinery and equipment production.[7] While these numbers are extremely crude, they are not likely to be far enough off the mark to invalidate the observation that, quantititatively, imported technology represents only a very small share of China's annual technology accretion.

Qualitatively, on the other hand, its significance is far more consequential. To understand just how consequential, we must look more closely at the way in which foreign technology ties into Chinese industry. For this purpose it is useful to distinguish among three different modes of industrial production that have gradually evolved in China.[8] They are ranked here in descending order of technological sophistication:

1. "Scientific laboratory industry"

    2. Heavy large-scale and medium-scale industry
       a. Centrally controlled basic and military industry
       b. Province and municipality-controlled medium- to small-scale industry.
    3. Local (rural) industry.

These modes differ sharply in character and in their need for and access to foreign technology, and it is useful to examine each separately.

C. *Modes of Chinese Industrial Production and Foreign Technology*

1. *Scientific Laboratory Industry*

This stands at the top of the sophistication pyramid and is a uniquely Chinese institution that grew out of Mao's insistence that all research be linked to production, and out of an educational philosophy that espouses "learning by doing." Hence, there is little purely basic research in China, and no research is officially sanctioned that is not clearly aimed at practical results and at meeting important, specific economic or societal needs. Going one step further, scientific institutes typically couple their research and development activities with manufacturing through a variety of organizational arrangements, *e.g.*, by setting up production workshops within their own institutes, by establishing separate pilot plants nearby, or by "adopting" and reorganizing existing "neighborhood factories" to enhance their production competence. These scientist-guided laboratory-workshops and plants produce surprisingly large quantities of sophisticated devices, especially in the field of electronics. For example, the Physics Department of Tsinghua University in Peking manufactures integrated circuits in its laboratory workshop, more or less by hand, but using sophisticated photo-reduction techniques, ultrasonic bonding, and optical systems produced by the Chinese Institute of Optics. The Institute of Electronics of the Academy of Science in Peking, which specializes in millimeter-wave and microwave research, produces klystrons, traveling-wave tubes, and carcinotrons.[9] In 1970, the Shanghai Institute of Computing Techniques adopted a "neighborhood" window-handle factory with an initial workforce of 20 housewives and taught it to produce magnetic cores, computer mainframes, and transistors under quite primitive conditions. A team of U.S. computer experts visited this factory and actually observed assembly work on an integrated circuit digital computer.[10]

Of course, these workshops and their scientist and institute sponsors are predominantly oriented toward achieving self-reliance in high technology and toward demonstrating that they can innovate and fashion the equipment and tooling they need without external assistance. Thus, their interests in foreign technology are limited to scientific information, technical literature, scientist exchange visits, and specialized instrumentation. Quantitatively, they are a small claimant on foreign technology.

2. *Heavy Large- and Medium-Scale Urban Industry*

This is the principal claimant and it appears at the next level of the pyramid. This category consists of two subgroups.

The Vertically and Horizontally Integrated Soviet-Style Basic and Military Industry Complexes. In most cases, these complexes are under the direct control of the central ministries, and, where not, Peking firmly determines their general direction. These industries include all of the large metallurgical, machine-building, automotive, aircraft, and electronic component plants originally obtained from the Russians but greatly expanded since. They also include essentially indigenous Chinese ventures, such as the massive petroleum extraction effort in the Taching oil fields. The main object of this subgroup is large-scale, standardized output, and its interest in foreign technology extends to anything that might enhance that output. But innovation policies in these large-scale plants tend to be conservative. Chinese design engineers are still relatively few in number and limited in experience, and their innovative zeal is more likely to be directed toward improvisation, adaptation, and marginal improvements in the production line, than toward the introduction of entirely new models or the design of complex, capital-intensive, ultra-modern plants. This important subgroup, therefore, stands to benefit most from the importation of complete, sophisticated plants with their emormous economies of scale. The integrated hot and cold steel rolling mill, for example, that is to be built by Japanese and West German consortia at Wuhan over the next three years will not only increase China's steel-making capacity by some 25 percent, but will also have a dramatic impact on cost of production and quality of product.

The Medium- to Small-Scale Industrial Enterprises. These are mostly under the control of province or municipality, and exist side by side with the large central plants, scattered throughout the country. Many of these enterprises have graduated from simple workshop or repair shop status by merging into larger entities. For example, the Canton Motor Vehicle Plant that manufactures the "Red Guard" 3½-ton truck started out in the early 1960's as the Huang-Fu Machinery Plant, which had been formed by combining a half-dozen small machine and repair shops. Such plants are highly dynamic and growth-oriented. They engage in a large amount of subcontracting and cooperative new-product development. When it was realized in 1970, for example, that semiconductor production required large numbers of single-crystal furnaces, the Shanghai municipality enlisted twelve factories and institutes in the design and assembly of such furnaces, and reportedly succeeded in getting the first furnace into trial production in thirteen days.[11] Since these provincial and municipal plants serve mostly local needs, their output is often not standardized, but their operations appear to be far more flexible and innovative than those of the large centrally-directed enterprises. The provincial and municipal plants seem constantly to be driving themselves, and being driven, to achieve higher levels of technology and to improve the quality and extend the range of their output. Although the provincial and municipal authorities enjoy a large degree of decision-making autonomy in organizing production and deciding how tasks are to be carried out, it is difficult to believe that such critical matters as the determination of priorities and the technology diffusion policy (including access to foreign technology) are not controlled by the center.

On this, however, the evidence is sketchy and contradictory. Audrey Donnithorne, in a 1972 article,[12] emphasized the declining importance of the center—the extent to which provinces, municipalities, and even counties *(hsien)* seemed to be developing along self-sufficient, autonomous lines, under the official injunction "to build small but complete industrial systems by self-reliance," and observed that these entities seemed to be trading with one another on almost mercantilist principles. She also noted that these local enterprises tended to expand or create new enterprises out of their own resources, rather than relying on planning coordination from the center and state investment grants.

While this kind of autonomous *intra*-municipality development and diversification has been going on, an equally important and more far-reaching process of diffusion has been taking place *across* provincial lines. That process is very much centrally initiated and state-funded. Often it takes the form of massive, nation-wide campaigns, such as the "general battle for radio and television equipment" that was launched by the central leadership in 1971. That campaign enabled every province, municipality, and autonomous region within two years to produce its own transistor radios and made it possible for twenty-six of them to achieve at least trial production of television receivers.[13] Such feats manifestly require central direction and central resource allocation.

A look at the automotive industry further demonstrates that nationwide diffusion of production technology does not take place through autonomous local action alone. Toward the end of the Cultural Revolution, the propagation of truck production became an important state objective. As provinces and municipalities throughout China organized themselves to manufacture trucks locally, their efforts were thoroughly dependent on the guidance, training and technology provided to them by China's second largest automotive plant, the Nanking Motor Vehicle Plant, which was selected as a kind of "lead plant." Its popular NJ-130 "Leap Forward" 2½-ton truck was designated as the prototype and it became the most widely copied truck model throughout China. By 1970, it was possible to identify (from Chinese press accounts) new manufacturers of this truck in at least nine provinces.[14] To a more limited extent, China's largest automotive plant, the Changchun No. 1 Motor Vehicle Plant in Manchuria, carried out a similar function by transferring the technology of its 4-ton and 4½-ton "Liberation" trucks to several other provinces.[15] Some recent data on Chinese motor vehicle production also reveal that, at least in that industry, there is a fair amount of production interdependence among plants across province lines.[16] For example, engine plants in Shanghai and Hangchow provide the 160 horsepower diesel engine that powers the "Yellow River" 7-ton dump truck made in Tsinan, and the Peking Motor Vehicle Plant that makes the "Long March" 10-ton all-terrain truck receives its big diesel power plant all the way from Sian (Szechwan). In short, the image of self-sufficient provincial "cellular" economies is more than a little overdrawn.

To what extent do these provincial and municipal enterprises benefit from foreign technology? As has been indicated, their principal source of new technology is a combination of self-help, improvisation, and a process of proliferation of know-how and exchange of experience within the country. But the most advanced plants also have direct access to technology from abroad. This is especially true of plants in such important industrial cities as Shanghai, Peking, Tsinan, Wuhan, and others. For example—looking again at the automotive industry—the "Long March" 10- and 12-ton trucks produced by the Hopei Changcheng Plant in Peking and the "Yellow River" 8-ton truck made at the Tsinan Motor Vehicle Plant are the result of extensive technological assistance provided in the mid-1960's by Czech manufacturers (Tatra and Skoda respectively). The Shanghai Truck Plant, in developing its 15-ton and 32-ton dump trucks, depended heavily on design data and technology obtained from the BelAZ automobile factory in Minsk, and learned much from a technology license for a French 32-ton truck purchased from Berliet in 1966. Most recently, in November 1973, the Gleason

Works of Rochester, New York, obtained a major contract for complete sets of sophisticated gear-grinding machinery, to be custom-built to the needs of six Chinese motor vehicle plants, at least four of which are in the medium- to small-scale category.

In short, both the large-scale central plants and the smaller-scale provincial and municipal plants are major "end users" of foreign technology. Collectively, their interest extends across the entire technology spectrum: critical materials that lie beyond China's present technical ability to produce (super alloys, special steels, composite materials); high-performance end-products that are urgently needed for the priority tasks of the Chinese economy (earth-moving and off-the-road vehicles for construction, drilling rigs and pipe for offshore oil exploration, dredges for port development, modern trucks and jet airliners for transportation, satellite ground stations for communication, and so forth); sophisticated equipment obtained as one-of-a-kind and two-of-a-kind prototypes for copying; and, most important, imports of complete plants to boost output in the key industrial branches (steel rolling, petrochemical and fertilizer production, power generating, petroleum extracting, and coal mining). The P.R.C.'s imports in all of these areas have increased significantly in the past several years.

3. Small-Scale Rural Industries

These lie at the bottom of the sophistication pyramid, but they are constantly growing and proliferating. They are not centrally planned or controlled, but rather are directed and coordinated almost entirely at the level of the county. Basically, the small-scale rural industries fall into five complementary categories: cement, iron and steel, electric power, synthetic fertilizers, and machine-building. Their output is mostly nonstandardized and of low quality; their principal aim is to serve the needs of agriculture within their own regions.

Such industries derive their technological advancement solely from a "trickle down" process of internal diffusion from higher to lower economic and administrative levels—from province to county, county to commune, commune to production brigade—with each higher level providing technical guidance, training, and equipment to the lower levels. The diffusion process is often highly organized and complex. For example, in 1970 Shanghai was assigned the task of designing and producing reasonably efficient, standardized packages of equipment for small-scale rural synthetic ammonia production. It took 10,000 people and a network of 400 plants in the Shanghai area two years, in a tremendous coordination effort, to turn out the machinery, instruments, and gauges required for such equipment packages.[17] By now, many other provinces employ this kind of management coordination technique. Rural industries are increasingly drawn into the network to supply the simpler components. These "lower echelon" industries have a strong incentive to upgrade their technical competence. Greater efficiency enables them to mesh more profitably with the production processes used at parallel and higher levels.

In the rural industry category, technology acquisition is an entirely internal process. It incorporates mobilization, basic technical education and on-the-job skill learning, and vertical and horizontal technology diffusion. It focuses on engendering mass participation and mass initiative. Foreign technology has no significant role to play in this process.

In sum, the highly structured process of internal diffusion is far more important as a source of technological advancement than the acquisition of technology from abroad. Foreign technology flows in only at the top half of the pyramid, to the most advanced plants and activities. Even there, new equipment, processes, and techniques are often acquired as much for the purposes of training, education, and emulation, as they are for the purpose of increasing output. The Chinese leadership seems willing to accept the cost of some decrement in productivity, some retardation of growth in the short run, to attain the broader social goals of "mass participation" and "self-reliance" in the long run.

II. THE IMPACT OF FOREIGN TECHNOLOGY

To analyze more particularly the significance of the contribution foreign technology makes, or could make, to Chinese development, we must consider separately the two most consequential forms of such imports: "prototypes" for learning and copying, and complete production plant and process equipment.

A. *Use of the Foreign Prototypes*

The procurement of a wide variety of one- and two-of-a-kind prototypes is a form of acquisition which the Chinese have developed into something of an art, often to the considerable annoyance or disillusionment of Western traders. Favorite occasions for such acquisitions are provided by industrial fairs and technology exhibitions held in Peking or Shanghai by major exporting countries.[18] At the conclusion of these exhibitions the Chinese are able to purchase display models of the most advanced equipment at bargain-basement prices, since exhibitors would prefer to avoid paying the return freight. Other opportunities to locate novel, sophisticated technology arise when Chinese technical missions are taken on plant visits abroad. In recent years, a great number of such missions have been roving the world, gathering free lessons in technology. In nine months of 1973, no less than 53 Chinese technical teams visited Japan alone.[19]

Recorded instances of successful Chinese prototype copying, done without any outside assistance, are legion. The Massey-Ferguson 35 h.p. tractor is one of the earliest examples, and the Hasselblad 500 C/M camera, one of the most recent. But prototype copying also has serious limitations. First, the prototype to be copied must be at the right level of sophistication—with respect to design engineering, fabricating skill, machining precision, and materials applications—relative to the competence the Chinese themselves have attained. If the item is too advanced, reverse engineering becomes too difficult. The relatively simple problem of hand-fashioning or custom-building a single duplicate is arduous enough. When the copier lacks design and manufacturing data, he must recreate the basic blueprints, the detailed engineering drawings, and, most important, the materials specifications. Devising adequate materials specifications often requires sophisticated metallurgical analysis, testing, and experimentation. The follow-up problem is equally difficult; the copier's level of fabricating technology must duplicate the metal casting, forming, shaping, joining, and finishing operations well enough to achieve the necessary endurances, tolerances, and dimensional accuracies.

The task becomes even more trying when the objective is not merely to fashion a single duplicate, but to achieve a series production run. Large-scale production adds an entirely new dimension of design standardization. It requires perfect interchangeability of parts and components, production tooling, plant layout, materials and work scheduling, and quality control. Again, without assistance from the originator, the copier's task is formidable and time-consuming. The prototype by itself reveals only *what* was produced, not *how* it was produced. And that raises the second major limitation.

For, when the copier has finally succeeded in series-manufacturing the item, he has merely demonstrated that, given time and effort, he can slavishly copy an existing design. He has not significantly enhanced his ability to design on his own.

The prototype does not explain the rationale behind the original designer's choices. Every major design feature of a complex, modern piece of equipment is the outcome of a large number of engineering compromises and trade-offs resulting from stress calculations, laboratory experimentation, and functional tests. "Understanding" the design to the point that the copier can ultimately improve upon it means knowing *why* these compromises were made and *how* the trade-offs were arrived at. The copier cannot learn this from studying the finished prototype. He must essentially retrace or reproduce the original designer's calculations and investigations. This is relatively easy if the copier is willing and able to obtain the original designer's assistance—his data and his experience. If the copier foregoes or rejects such assistance, as the Chinese have done throughout the post-Soviet period, his problem becomes far more difficult. The degree of difficulty will depend largely on the level of design experience and production know-how that the copier already has, *i.e.*, the breadth of the technological gap that separates him from the originator.

The Chinese are not unaware of these limitations. While they have engaged in copying on a grand scale and will no doubt continue to do so, they acknowledge that too much reliance on this form of acquisition would condemn China's technical level to permanent inferiority, ". . . because others are continuously advancing. . . . [p]urchasing sample machines from others can only be for the purpose of increasing our knowledge and knowing how others have taken their road. We cannot open up a road for ourselves merely by copying from others."[20]

B. *Complete Plant and Process Imports*

A far more rewarding, but also more expensive, form of technology import is the "turn-key" production plant or comprehensive equipment package, complete with the technical data and advisory assistance to set it up. The Chinese resorted to this form of acquisition only on a modest scale in the post-Soviet period of the 1960's. Even when acquiring these packages they often deprived themselves of the full benefit of the plants by refusing to accept—on the grounds of self-reliance—the kind of on-site foreign assistance in, and supervision of, plant assembly and shake-down that would have significantly shortened the absorption period.

Since the Cultural Revolution, however, and especially in the past two years, the Chinese have expanded their plant purchases dramatically. Tables II and III give an approximate breakdown of recent P.R.C. plant purchases by type of plant and by country of origin. The purchases shown cover the period from January 1972 through May 1974, and represent contracts concluded, *not* plants delivered. Actual deliveries will be spread over a period of several years, in some cases as many as four years. Because the estimates are based on incomplete and often contradictory press and trade publication reports, they must be treated with some reserve.[21]

TABLE II. P.R.C. PURCHASES OF COMPLETE PLANTS
(BY TYPE)

Contracts Concluded January 1972 through May 1974

TYPE OF PLANT	NUMBER OF UNITS	ESTIMATED COST *(Millions U.S. $)*
IRON AND STEEL PLANT		512
Rolling Mills	4	
Iron Works	1	
POWER-GENERATING PLANT		303
Complete Stations	3	
Turbines and Generators	43	
PETROLEUM EXPLORATION AND EXTRACTION PLANT		120
Offshore Drilling Platforms	4	
Oil Rigs	2	
Survey and Supply Vessels	24	
PETROCHEMICAL AND SYNTHETIC FIBER PLANT		783
Intermediate Product	28	
Synthetic Fiber	10	
CHEMICAL FERTILIZER PLANT		492[a]
Ammonia	16	
Urea	14	
OTHER PLANT		133
		2,342[b]

[a] This figure excludes value of four 1972 Japanese fertilizer plants for which no cost data are available. Actual total, thus, may be some $50-60 million higher.
[b] Differences between totals and sums of individual items are due to rounding.

TABLE III. P.R.C. PURCHASES OF COMPLETE PLANTS
(BY COUNTRY)

Contracts Concluded January 1972 through May 1974

COUNTRY	COST (Millions U.S. $)	SHARE PERCENTAGE
Japan	1,029	44
France	540	23
West Germany	293	13
United States	208	8
Italy	103	4
Netherlands	90	4
U.S.S.R.	25	1
United Kingdom	25	1
Denmark	20	1
Belgium	5	Negl.
Sweden	4	Negl.
TOTAL	2,342[a]	100[a]

[a]Difference between total and sum of individual items is due to rounding.

Nevertheless, the tables provide a fair indication of the major thrust of the plant acquisitions. Acquisitions are centered on a few basic areas which are necessary to China's growth and to feeding and clothing its people: petrochemicals, largely for the textile industry; fertilizers for agriculture; and the fundamentals of steel, power, and petroleum. All of the plants to be delivered are ultramodern and represent high-technology production equipment. In the branches of industry they affect, the plants will enable China to "leap forward" in production efficiency and product quality. However, many other branches of industry are equally in need of a technology transfusion, and appropriate plant acquisitions could make a big difference. The automotive and aircraft industries are two cases in point.

In the automotive industry, China has only two large-scale production plants—Changchun and Nanking. These two produce at least three-quarters of the roughly 120,000 trucks China turns out annually. But the models they produce are ancient. The production models are essentially replicas of the thirty-year-old ZIS-150 and GAZ-51 models the Chinese inherited from parent plants in Moscow and Gorki through Soviet technological assistance in the mid-fifties.

The Soviet models in turn were copies of Ford and International Harvester trucks that the U.S. had provided for the Russians under Lend-Lease in World War II. They are functional, of course, but grossly deficient in productivity, maintainability, and durability.[23]

Interestingly, among the large number of small-scale provincial truck plants that were described earlier (there are some 37 in all), the most advanced are able to manufacture trucks which are considerably more modern, with overhead valve gasoline engines and with higher compression diesels. However, these plants are mostly amalgamations and mergers of small workshops or municipal repair shops, and thus cannot produce in significant volume i.e., volume larger than 1,000 or 2,000 trucks per year).

The Chinese are keenly aware of their problem. They have been importing trucks in large numbers and in a variety of models from more than a dozen countries, but especially from France, Germany, and Japan. In 1973, they imported more than 15,000 from Japan alone. But this widely scattered importation is very costly, and the enormous diversity of models creates a nightmarish problem of maintenance, logistics, and spare parts supply. Moreover, to meet its massive needs for transportation and construction, China requires a much larger fleet of more capacious and efficient heavy vehicles. Importing a modern production plant offers a relatively quick solution. Accordingly, the Chinese have been negotiating with Toyota to acquire a $380 million integrated automotive plant and with Volkswagen to produce the VW Safari jeep under license. These acquisitions would constitute a tremendous jump for the Chinese—at least as great as, if not greater than, the change in the Soviet automotive industry that followed the comparable Fiat-Togliatti plant transfer to the Soviet Union a few years ago.

What the Chinese lack is not the ability to build trucks. They manage quite well with custom-building, hand-machining, and small-scale "batch-type" production. What they have not mastered are the techniques of modern continuous-flow manufacturing processes, precise automation technology and, most importantly, what is sometimes called management technology. It is in these technological areas that package plant imports can be most helpful. The imports carry with them not only novel production systems and fabricating techniques, but also efficient plant layout, flow patterns, embodied production organizations, and implicit management systems.

The aircraft industry represents a second example of the potential value of such imports. In China, this industry is oriented almost entirely toward military production, yet has not had a very high priority. In the military sphere, the Chinese leadership has concentrated for many years on a rather narrow set of priorities.[23]

Somewhat too simply, the priorities might be reduced to three: nuclear weapons, rocket propulsion, and electronics—all self-evidently related. This concentration has meant that China was allowed to fall far behind in many other areas of military production. Aero-engines are a good example; China worked hard on airbreathing propulsion during the late 1950's and early 1960's. But the higher-priority rocket propulsion field subsequently drew away some of the best scientists, engineers, and other scarce resources, leaving aero-engine technology in a state of retarded development. As a result, a big gap now separates China's aero-engine design and production capabilities (exemplified by the mid-1950's generation turbojets in their inherited Soviet-designed fighters and medium bombers) from the sophisticated current generation turbofans of Rolls Royce, Pratt and Whitney, and General Electric that power the major Western aircraft. Western aeronautical experts report that the Chinese themselves judge their aero-engine technology to be at least twenty years behind the West in terms of all the relevant performance criteria. Such a substantial gap cannot be overcome merely by independent, incremental upgrading or by importing some advanced engines as prototypes for copying.

As in the automotive industry, large advances can only come through direct technological assistance from abroad. Indeed, the Chinese have been negotiating with Rolls Royce (1971) Ltd. to acquire unrestricted license production rights for Rolls Royce Spey engines, complete with extensive technical assistance from Rolls Royce engineers. Acquiring that technology would bring the Chinese ten years forward in relatively short order into the more advanced turbofan era of the early sixties. Of course, this would still leave them about ten years behind the most advanced, high-compression, low fuel consumption, high-bypass ratio engines now being turned out in the West. Nevertheless, the practical consequences of the ten-year jump would mean a significant advance for their future aircraft performance.

III. TWO DILEMMAS

From what has been said, it should be clear that China's potential economic gains from foreign technology are large and that its appetite for importing technology has grown vastly. Not only have these imports spurted quantitatively; almost every day brings new reports of Chinese feelers, negotiations, and contract closings over an ever widening range of technologies and processes.

There are, however, two important obstacles, or dilemmas, that confront the Chinese leadership in expanding its technology import drive. One is simply China's "ability to pay"—the ability to expand exports in order to earn the foreign exchange necessary to pay for imports. Although the Chinese have succeeded in enlarging their range of exportable light industry products, the world economic recession has caused a falloff in demand for Chinese exports. Also, they are now beset with materials shortages, capacity limitations, and transportation bottlenecks which will limit the rate at which exports can be expanded. At the same time, the relentless growth of China's population will continue to require it to import large quantities of cereals, fertilizers, and other food-related raw products, imposing a persistent drain on its foreign exchange resources.

So far, the Chinese have eased this problem by backing away from their ultraconservative bilateral payment-balancing policies. Seeing all too clearly that paying cash is not regarded in the capitalist world as an indicator of financial probity, they are now willing to accept deferred payment terms, governmentally subsidized credit, and other schemes for low-interest borrowing. They have been receiving every encouragement in this direction from the international financial community, especially from the Japanese. The latter have, for example, provided China with a large trade credit by opening a yuan account in the Bank of Japan and allowing its yuan reserves to build up.

In the longer run, however, China's export earnings will have to grow sharply if its imports are to continue to expand. There may be a dramatic solution: China's huge petroleum resources, which might well turn out to be the key to China's foreign exchange earning problem. On the other hand, petroleum exploration, extraction, and refining require huge investments and highly complex technology, which would again necessitate resort to foreign technology imports. There is an obvious circularity here: to expand technology imports, China must increase its exports; to expand exports, China must increase its technology imports!

One resolution of the dilemma might be for China to enter into joint ventures or contingent service contracts with international petroleum exploration and drilling firms. The Chinese, however, have firmly rejected such a course. They evidently recognize that this would risk sharpening a second dilemma—the need to preserve at least a modicum of the Chinese self-image of self-reliance.

The intrusion of foreign influences looms once again as a threat. With large-scale influx of Western visitors, greater exposure of Chinese technicians and functionaries to capitalist ways abroad, reacceptance of the relevance of foreign expertise and technology to Chinese development, and the noticeable revival of the pragmatic Liuist line, the Maoists must be deeply disquieted as they seek to preserve the purity of the revolution. The trend of the last two years has been a steady and highly visible drift away from past "self-reliance" strictures and dependency-avoidance policies, toward a more open, flexible relationship with the outside world. The Maoists can only see this as a threat to contaminate the "new Maoist man" by bourgeois influence and backsliding into revisionism.

The recent anti-Confucious-Lin Piao campaign is a reminder that the "struggle between the two lines" continues; and our earlier chart (Figure 1 *supra*) tells us that trends in technology policy are easily reversed. For the moment, the existing policy seems firmly established, and Chinese trade officials go out of their way to emphasize that it will not be reversed.[24] But the leadership must no doubt tread gingerly and avoid pushing the liberalizing trend too fast, for fear that what has been an educational campaign of purification might turn into a purgative one. In shaping future technology policy, the leadership must view this danger both as a dilemma and a constraint.

NOTES

[1] *See* Eckstein, *Economic Growth and Change in China: A Twenty-Year Perspective* in THE CHINA QUARTERLY 220-241 (Apr.-Jun. 1973). *See also* Whitson, *China's Quest for Technology* in PROBLEMS OF COMMUNISM 16-29 (Jul.-Aug. 1973).

[2] *See* Hall and Johnson, *Transfer of United States Aerospace Technology to Japan* P-3875 (Rand Corp., Jul. 1968), for a good description of this latter experience between the Lockheed Aircraft Corporation and North American Aviation on the one hand, and Mitsubishi Heavy Industries and Kawasaki Aircraft Company on the other.

[3] *See* M. GARDNER CLARK, THE DEVELOPMENT OF CHINA'S STEEL INDUSTRY AND SOVIET TECHNICAL AID (1973), especially chapters 3 and 9, for an excellent account of the impact of Soviet assistance.

[4] *See* Eckstein, *supra* note 1, at 240.

[5] 1 U.S.-CHINA BUSINESS REVIEW 33 (No. 2, Mar.-Apr. 1974).

[6] Arthur Ashbrook ventures a figure of $128 billion for China's GNP in 1971 at 1970 prices, *see China: Economic Policy and Economic Results, 1949-1971*, PEOPLE'S REPUBLIC OF CHINA: AN ECONOMIC ASSESSMENT (1972), at 47. Allowing for real growth and dollar price inflation, the 1973 figure might be on the order of $170 billion. A figure of $172 billion, derived from U.S. Government sources, is given in U.S.-CHINA BUSINESS REVIEW, *supra* note 5, at 33.

[7] Ashbrook estimates China's gross investment at 18% of GNP in 1971, *supra* note 6, at 45. Taking net fixed capital formation as 16% and the machinery and equipment share as accounting for half of that (based on estimates for 1952-65 in an unpublished manuscript by Kang Chao), one obtains a 1973 machinery and equipment figure of $13.6 billion.

[8] The categories are differentiated quite sharply here, in order to underline the distinct character of each. In fact, there is a fair amount of overlap between the categories and a melding of each into the other.

[9] Lubkin, *Physics in China*, PHYSICS TODAY 26, 27 (Dec. 1972).

[10] Cheatham, Jr., *et al.*, *Computing in China: A Travel Report*, 182 SCIENCE 136 (Oct. 1973). *See also* Szuprowicz, *Computers in Mao's China*, NEW SCIENTIST (Mar. 15, 1973).

[11] *China's Young Electronics Industry*, CHINA RECONSTRUCTS 8 (Feb. 1974).

[12] *China's Cellular Economy: Some Economic Trends since the Cultural Revolution*, 1972 CHINA QUARTERLY 605 ff. (No. 52, Oct.-Dec. 1972).

[13] *China's Young Electronics Industry*, *supra* note 11.

[14] Wuhan (Hupeh), Nanchang (Kiangsi), Changte (Hunan), Taiyuan (Shansi), Liuchow (Kwangsi), Paotow (Inner Mongolia), Chengchow (Honan), Foochow (Fukien), and Fushun (Liaoning). By 1972, the Wuhan and Nanchang plants had attained a sufficiently high technical level to warrant being listed in the Technical Handbook for P.R.C. Motor Vehicles as independent producers of this model truck, each with its own brand name.

[15] Hsining (Tsinghai), Kunming (Yunnan), and Taiyuan (Shansi).

[16] *Technical Handbook for P.R.C. Motor Vehicles* (Aug. 1972), in Translations on People's Republic of China No. 243, J.P.R.S. 60262 (Oct. 12, 1973).

[17] *See* J. Sigurdson, *Rural Industry and the Internal Transfer of Technology in China* (paper presented at the University of Sussex Workshop, Jun. 1972).

[18] According to CHINA TRADE REPORT 8 (Jan. 1974), no less than six countries held such exhibitions in 1973 alone.

[19] CHINA TRADE REPORT (No. 322, Sept. 1973).

[20] Shen Hung, *Let Us Become Revolutionary Promoters in Product Design Work*, Kuang-ming Jih-pao, Apr. 8, 1965, in 3441 SURVEY OF THE CHINA MAINLAND PRESS 9 (Apr. 21, 1965).

[21] The author is indebted to Miss Jeanette Koch of the Rand Corporation for a detailed and painstaking compilation of the plant purchase data upon which these estimates are based.

[22] These deficiencies are reflected both in the performance indicators derived from Chinese truck specifications (compression ratios, fuel consumption, ratios of weight to horsepower, etc.) and in the observations of Western automotive experts who have toured Chinese plants.

[23] The narrowness of this concentration began to become apparent in the 1950's. It is foreshadowed by the seven highest priority fields of research singled out among the 57 *important tasks* listed in the Twelve-Year Science Plan (1955-67) adopted in mid-1956: atomic energy, semiconductors, electronics, computer science, automation, high-speed fluids, and turbine propulsion. *See* Keiji Yamada, *The Development of Science and Technology in China: 1949-65*, 9 THE DEVELOPING ECONOMIES 518 (Dec. 1971).

[24] *See* the report by veteran China trader Harned Pettus Hoose, The Washington Post, Apr. 13, 1974, § B at 6, col. 5.

Chinese Perceptions of Social Imperialism and Economic Dependency: The Impact of Soviet Aid

DENNIS M. RAY*

In the aftermath of the Korean War, American policy makers characterized the activities of the Soviet Union in China as constituting a new form of imperialism hidden beneath a socialist facade. Nearly a generation later, in the aftermath of the Cultural Revolution, the Chinese themselves describe Soviet activity in China during this period as a form of "social imperialism." The purpose of this paper will be to examine some of the implications of Chinese reliance on Soviet aid during the First Five-Year Plan period (1953-1957). How do the Chinese now perceive their relationship with the Soviet Union during this period? What are the objective bases of these Chinese perceptions? How can we explain the change in Chinese calculations about the utility of Soviet aid?

I. CHINESE PERCEPTIONS OF SOCIAL IMPERIALISM AND ECONOMIC DEPENDENCE

The Chinese in recent years have begun to compare their international status to that of the various client states of Asia, Africa, and Latin America. In an important statement to the plenary meeting of the Third UNCTAD Conference, Chou Hau-min gave an authoritative review of contemporary Chinese perceptions:

> In the past the Chinese people suffered long from imperialist oppression. For over a century, the imperialist powers repeatedly launched wars of aggression against China. They divided China into their spheres of influence, interfered with China's internal affairs, backed the reactionary authorities, subjected the Chinese people's revolutionary struggle to bloody suppression, engineered civil wars among warlords, controlled China's customs, shipping and insurance, manipulated China's financial and monetary affairs and extorted privileges of running mines and factories, building railways, inland navigation. . . .[1]

*Associate Professor of Political Science, California State University at Los Angeles.

Similarly, oppression and plunder by imperialism and colonialism explain the economic backwardness of the Third World:

> The economy of the colonies and dependent countries was turned into a "single-product economy" as a result of lopsided development under the man-made "division of labour" in the colonial interests of imperialism. These countries were reduced to sources of raw materials and markets of manufactures monopolized by colonial and metropolitan countries, and were subjected to ever more cruel exploitation.[2]

In contrast to the exploitation practiced by other great powers, the Chinese hold that each country "has the right to dispose of its natural resources with a view to developing its natural economy and expanding its foreign trade."[3] Further, this expansion of trade with developing countries must not be a tool of imperialist exploitation. The Chinese attitude on international trade relates to more than an exchange of goods; such trade ought to take the "important form of mutual support and mutual help in [the] struggle against imperialism and for complete independence"[4] and

> [c]onform to the requirements and possibilities of both sides and promote both sides' economic development. [The Chinese] firmly oppose the imperialists who, under the disguise of trade, control and plunder other countries, and seek by various selfish means to seize important resources, extort huge profits and obstruct the economic development of other countries.[5]

The Chinese also distinguish between the generous aid of socialism and the "imperialist aid" of the "neo-imperialist exploiters," the latter being but a means of aggression. Thus, "[b]y means of aid they export capital, dump their products, plunder raw materials, and even encroach upon the sovereign rights and intervene in the internal affairs of other countries, thus turning the aid-receiving countries into their satellites and colonies."[6] Socialist aid, on the other hand, comes from "the revolutionary people of various countries in the world—especially those in the socialist camp. The aid among the people of various socialist countries is mutual. Hence, this kind of aid is in fact international economic cooperation."[7] The interest on long-term economic loans is but another form of imperialist exploitation. Accordingly, age-old imperialism and colonialism have been replaced by a more subtle form of imperialism which creates dependence through unequal trade and usurious long-term loans.

The Chinese preoccupation with trade and aid as instruments of imperialism highlights the absence of talk about direct foreign investment, which is the most significant instrument of neo-imperialism. We cannot know the extent to which Chinese rhetoric reflects a sense of former dependence on the Soviet Union or represents skillful public relations designed to express an essential oneness with the exploited countries of Asia, Africa, and Latin America.[8] However, Chinese writing on the question of social imperialism leaves little doubt that there is deep resentment towards the Soviet Union which reflects the political context of Sino-Soviet relations during the 1950's. Perhaps the most efficient way of summarizing the Chinese perceptions of social imperialism is to pose a series of questions and answer each with the appropriate Chinese perception.

What are the sources of social imperialism? According to a joint editorial of the *People's Daily*, *Red Flag*, and the *Liberation Army Daily*, revisionism and the capitalist road are the key sources of social imperialism.

> If we examine this question from the standpoint of Marxism-Leninism, and especially in the light of Comrade Mao Tse-tung's theory of continuing the revolution under the dictatorship of the proletariat, we shall be able to understand that this was mainly a product of the class struggle in the Soviet Union, the result of the usurpation of party and government leadership by a handful of party persons in power taking the capitalist road there, in other words, the result of the usurpation of the political power of the proletariat by the Soviet bourgeoisie. At the same time, it was the result of the policy of "peaceful evolution" with world imperialism. . . .[9]

What type of international order or system of international stratification do the social imperialists pursue? The Chinese perceive an evolving international system characterized by a superpower oligarchy in which American imperialists and the Soviet social imperialists collaborate in the counter-revolutionary domination of all other countries.

> To realize its wild ambition of struggling for hegemony and redividing the world with US imperialism, the Soviet revisionist renegade clique has all along been colluding and, at the same time, contending with US imperialism in a vain

attempt to sabotage the Vietnamese people's war against US imperialism and for national salvation. So did Khrushchev and it is all the more so with Brezhnev and company. They have been nakedly engaged in the plot of sham support but real betrayal and have made dirty deals privately with US imperialism, in a futile attempt to stamp out the revolutionary flames of the Vietnamese people and ruin the fruits of victory of the Vietnamese people's revolution. Numerous facts show that the Soviet revisionist renegade clique and US imperialism are jackals of the same lair and the common enemy of the Vietnamese people and the people throughout the world.[10]

Though expressed in a highly inflammatory fashion, the observation that Soviet-American relations now involve conflict and collaboration is quite correct. According to the Chinese, U.S. imperialism and Soviet revisionism are also "stepping up arms expansion and war preparations in Europe."

By using two opposing military blocs, they have carried out, each in its own sphere, military control, interference and occupation in a number of West and East European countries, seriously encroaching on their independence and sovereignty. To divide spheres of influence and contend for hegemony in Europe, the two superpowers are collaborating and at the same time contending with each other just as they do in the Middle East and other parts of the world.[11]

No doubt the superpower oligarchy is intended to give the Soviet Union unchallenged hegemony within the Communist bloc, the "new tsar" being "free to invade and occupy the territory of other countries."[12]

How do the social imperialists dominate their socialist allies? The Chinese analysis of the goals and methods of social imperialism closely parallels early American analyses of the Cold War.

The fundamental objective of the Soviet revisionist renegade clique's control and occupation of some East European countries is not only to turn these into its colonies and dependencies where it could do whatever it likes and plunder at will, but also to use this area as a base for further expansion abroad. . . .[13]

Social imperialism, like the more common theories of capitalist imperialism, has a deep economic basis. The Chinese see interdependence and international economic specialization as sources of domination and exploitation. "Production specialization" allows the Soviet revisionists to control the foreign trade of other member countries of the Council for Mutual Economic Aid (C.M.E.A.).[14] Like U.S. domination of Latin American trade, the foreign trade of Eastern Europe has "fallen into the clutches of the Soviet revisionists who manipulate and influence those countries' foreign trade at will."[15] The Soviet revisionists use their position of political and military dominance to manipulate the terms of trade in their favor. "It should be pointed out that Soviet revisionism's so-called 'aid' and 'loans' to the 'CMEA' member countries are not in cash but are unsalable products and equipment sent to these countries at exorbitant prices."

> "Co-ordination" of economic plans means that the national economic plans drawn up by the CMEA states themselves should be co-ordinated on the basis of the principle of the "international division of labor" and according to the needs of the Soviet revisionist social-imperialists. Everything needed by the Soviet revisionists must be included in the plans and produced according to the time, quality and quantity stipulated; everything they do not need must be produced in reduced quantity or not produced at all. In this way, the national economic plans of other CMEA states are entirely geared to the predatory needs of the Soviet revisionist social-imperialists. National independence and sovereignty have completely disappeared; what is left for all to see are the undisguised relations between Soviet revisionism as a suzerain state and its colonies.[17]

The Soviet Union directly controls the vital branches of the national economies of C.M.E.A. countries through various functional agencies of what the Chinese cynically call "organizations for economic co-operation."[18]

How is this system of economic domination maintained and rationalized? According to the Chinese, Soviet economic exploitation of Eastern Europe is based on the "fascist theories" of limited sovereignty and the international dictatorship of the proletariat.

> In the name of the "international division of labor" and "specialization," it [the U.S.S.R.] strives to achieve so-called

"economic integration" in the "community," subjecting the
economy of these countries to its own needs, turning them
into its economic appendages and plundering their wealth. It
has converted the "Warsaw Treaty Organization" into an
instrument for realizing its social-imperialist designs.[19]

The Soviet Union has adopted the "most despotic and vicious
methods to keep these countries under strict control" and like the
U.S., it is "acting as a world gendarme."[20]

These Soviet policies have been gathered under the Brezhnev
Doctorine. Speaking in Warsaw on November 12, 1968 to the Fifth
Congress of the Polish United Workers Party, Brezhnev emphasized
the need for "strict respect" for sovereignty of other socialist
countries but added:

When internal and external forces that are hostile to
Socialism try to turn the development of some socialist
country towards the restoration of a capitalist regime, when
socialism in that country and the socialist community as a
whole is threatened, it becomes not only a problem of the
people of the country concerned, but a common problem
and concern of all Socialist countries. Naturally an action
such as military assistance to a fraternal country designed to
avert the threat to the social system is an extraordinary step,
dictated by necessity.[21]

Such a step, Brezhnev added, "may be taken only in case of direct
actions of the enemies of Socialism within a country and outside it,
actions threatening the common interests of the Socialist camp."[22]

The Chinese have made five major criticisms of the Brezhnev
Doctrine, which they view as an "outright doctrine of hegemony."
First, the theory of "limited sovereignty" is criticized on the grounds
that what the Soviet leaders call the interests of socialism are actually
the "interests of [Soviet] colonialism."[23] The Soviet Union imposes
its "supreme sovereignty" on other countries and peoples so that the
"sovereignty of other countries is 'limited', whereas [the Soviet
Union's] own power is 'unlimited.'"[24]

Second, the Chinese criticize the theory of the "international
dictatorship" as a facade for rationalizing military intervention. The
Chinese condemn the Soviet Union for putting up "the signboard" of
"aid to a fraternal country" and using it to "bully" other countries
such as Czechoslovakia. The Chinese ask the Soviet Union:

What difference is there between this and the invasion of

China by the allied forces of eight powers in 1900, the 14-nation armed intervention in the Soviet Union and the "16-nation" aggression organized by U.S. imperialism against Korea... [?] [25]

Third, the theory of "socialist community" is seen by the Chinese as a synonym for a colonial empire with the Soviet Union as a metropolitan state. This attempt at domination subverts the relationship which should exist between genuine socialist states, built on principles of complete equality, respect for state sovereignty and independence, non-interference in each other's internal affairs, and the internationalist axiom of mutual support. [26]

Fourth, the theory of "international division of labour" denies national economic autonomy. The Chinese quote this statement from a report by A.N. Kosygin to the 23rd Party Congress on April 5, 1966:

This co-operation enables the Soviet Union to make better use of the international division of labour. We shall be able to purchase in these countries increasing quantities of their traditional export commodities—cotton, wool, skins and hides, dressed non-ferrous ores, vegetable oil, fruit, coffee, cocoa beans, tea and other raw materials, and a variety of manufactured goods. [27]

The Chinese suggest that this "traditional export commodities" list might have been more complete if petroleum, rubber, meat, vegetables, rice, jute, cane sugar, and similar products had been added. [28] The "international division of labour" is a means for infiltrating, controlling, and plundering the Asian, African, and Latin American countries.

Fifth, the theory that "our interests are involved" is equated with American policy of *Pax Americana* as expressed by Lyndon Johnson and a generation of high American officials. The Chinese rhetorically ask whether a country can send its gunboats everywhere to carry out intimidation and aggression because it "has extensive international contacts." Indeed, the use of national interest is a poor disguise for great power aggression.

What is the relationship between social imperialism and the Third World? Like its forerunner, capitalist imperialism, social imperialism exploits the nations of Asia, Africa, and Latin America. The Chinese explain Soviet policy in the Third World in terms which echo Hobson-Leninist explanations of capitalist imperialism.

The Soviet revisionist renegade clique's expansion in Asian,

African and Latin American regions reveals its social-imperialist nature of aggression as well as its feebleness which is characteristic of a paper tiger. Its "aid" to Asian, African and Latin American countries consists mostly of items for heavy industry, such as mining, metallurgy and power plants. This is because the lopsided development of its economy has resulted in large stockpiles of machines and equipment—products of heavy industry—and it is anxiously looking for markets abroad to dump these outdated machines in an effort to extricate itself from the difficulties in production at the expense of the Asian, African and Latin American people.[29]

Chinese allegations against Soviet policies in the Third World are virtually identical with radical criticisms of American policies in the same area. Consider the following categories:

Economic aid. In providing "aid," Soviet revisionism aims not only at fleecing Asian, African and Latin American people; what is more important, it wants to dominate the recipient countries politically so as to establish a colonial rule. . . . Its aid is adapted to and closely co-ordinated with its counterrevolutionary global strategy.[30]

Military aid. Through its military "aid," Soviet revisionism controls the armed forces and key military departments of the recipient countries, takes their military training and operation into its own hands, enjoys military privileges, and establishes military bases there.[31]

Technical assistance and transfers of technology. The Soviet revisionists dump old machines and equipment in Asia, Africa, and Latin America, usually at prices 20 or 30 percent higher than those on the world market. Many of the machines and equipment supplied by the Soviet revisionists are long out-of-date.[32]

Long-term loans. Although the Soviet revisionists only ask a nominal 2.5 per cent rate of interest on their loans, the actual high rate of interest is felt in the high prices for the goods they supply. This is in essence disguised usury. Moreover, the interest is to be paid a year after delivery of the equipment. The Soviet revisionists who use "aid" as a means of dumping also make it a rule that their loans must be spent on Soviet goods. They really leave no stone unturned in bleeding the people white.[33]

TABLE I. CHINESE CONCEPTUALIZATION OF SOCIAL IMPERIALISM

CRITERIA	WITHIN COMMUNIST BLOC	WITHIN THIRD WORLD
Economic and Political Causes	Revisionism Great power chauvinism	Lopsided industrial development Need for foreign markets
System of International Stratification	Superpower oligarchy (peaceful coexistence and spheres of influence)	Indirect neo-imperialist domination
Economic Goals	Economic integration and Specialization through international division of labor	Markets and access to primary goods
Economic Means	C.M.E.A. (integration into Soviet international system) Manipulation of terms of trade Economic dependence on Soviet Union	Loans Technical assistance
Military Means	Warsaw Pact (military integration) Military integration	Arms sales Military training Concessions of military Bases
Sanctions	Military intervention	Withdrawl of aid (implied)
Ideological Props	Limited sovereignty International dictatorship Socialist community International division of labor Our interests are involved	Aid and assistance other than that coming from capitalist powers

Some reflections. The rhetoric which the Chinese use in criticizing social imperialism, which is summarized in Table I, has several levels of meaning. At a superficial level, we might dismiss Chinese rhetoric as a propaganda ploy to discredit Soviet behavior within the world communist movement and throughout the Third World. At another level, it expresses the Chinese anxiety about the direction of Soviet society and the use of Soviet power abroad, especially against China.[34] Chinese reaction to the Soviet invasion of Czechoslovakia cannot be divorced from China's anxiety about a potential Soviet invasion into China. At still another level, the Chinese resentment of Western and Russian (the frequent use of "new tsars") imperialism in China. Having been a victim of Western imperialism and Japanese aggression, the Chinese have a very high sense of empathy for the contemporary victims of all forms of great power imperialism. More immediately, Chinese rhetoric seems to express Chinese perceptions of their own experience with the Soviet Union. When the Chinese criticize Soviet economic loans as usurious, they are probably expressing resentment for the economic hardships experienced in paying off Soviet loans made during the Korean War. Chinese criticism of Soviet technical assistance as a way of dumping obsolete equipment at a good price is, indeed, related to their own experiences. At still another level, Chinese rhetoric may be a mechanism for legitimizing (and rationalizing) Maoist policies of national economic autonomy and self-reliance. The vivid accounts of the "plunder" of East Europe by social imperialism, if accepted, make the policies of self-reliance look very good. Finally, the rhetoric of opposition to social imperialism seems to be an attempt to place the reality of Soviet foreign policy and Sino-Soviet relations into a conceptual framework which not only updates conventional Marxist-Leninist tenets but which also has propaganda appeal in the Third World.

In order to evaluate the descriptive power of these Chinese perceptions, we need to explore some basic aspects of Chinese relations with the Soviet Union in the 1950's. Were the Chinese becoming economically and technologically dependent on the Soviet Union?

II. THE STRUCTURE OF ECONOMIC
AND TECHNOLOGICAL DEPENDENCE

A. *The Meaning of Economic Dependence*

While the concept of dependency has its origins among students of U.S. foreign policy in Latin America, it has wider applicability. As the concept will be used here, dependence is created not by military intervention or gunboat diplomacy, control mechanisms more readily associated with prolonged occupation and the concepts of colonialism and imperialism. Rather, dependence refers to day-to-day and peaceful economic relations between dominant and subordinate states. Dependence is a situation in which the economy of one country is conditioned by the needs and interests of another country. Economic development in the dependency is a reflection of the growth and expansion of the hegemonic power.[35] There results an international stratification among dominant and subordinate states in which decisions made in the dominant state determine the pace, direction, and content of economic growth and development in the subordinate state. The development alternatives open to the subordinate state are defined and limited by its integration into and functions within the world market.[36]

This system of international stratification is not necessarily malevolent, for it may have a strongly paternalistic, even benevolent, quality. There are a number of positive economic returns to the dependency in terms of capital, production, and technology. However, the beneficence is at best a "trickling down of wealth and prosperity." Accordingly, great wealth among the elite in the dominant country brings moderate wealth to the middle classes in the dominant country and to the elite in the subordinate country.[37] This in turn may eventually uplift the downtrodden in the Third World—if a number of optimistic assumptions about economic growth, income distribution, and population growth rates are made.

B. *The Meaning of Technological Dependence*

The transfer of technology from one country to another can easily become addictive for the recipient country. Plants and machinery constructed with a particular type of technology are not readily adaptable to factories constructed on a different technology. Multi-million dollar industries can be crippled if for some reason a foreign supplier decides to withhold parts. While foreign ownership can be quickly terminated by expropriation, technological dependence cannot be so easily ended:

> Technology is so strong a factor that if its stream runs in only one direction it can determine not only the quantity and quality of production, but the lines and methods of production as well. Patents are only frontier markers of the effective borderlines against intruders. Whoever controls technology can determine the market within which products developed on the basis of that technology can be sold and

used. Therefore, the stream of technology is equivalent to the stream of control.[38]

Technological dependence may be a universal phenomenon but it has its greatest impact on the countries of the Third World, because their technical incapacity to produce capital goods requires them to import modern technology. Underdevelopment is characterized by a structural incapacity to produce the capital goods required for economic growth. The conventional answer to this problem in recent decades has been to adopt foreign techniques. While the short-term gains appear to be very great, the underdeveloped country virtually surrenders to the dominant country—or its leading corporations—the direction and pace of development. Radical critics of technological dependency argue that it fosters international and local inequality, unemployment, regional and social polarization, social marginality, decapitalization, foreign indebtedness, and restricted growth.[39]

III. CHINA'S DEPENDENCE ON THE SOVIET UNION

A. *Military-economic Dependence*

China's experience with the Soviet Union provides some useful insight into the nature of dependence. China's case, however, may be somewhat unique, for economic dependence seems in the first instance to have been created by Soviet military aid.[40] On February 14, 1950, a Treaty of Friendship, Alliance, and Mutual Assistance was signed in Moscow. An economic development loan of $300 million from the Soviet Union was included in the agreement.[41] The protocols for military assistance were not published, but it is clear that arrangements were made for the Soviet Union to supply material and training, since a Soviet military mission was established in Peking and an estimated 3,000 Soviet military advisers were sent to China.[42]

With China's entrance into the Korean War, military expenditures grew to 48 percent of the Chinese budget by 1951.[43] The military aid program was comprehensive and expensive since the Chinese were compelled to *purchase* military supplies received from the Soviet Union. Given the circumstances in Korea, the Chinese had no real choice but to accept the Soviet terms. And even beyond the immediate threat posed by the American presence in Korea, modernization of the Chinese military establishment required production, logistics, and communications systems that would have been impossible for China to obtain elsewhere.[44]

In the process of responding to the American encroachment along the Yalu River and later of modernizing its military forces,

China incurred heavy debts to the Soviet Union. While estimates vary, these debts may have amounted to as much as two billion dollars[45] of which perhaps one-half was covered by Soviet credits.[46] School children reportedly were asked to canvass their neighborhoods for funds to be spent on Soviet tanks and aircraft in 1953.[47] An early indication that the Chinese resented mortgaging their future to the Soviet Union was provided by General Lung Yun, who publicly declared that it was "totally unfair for the People's Republic of China to bear all the expenses of the Korean War."[48] He noted that the United States had forgiven Allied debts in World Wars I and II while the Soviet Union had not forgiven the Chinese debt. He also noted that the Soviet Union had dismantled industrial equipment in Manchuria and shipped it back to Russia. None of this seemed to reflect fraternal comradeship.

Not only were the debts a heavy burden on the Chinese economy, but the Chinese obligation to repay and service her debts to the Soviet Union seriously limited the ability to expand trade with nations outside the bloc. This was at a time when China's balance of payments deficit with Eastern Europe demanded the use of non-bloc currencies. Certainly this foreign exchange requirement could not be met by trade with other underdeveloped countries, which had been conditioned by the Soviet Union to expect that their imports could be paid for by exporting primary products.[49]

As China moved towards military modernization, the flow of Soviet weapons diminished. Unfortunately, however, the balance of payments damage had already taken place. From 1950 to 1955, Chinese imports from the Soviet Union had consistently exceeded exports; but by 1957 China had to export more to the Soviet Union than she imported in order to meet her obligations. The Chinese export surplus totaled 1,900 million rubles from 1956-1958 and persisted in 1959 at a level of 600 million rubles.[50] This reversal in China's trade balance with the Soviet Union reflected the exhaustion of Soviet economic aid credits, which had amounted to only 1,720 million rubles between 1950 and 1954. To put it another way, Chinese exports not only paid for China's imports of Soviet machinery; they also repaid financial obligations to the Soviet Union—partly incurred by the earlier economic credits but mainly incurred by military aid credits.[51]

B. *China's Technological Dependence*

The full impact of Soviet trade and Soviet loans cannot be communicated by numbers. The Chinese received plans, blueprints, technical assistance, technical training, and spare parts from the

Soviet Union. Indeed, the Russians claimed, undoubtedly with some self-congratulatory exaggeration, that "... there is not a single branch of industry in the Chinese People's Republic that does not produce goods from blueprints, technical specifications, technological documentation devised in the USSR and transmitted to China."[52] This section will examine this claim by investigating four forms of technical assistance (dependence): (1) Chinese students in the Soviet Union, (2) Soviet technicians in China, (3) Chinese delegations in the Soviet Union, and (4) the exchange of scientific materials.

1. Chinese Students in the Soviet Union

There is no way of knowing precisely how many Chinese studied in the Soviet Union, for the figures simply are not consistently presented. One Soviet source claims that between 1951 and 1962 more than 8,000 Chinese citizens received on-the-job training in the U.S.S.R.[53] During the same period, over 11,000 Chinese undergraduates studied in Soviet educational institutions, and approximately 1,000 scientists of the Chinese Academy of Science received advanced training in the research institutes of the Academy of Sciences of the U.S.S.R.[54] Thus, some 20,000 students, technicians, and scientists had received advanced training or education in the Soviet Union, according to Soviet sources.

The Chinese sources are reviewed by Leo Orleans. He finds that between 1949-1950 and 1954-1955, some 5,000 Chinese students were sent out of the country for study.[55] Another source reports that between 1950 and 1957 over 6,000 students and postgraduates studied in the Soviet Union.[56] By 1959, that cumulative figure had risen to 14,000, according to another Chinese source.[57] The meaning of the Chinese use of the term "student" is not entirely clear, however. In addition to the 6,000 students who had studied in the Soviet Union by 1958, some 7,000 teachers had received some training and education in the Soviet Union. This latter figure, when added to the 14,000 students, gives a total figure of 21,000, which is reasonably close to the Soviet figure.[58]

If we consider technology a commodity, specialists trained in the Soviet Union are China's purchasing agents of foreign technology. Having been trained in Soviet technology, they would no doubt show a natural preference for and desire to continue using Soviet technology.

2. Soviet Technicians in China

As with the number of Chinese studying in the Soviet Union, the number of Soviet technicians and scientists who were in China is open to dispute. The Soviet Union claims that between 1950 and 1960 more than 10,000 highly skilled Soviet specialists were sent to China.[59] An authoritative Chinese source states that by the end of 1958 there were 7,000 Soviet technicians in China.[60] The total number of Soviet specialists, scientists, technicians, and military advisers may have been significantly more than the cited figures indicate. Kuo Mo-jo expressed in non-quantitative terms the extent of the Soviet contribution to Chinese technological development in May 1957:

> In several years since the liberation, our science, like other branches of the national economy, has been making rapid progress. This is chiefly attributable, apart from the devoted efforts of our own scientists and technicians, to aid given us by the scientists of the Soviet Union. . . . Again, in the formulation of long-term plans for scientific development, the Soviet Academy of Sciences has sent us more than 10 of the finest scientists of the Soviet Union to assist us. Large numbers of Soviet experts in China, and experts of other fraternal countries, too, have taken part in the task.[61]

After 1957, however, the number of Soviet experts in China began to decline sharply. Gerald Clark of the North American Newspaper Alliance wrote after a 1958 visit to China that while there were tens of thousands of Soviet technicians in China in 1956, there were no more than 4,000 by 1958.[62] Whatever their exact number, Soviet technicians in China had a far-reaching influence.

3. Chinese Delegations

There was a considerable amount of scholarly and technical contact in the 1950's between Chinese groups and their counterparts in the Soviet Union. Between 1949 and 1956, over 100 delegations with a total of 1,900 Chinese scholars visited the Soviet Union. [63] Accounts in Chinese sources indicate that several times that number of machinists, engineers, and technicians visited the Soviet Union before 1960.[64] In addition, Chinese scientists participated in Soviet professional meetings and toured scientific installations in the Soviet Union. For example, in 1956 the Chinese Academy of Science sent a mission to the Soviet Union to study the conditions of research work in titanium metallurgy, automation, electronics, electrical engineering, and machinery.[65]

4. Exchange of Scientific Materials

A vast array of written scientific and technical materials came to China from the Soviet Union. The Chinese placed great emphasis on the translation and publication of Soviet scientific and technical literature. From 1949 to 1955, for example, 3,000 Soviet technical books were published with a total printing of 20 million copies.[66] In 1956 the Soviet Academy of Sciences sent about 70,000 books to China while an interlibrary loan arrangement was established with the Lenin Library in Moscow and another library in Leningrad.[67] According to Soviet sources, the Soviet Union provided China with over 24,000 complete sets of scientific-technical documents, including 1,400 designs for major enterprises, between 1954 and 1959.[68] From the Soviet perspective, the exchange was an act of comradely benevolence. As one Soviet writer put it:

> Essentially, all this documentation was transmitted to the CPR gratis even though, according to the estimates of foreign experts, it is worth billions of dollars. The important thing is not so much the value as the fact that nowhere would the CPR have been able to obtain the scientific-technical documentation in the volume necessary for extensive economic construction and, moreover, documentation that would be consistent with the latest advances in science and technology. Not one of the highly developed capitalist countries was willing to help China eliminate its economic backwardness. But even if the capitalist countries had agreed to do so, the CPR would either have had to pay enormous sums of foreign currency (which China did not possess at the time) for this scientific-technical aid or would have had to sacrifice its political and economic independence.[69]

Thus, the Soviet Union believed that China was receiving a great deal of technical assistance for nothing. The Chinese, on the other hand, became increasingly aware of the political costs of this "free" technical assistance.

C. Industrial Location and Transportation: Symptoms of Economic Dependence

A potential symptom of Chinese economic dependence on the Soviet Union is the physical distribution of the approximately 200 major industrial enterprises which the Soviet Union helped construct in China.[70] While considerable growth has taken place in the established industrial centers, China's general policy toward industrial location has been dispersion, as evidenced by the emergence of new industrial cities.[71] However, Soviet aid projects attempted to skew the dispersion policy by shifting the focus of industrialization toward the Soviet border. Yuan-li Wu, in a major study of industrial location in China, shows that Soviet aid was an important element in the determination of location policy although he does not see that influence contradicting China's location policy of shifting industry away from the coastal provinces.[72] If we assume Sino-Soviet amity, industry located along the Soviet border might be considered consistent with the security goals implicit in shifting industry away from the eastern coastal regions. However, if we acknowledge the potential for Sino-Soviet conflict, the focus of Soviet aid projects only responds to the letter of China's security interests, not the spirit of those interests.

The data presented in Table II compares the distribution of 132 Soviet aid projects with a frequency distribution of 328 production locations for industrial groups in 26 provinces and autonomous regions. If the Soviet Union considered geographic propinquity a factor in international political and economic influence, as the whole

TABLE II. THE RELATIVE BIAS
OF INDUSTRIAL LOCATIONS AND AUTONOMOUS REGIONS
ON OR NEAR THE SOVIET BORDER

PROVINCE (N=7)	DISTRIBUTION OF SOVIET AID FOR INDUSTRIAL PROJECTS (N=132)	FREQUENCY DISTRIBUTION OF PRODUCTION LOCATIONS BY INDUSTRY GROUPS (N=328)
Liaoning[a]	37	16
Kirin	8	15
Heilungkiang	20	15
Ningsia	0	3
Kansu	5	7
Sinkiang	2	8
Inner Mongolia	7	15
TOTAL	79	79
As percent of sample	60%	24%

Source: YUAN-LI WU, THE SPATIAL ECONOMY OF COMMUNIST CHINA, 242, 237 (Tables C-3, B-3, 1967). Based on the following sources: Yeh-hui Haiao, *Fei-O Ching-chi Kuan-hai chih Yen-chiu* [A Study of Sino-Russian Relations], 2 FEI-CHING YEN-CHIN [Communist China Research] 63-64 (No. 6, 1963); and a variety of sources listed at 233.

[a]While not adjacent to the Soviet Border, Liaoning was included in the sample because it is an integral part of northeast China and it has been historically and remains somewhat geographically detached from the locus of Chinese authority.

thrust of Soviet foreign policy seemed to reflect, then the data suggests that the Soviet industrial aid projects were located so as to maximize the potential for further influence. The concentration of Soviet aid projects in the northeast is particularly significant. This area, formerly known as Manchuria, has proven vulnerable to foreign penetration and has been a major target of Russian interest.

While Soviet aid projects have been concentrated along the Soviet border and, in other cases, in the northern section of China, the evidence does not really support the conclusion that Soviet aid has consequences incompatible with China's location policy. Among the primary criteria for location of new industry are these: (1) new projects should be near raw materials and energy resources, (2) new projects should be near markets to cut down on the demand for transportation, (3) new industry should be widely dispersed so as to reduce the gap between the industrial and rural sectors of society, (4) new industry should be widely dispersed so as to achieve a better balance between industry and agriculture in each major economic region of China, and (5) new industry should be dispersed and inland so as to maximize security considerations.[73] The Soviet advice for locating new plants may have been self-serving, but it was simply integrated into a national strategy of dispersion and relocation.[74]

Another possible barometer of Soviet influence is the evolution of China's transportation system since 1949. Much of the new railway construction during the 1950's was aimed at connecting China with the Soviet Union. An indirect indication of this is provided in Table III, which compares the amount of railway construction in the border provinces with the rest of China.

In order to measure the relative influence of the Soviet Union on railway location, four possible location strategies were examined. These are: railway construction concentrated in (1) the interior, (2) the coastal provinces, (3) the Soviet border regions, and (4) the non-coastal regions (including the Soviet border regions). It was assumed (the null hypothesis) that in the absence of any explicit policy or special pressure, railway construction in the post-1949 period would follow the pattern established before 1949.[75] This is not necessarily a good assumption since industrial and railway construction before 1949 reflected Western pressure and Japanese military occupation. However, it does provide a convenient way of testing the variance from the previous locational pattern.

The data presented in Table IV suggest that Soviet aid exerted no special influence on railway location since there was little deviation from the 1949 pattern in the number of railway kilometers located in the border region. The data do support the conclusion that railway construction was pushed in the interior regions of China. Still, since more kilometers of railway lines are in operation in the Soviet border

TABLE III. LENGTH OF IDENTIFIED RAILWAY IN
OPERATION IN PROVINCES AND AUTONOMOUS REGIONS
ON OR NEAR THE SOVIET BORDER AND IN THE
REST OF CHINA, 1949 AND 1963 (IN KILOMETERS)

| PROVINCE | TOTAL | | CHANGE | TRUNK | | BRANCH | |
	1949	*1963*		*1949*	*1963*	*1949*	*1963*
Lianoning	2,273	3,096	823	----	2,283	----	813
Kirin	2.046	2,749	703	----	2,295	----	454
Heilingkiang	2,926	4,132	1,206	----	3,445	----	687
N.E. Subtotal	7,245	9,977	2,732	----	8,023	----	1,954
Ningsia	----	470	470	----	470	----	----
Kansu	74	2,153	2,079	----	2,077	----	76
Sinkiang	----	707	707	----	707	----	
Inner Mongolia	1,073	2,764	1,691	----	2,684	----	80
Total Border Regions	8,392	16,071	7,679	----	17,418	----	2,366
All of China	17,036	34,235	17,199	----	30,350	----	3,885
Non-Border Regions	8,644	18,164	9,520	----		----	

Source: YUAN-LI WU, THE SPATIAL ECONOMY OF COMMUNIST CHINA, 252-261 (Table E-1, 1967). Data based on LING HUNG-HSUN, GENERAL SURVEY OF RAILWAYS IN CHINA (1950) and other unidentified sources.

region than anywhere else in China, we must conclude that the pattern of railway location supported the pre-existing "north China" pattern.

D. *Summary of Findings*

In applying the dependence model to China's relationship with the Soviet Union, five types of evidence have been examined:

1) Soviet loans which may have represented a form of financial penetration;
2) Soviet scientists and technicians in China;
3) Chinese scientists, technicians, and students in the Soviet Union;
4) Technological dependence based on the flow of books, blueprints, and plans coming from the Soviet Union; and
5) Geopolitical factors such as the location of industrial plants and new railway lines.

TABLE IV. SECONDARY ANALYSIS OF DATA ON RAILWAY DISTRIBUTION IN CHINA, 1949—1963 (IN KILOMETERS)

CRITERIA	ALL OF CHINA[a]	INTERIOR[b]	COASTAL[c]	SOVIET BORDER[d]	NON-COASTAL[e]
1949	17,036	3,783	7,134	8,392	9,902
1963	34,235	9,475	11,785	16,071	22,450
Increase	17,199	5,692	4,651	7,679	12,548
Increase (%)	101%	150%	65%	91.5%	126.5%
1949 Kilometric Proportion of 1949 Total	100%	22.2%	41.8%	49.2%	58.2%
Expected	34,235	7,640	14,310	16,860	19,925
Actual	34,235	9,475	11,785	16,071	22,450
Deviation from Expected	0	+1,835	− 2,525	− 789	+ 2,525
Deviation (%)	0	24%	17.7%	4.9%	12.7%

Source: YUAN-LI WU, THE SPATIAL ECONOMY OF COMMUNIST CHINA, 252-61 (Table E-1, 1967).

[a] Column 1 = col. 3 + col. 5;

[a] Column 1 = col. 4 + col. 2 + col. 3—Liaoning (which is classified both a coastal and Soviet border province).

[b] *Interior:* All provinces and autonomous regions not on the coast or contiguous with the Soviet Union: Shansi, Anhwei, Honan, Hupeh, Hunan, Kiangsi, Shensi, Szechwan, Yunnan, Kweichow, Tibet, and Tsinghai.

[c] *Coastal:* All provinces which are at some point contiguous with the Pacific Ocean: Kwangsi, Kwangtung, Fukien, Chekiang, Kiangsu, Shantung, Hopeh, and Liaoning.

[d] *Soviet Border:* All provinces contiguous with the Soviet Union plus Liaoning, which has a high level of geographic propinquity with the Soviet Union: Liaoning, Kirin, Heilungkiang, Ningsia, Kansu, Sinkiang, and Inner Mongolia.

[e] *Non-Coastal:* All provinces and autonomous regions not contiguous with the Pacific Ocean: Shansi, Anhwei, Honan, Hupeh, Kiangsi, Shensi, Szechwan, Yunnan, Kweichow, Tibet, Tsinghai, Kirin, Heilungkiang, Ningsia, Kansu, Sinkiang, and Inner Mongolia.

What is the meaning of this evidence? If the creation of a dependency relationship was the goal of Soviet policy, why did the Soviet Union extend only short-term loans to China? Would it not have been to the Soviet advantage to have extended the period of Chinese indebtedness over many decades with long-term loans?

The exchange of scientific and technical personnel and materials does illustrate the degree to which the Chinese depended on Soviet assistance. But this does not represent the kind of permanent subordination that characterizes the technological dependency of foreign subsidiaries on American multinational corporations, for example. Unlike foreign employees of American corporations, Chinese scientists and technicians returned to their Chinese laboratories and enterprises, places independent of Soviet authority and control.

E. *Dependency Theory and Sino-Soviet Relations*

The commodity composition of Sino-Soviet trade weakly follows the classic dependency pattern; however, the evidence does not support the conclusion that the Chinese had adopted a strategy of import substitution.[76] While the Chinese did, indeed, export primary goods and import industrial goods, the industrial goods were capital, not durable consumer goods. Capital goods would, in time, give China the capacity to produce independently capital as well as consumer goods. This pattern appears more a temporary expedient than the beginning of a permanent and fixed relationship.

If China's economic relationship with the Soviet Union were one of dependency, we should expect to find these kinds of actions on the part of the Soviet Union:

1) Attempts to establish permanent production facilities within the People's Republic of China;
2) Assured Soviet access to Chinese natural resources;
3) Long-term loans which establish financial dependence;
4) Unequal flow of economic resources in favor of the Soviet Union;
5) A pattern of import substitution;
6) A "brain drain" to the Soviet Union;
7) Soviet policy-makers shaping important Chinese economic decisions; and
8) Economic relations used by the Soviet Union to influence Chinese political and military policy.

On the whole, these things do not emerge in Sino-Soviet relations. While the dependency model has heuristic value in analyzing Sino-Soviet relations during the 1950's, those relations are far more subtle and complex than the dependency model suggests.

As Chinese criticisms of "economic integration" suggest, the phrase can have two very different meanings. The integration of two equal partners is not to be confused with the integration of unequal partners in a hierarchical relationship. The *context* of economic integration is perhaps as important as the content and magnitude of such interactions. The Soviet Union had economic alternatives; the Chinese did not.[77]

> The essential thesis developed here is that in light of the under-developed state of the economy and China's greater economic dependence on Russia, rather than vice versa, both the costs and the benefits of the relationship were far more significant to China than for Russia. Such a pattern of dependence provided the Soviets with superior bargaining power in the economic sphere. . . . [78]

The Soviet Union entered these economic interactions as the overwhelmingly dominant leader of the Communist Bloc. Since the American policy of containment effectively excluded China from normal relations with the rest of the international community, the social context of Sino-Soviet interactions was not really one of equality but of hierarchy. This was certainly understood by the Chinese when they referred to the special tasks and obligations of all members of the Communist camp.[79] For example, in 1956 it appears that the Chinese accepted a subordinate position in the hierarchy of authority established by the Soviet Union, for Chou En-lai reported to the Eighth Party Congress that

> [a]s a member of the socialist camp, our country assumes its own share of obligations; we must fulfill this share of obligations. We have the duty towards all the brother nations to supply them with quantities of agricultural products, animal products, mineral resources and certain machine equipment and industrial commodities required in building socialism. We must strive to increase production or adequately reduce domestic consumption to guarantee the supply of these commodities.[80]

The degree of equality or hierarchy in any relationship is at least partially in the eyes of the beholder. Dependency may be not so much a precise empirical condition as a subjective state of mind. In this sense, dependency compares with other concepts which have dominated our thinking about international relations in the last 25 years. Neither security nor deterrence have precise empirical meanings; they are concepts which depend greatly on the subjective perceptions of the participants in the relationship. Thus, to understand dependency in Sino-Soviet relations, we must examine China's perceptions of that relationship. Figure 1 attempts to express this idea.

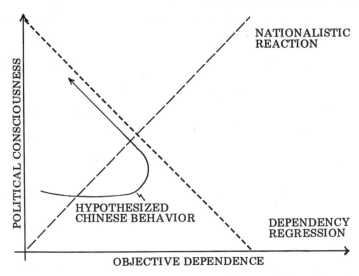

Figure 1. Political Consciousness and Objective Dependence Hypothesis.

Notes: The dashed line with the positive slope represents a nationalistic reaction line. Assuming elite political autonomy, a country's political consciousness will be raised as it becomes more economically and objectively dependent upon another country.

The dotted line with the negative slope is a dependency regression line. In the absence of elite autonomy, objective dependency is associated with a declining level of political consciousness.

In most dependent countries elite behavior conforms to the dependency regression line with extremist groups on the political left and political right following a pattern of behavior similar to the nationalistic reaction line.

The solid line with an arrow represents, in very rough terms, the progression of Chinese behavior over time. The Chinese embarked on the policy of "leaning to one side" with a fairly high level of political consciousness, but also with limited international options. The First Five-Year Plan increased their dependency without having a decisive effect on the level of political consciousness in China. However, Chinese behavior was in the direction of the dependency regression line. The Great Leap Forward and the People's Commune Movement represented a decisive turn in Chinese policy and behavior, designed to achieve a high level of self-reliance.

Dependency is a relative concept in the sense that the degree of dependency is not determined solely by economic data. Cuban policy after the revolution, Chilean policy under Allende, Rumanian economic policy, and China's policy of self-reliance after the First Five-Year Plan all indicate that a strong leadership can terminate a dependency relationship. These deviant cases tentatively suggest that there has perhaps been too much economic determinism in writing about dependency. To adapt a Maoist phrase, in cases where the national leadership is strong and independent, politics commands economics.[81]

IV. CHINA'S RECOGNITION OF DEPENDENCE

A. *Possible Reasons for Chinese Disenchantment*

Whatever the empirical evidence of Chinese dependence, the subjective meaning of the evidence was important to the Chinese. Sometime after 1955 there was growing awareness within the Chinese Communist elite of their dependence on the Soviet Union. While it is beyond the scope of this study to delineate the intra-Party differences in these perceptions, this section will attempt to explain why the Maoist segment of the Chinese elite became disenchanted with Soviet aid and increasingly conscious of the costs and liabilities of dependence. Eight explanatory hypotheses will be explored.

Hypothesis 1: Ethnocentrism. Ethnocentrism is a cultural condition which is not necessarily constant over time. In 1949 the Chinese had few options other than reliance on the Soviet Union for diplomatic support, economic assistance, and military alliance. The American involvement in Korea and the subsequent need for a Chinese response to the American/U.N. military movement towards the Chinese border did little to enhance China's options. Whatever the long-term influence of ethnocentrism on the Chinese Communist elite, the objective need for Soviet assistance outweighed whatever psychic costs were involved. By the late 1950's, however, China's consciousness of a separate cultural identity could more readily assert itself after nearly a decade of remarkable economic growth. Thus, the positive economic benefits of dependence created conditions which increased the consciousness of dependence within the Chinese Communist elite. Once the material conditions within China improved or the international context of Chinese foreign policy vis-à-vis the United States began to change, it became inevitable that the Chinese would find their hierarchical relationship with the Soviet Union increasingly unacceptable.

Hypothesis 2: The history of the Chinese revolutionary movement. The history of the Chinese Communist revolutionary movement may also have been a conditioning factor in the eventual Chinese rejection of dependency. One of the central lessons of China's civil war experience was the importance of self-reliance. To some extent, the remarkable turnabout in the relative fortunes of the Kuomintang and the Communists hinged on the issue of self-reliance.

The Communists were forced to be self-reliant by the exigencies of geography and conflict. After the American entry into the war against Japan, the Kuomintang lost whatever incentive they had to be self-reliant.

Another important historical factor may well have been the assertion of Mao Tse-tung's leadership in spite of the opposition of the Comintern. In no way could Mao Tse-tung be construed as the hand-maiden of Soviet interests in China. Indeed, at several junctures, his policy preferences rejected Soviet advice on how to conduct a revolution and a civil war in China. How people make utility calculations is affected by their experiences, and Mao Tse-tung's experiences definitely emphasized the importance of self-reliance. This linkage between revolutionary experience and developmental policy was made by a Chinese economist about a year before the Cultural Revolution. He wrote:

> Comrade Mao Tse-tung's thought on self-reliance is applicable not only to a war of resistance against foreign aggression, but also to the revolutionary civil war. It is applicable not only to the construction of bases before the victory of the revolution, but also to socialist construction after the victory of the revolution.[82]

Hypothesis 3: Factor endowments. China's factor endowments made the Soviet model of development, which emphasized heavy industry at the expense of agricultural development, something less than optimal. The rejection of the Soviet model inevitably raised issues about China's economic and technological relationship with the Soviet Union. If, for example, Soviet aid adversely influenced China's allocation of capital resources between industry and agriculture, a new inter-sector allocation strategy would necessarily imply a new relationship with the Soviet Union. Moreover, the Soviet model of centralized planning and administration might have run counter to the Maoist emphasis on mass labor mobilization, and the Soviet preference for coercive organizational tools of social control might have frustrated the Chinese need to build on the commitment and industry of the Chinese people. To the extent that the Chinese were conscious of the fact that Soviet aid distorted their development programs, they would perceive China as dependent on the Soviet Union.

Hypothesis 4: Organization. Since the Cultural Revolution, we understand more clearly that the Soviet organizational model was unacceptable to Mao Tse-tung. His emphasis on egalitarianism, elite-mass integration, intensive local-level political participation, and regional decentralization operated against staying in the Soviet organizational mode. This orientation probably sensitized Mao and his associates to the indirect costs of dependency more readily than those with a more elitest or bureaucratic orientation.

Hypothesis 5: Adverse economic terms. A significant economic barometer is the trade balance between China and Russia. This balance was altered significantly in 1955-1956, so that Chinese exports to the Soviet Union exceeded imports from the Soviet Union. According to William E. Griffith,

> [f]rom 1955 to 1956 the Chinese began to repay their debts by substantially increasing their deliveries, whereas the Soviets reduced their exports. . . . Soviet exports to China thus declined markedly from 1956 through 1958, while Soviet-Indian trade jumped more than 500 percent in 1956 and nearly doubled again by 1958. Similarly, the temporary upsurge of Soviet exports during the 1959 and 1960 period again coincided with a simultaneous slump in exports to India.[83]

There is some evidence—at least in the *post factum* sense—that the Chinese became very conscious of the adverse terms of Soviet loans and Soviet trade. Fraternal comradeship was increasingly perceived as a form of indirect economic exploitation. Since the Chinese had at least some interest in securing assistance from the Soviet Union, they were reluctant to express dissatisfaction about the terms of their economic interactions with the Soviet Union until after 1960. Unfortunately, it is difficult to judge whether such accusations reflect current hostility or earlier assessments of the harshness of Soviet economic policies. Oleg Hoeffding writes that:

> . . . as to trade and financial relations . . . one gets the impression that the Chinese grievances stem not from agreements "torn up," [in 1960] but from old agreements harsh in the first place and literally enforced, and from agreements newly negotiated—against the background of political tension and economic crisis—which must have struck the Chinese as niggardly, Shylock-like, and fratricidal rather than fraternal.[84]

Illustrative of the literal enforcement of the terms of the Sino-Soviet agreements was the fact that the Soviet Union insisted on collecting debt service installments from China even in 1958 and 1959 when China's need to finance its imports from the Soviet Union was straining Chinese export resources to the limit. To add insult to injury, Mongolia and North Vietnam among other countries were at the same time treated to a bounty of Soviet economic credits and even waivers or deferments on payments of debts previously incurred.[85]

The transformation of Chinese perceptions is summarized in Table V. The "generous donor" gives "socialist aid" while the "neo-imperialist exploiter" gives "imperialist aid." True socialist aid is "based upon proletarian internationalism" and is extended or accepted by a country, "not for its own interests but for the common interests of the international proletariat."[86] Social imperialist aid is designed to "prohibit the fraternal countries from developing their economy independently under the signboard of. . .'economic mutual aid'" and thereby force recipients to supply raw materials and serve as a market for exported industrial goods.[87] In essence, the Chinese now apply to themselves the same noble attributes they once attributed to the Soviet Union. They also apply the same pejoratives to the Soviet Union they once reserved only for the United States and other capitalist powers.

TABLE V. CHINA'S PERCEPTION OF INTERNATIONAL ASSISTANCE

TIME	RECIPIENT	GENEROUS DONOR	NEO-IMPERIALIST EXPLOITER
1949– 1958	China	Soviet Union	U.S. Capitalism
1960– 1974	Third World	China	U.S. Capitalism Soviet Social Imperialism

Hypothesis 6: National Security. Another factor, which may have reinforced the subjective perception of dependence more strongly than it caused the perception, is the question of national security. This issue has at least two ramifications in the context of China's cognizance of dependence on the Soviet Union. First, the Chinese were somewhat dependent on the Soviet Union for information about nuclear weapons development, material inputs, and technical assistance.[88] In 1963 the Chinese claimed:

As far back as June 10, 1959, when there was not yet the slightest sign of a treaty on stopping nuclear tests, the Soviet government unilaterally tore up the agreement on new technology for national defense concluded between China and the Soviet Union on October 15, 1957, and refused to provide China with a sample of an atomic bomb and technical data concerning its manufacture. This was done as a presentation gift at the time the Soviet leader went to the United States for talks with Eisenhower in September.[89]

Second, the Chinese realized after the Quemoy Crisis of 1958 that their foreign policy options were constrained by dependence on the Soviet nuclear umbrella. The Soviet nuclear monopoly plus unreliability of the Soviet deterrent undoubtedly prompted the Chinese leadership to think through a whole series of questions about China's technological and economic dependence on the Soviet Union.

Hypothesis 7: International Stratification. The Maoist leadership probably became increasingly conscious of the evolution of a hierarchical relationship between themselves and the leadership of the Communist Party of the Soviet Union. Countries which have been humiliated and suppressed are more sensitive to hierarchical and status distinctions than other countries, especially when the humiliation is juxtaposed against historical grandeur. Not surprisingly, the most perceptive analyses of international stratification have come in recent years from Chinese sources. The Chinese are extraordinarily sensitive to the collective status deprivation suffered by China in the last 100 years at the hands of the West and Japan.

On most matters, the Chinese are pragmatic, but on the question of status they have proven unbending. Chinese reactions to the Test Ban Treaty and to the Non-Proliferation Agreement reflect not only short-term Chinese national interests but the long-term sensitivity of a "have not" to the prerogatives of a great power. The primacy that the Chinese give to the question of "principle" in border negotiations may have similar origins. Finally, Chinese statements about Soviet behavior and foreign aid programs reflect a high sensitivity to the status costs of international economic dependence. At some point (probably late in 1957), the Chinese decided that Sino-Soviet economic relationships were not based on equality, reciprocal benefit, mutual respect, or non-interference.

Hypothesis 8: Co-optation. Reliance on Soviet loans and technical assistance had a number of social and political ramifications within China. For example, sending students to the Soviet Union probably reinforced the elitest qualities of Chinese education. Special examinations were held by the Ministry of Higher Education to insure the quality of students going abroad, which inevitably excluded bright but unpolished youth from the countryside. The Kao Kang affair indicated the possibility of a member of the Chinese Communist leadership being co-opted by ambition and probable Soviet support. The removal of Peng Teh-huai illustrated, in part, the dangers of Soviet-style professionalism, at least from the perspective of the Maoist revolutionary style.

In a sense, the political culture of China's revolution was being corrupted by the symbols and methods of Soviet communism. In this context, there is a real affinity between DeGaulle's reaction to French dependency on the United States and Mao's reaction to Chinese dependency on the Soviet Union. It is not simply a question of economics or technology or even politics; it is a question of culture and identity.

B. *The Chinese Leadership and Co-optation*

Since co-optation may be the central factor in Mao Tse-tung's reaction to continued reliance on the Soviet Union, it might be appropriate to examine the process at some length. In his classic study of the Tennessee Valley Authority (T.V.A.), Philip Selznick defined co-optation as "the process of absorbing new elements into the leadership or policy-determining structure of an organization as a means of averting threats to its ability or existence."[90] Authorities normally prefer to limit participation in policy-making to those elements most susceptible to control, but co-optation involves yielding access to the most difficult and threatening partisans.

Economic dependency in the Third World, with or without industrialization in the dependent country, tends to transform the local elite into a clientele social class. While the indigenous ruling class possesses political sovereignty, it performs important functions on behalf of foreign interests. In exchange, the foreign interests and/or their governments insure wealth, power, and privilege to the colonials.[91] The local ruling elite becomes the junior partner of the metropolitan interests.

Since the basis of China's special relationship with the Soviet Union was politically and ideologically based rather than a product of corporate economics, members of the Chinese Communist Party, not the industrial bourgeoisie, might be expected to be potential targets of co-optation. However, Party leaders and cadres in China had established a high degree of autonomy in their long years of revolutionary and civil strife. Moreover, their interaction with the Soviet Union was relatively restricted and focused on political and ideological matters, issues which are more subject to conflict.

Consequently, the groups most subject to co-optation in China were the bourgeoisie, the technocrats, certain types of intellectuals, and the professional military officer corps. As Table VI suggests, the operative process in co-optation is emulation, which is a form of inter-elite psychological dependence.[72] Selected strategic elites in China emulated the role performance, organizational style, and activities of their counterparts in the Soviet Union.

TABLE VI. SOVIET CO-OPTATION OF STRATEGIC ELITES IN CHINA

ELITE	SOURCE OF CONTACT	DISTORTED INTEREST	OPERATIVE PROCESS
Bourgeoisie	Visits, Study	Disregard for mass line and mobilization techniques	Emulation
Technocrats	Visits, Training, Advisers	Commitment to serve the people	Emulation
Military Professionals	Training, Advisers, Technology	Commitment to serve the people	Emulation

Co-optation across national boundaries is best understood as a process in which the goals of the local elite and satellite classes are shaped to conform to the political and economic needs and styles of foreign interests. There are two requirements for the successful accomplishment of this process. First, the local elite must imitate the political style of the hegemonic elite. This is done through "demonstration effect" and a variety of rewards and bribes. Second, the local elite are shown that the best way to achieve the new goals is cooperation with foreign interests. The lesson to be learned is that the pursuit of goals in conflict with those of the dominant country involves unacceptable costs, particularly in contrast to the rewards of cooperating with the dominant country. The two requirements are interactive and mutually reinforcing.[93] A preliminary attempt has been made to explore this hypothesis more fully. A sample of 31 titles were selected from the bibliography of the *Journal of Asian Studies* (1958-1971). The articles were selected on the basis of whether their titles gave some indication of criticism of intellectuals, scientists, and technocrats. The result of the research was the identification of six themes which reflect some perception of dependence upon, or co-optation by, the Soviet Union of strategic elites within the People's Republic. Each theme also suggests a desire on the part of the Chinese leadership to regenerate revolutionary ardor.

1. *Adherence to the foreign slave mentality.*

This theme represents an explicit criticism of those strategic elites whom the Maoist leadership viewed as being co-opted by the Soviet Union, and implies acceptance of the goals and methods of a foreign country. For example,

> [t] he revisionist line of China's Khrushchev and his agents in scientific circles promoted an attitude of slavishness and crawling behind foreign science so that the work on the telescope was greatly hampered.[94]

Chinese intellectuals, scientists, and technocrats who had been sent to the Soviet Union for advanced training or who had closely worked with Soviet personnel in China were the most likely victims of the foreign slave mentality. Indeed, these strategic elites had been conditioned by earlier Chinese policies and by the Soviet personnel with whom they interacted to believe that Soviet methods, attitudes, and goals were correct and superior with respect to development. Why else would their government have sent them to study these methods? Once China embarked upon a policy of self-reliant development, this attitude became a major liability.

2. *The use of experts.*

To advocate the use of experts was, in the eyes of the Maoists, to assert a principle that was in direct opposition to certain central tenets of the Chinese revolution, that a revolution should be carried out for and by the masses. In various criticisms, the linkage between experts and things foreign was invariably very strong. Advocating the use of experts was synonymous with believing that foreigners could aid China in her development better than the Chinese people themselves:

> The more than 30 workers and technicians of the Hukuang Scientific Instruments Factory average only 25 years of age. Together with workers in the factory, they thoroughly repudiated. . .the slavish ideology of the plant's few reactionary bourgeois "experts" or [those who] worshipped everything foreign.[95]

Liu Shao-ch'i was criticized for being concerned that once China was "divorced from foreign data or experts, there is no way to master new techniques and for the Chinese people to make innovations."[96] Whether Liu actually represented this view is not crucial in the context of this paper; that it was expressed within the Chinese leadership reflects a high level of co-optation with little respect for the inherent capabilities of the masses in which Mao so strongly believed.

3. *The one-sided pursuit of high standards.*

Anyone who one-sidedly pursued high standards must, according to Maoist criticisms, be doing so from foreign influence rather than revolutionary Chinese experience.

> Affected by the knowledge they acquired from foreigners before 1957, some designers appeared to have certain undesirable tendencies, such as the adoption of foreign frameworks and one-sided pursuit of high standards.[97]

> Last year, an inspection of the designing revolutionization movement revealed some of the following tendencies: one-sided seeking of big and comprehensive projects; pursuit of high standards, style and beauty. . .and uncritically worshipping foreign and ancient designs.[98]

No evidence was uncovered to directly link one-sided pursuit of high standards and interaction with Soviet specialists or training in the Soviet Union. However, the charges remain.

4. *Being divorced from politics, practice, and the masses.*

The very essence of the Maoist revolutionary experience can be defined in terms of politics, practice, and integration with the masses. Contrary attitudes are taken to deny revolutionary China and embrace identification with a foreign country, particularly the Soviet Union.

> [Bourgeois technical authorities] planned to oust all technicians who were not university graduates from the research institute, so that they might build a research unit consisting of purely foreign students and university graduates with the bourgeois "authorities" as the "leading body" in a vain attempt to exclude the worker-peasant masses from the door of science and technique.[99]

If the phrase "China's Khrushchev" is more than a clever tactical device to discredit a political opponent, and is a symbolic rejection of things foreign and things Soviet, then the following is suggestive:

"... China's Khrushchev and his pawns did everything within their power to lead the research work in farm machines and tools astray and away from the masses."[100] In contrast, the Maoist or true revolutionary approach advocated "[t]aking the direction pointed out by Chairman Mao, [for which] research workers left their laboratories and went to live and labour with factory workers . . . ."[101] The Soviet technicians' purpose in China was not to urge the masses on to greater technical accomplishments, but to aid and instruct Chinese scientists, technicians, and other specialized personnel. From a Maoist perspective, the scientists and technicians who came into daily contact with Soviet personnel must surely have been pulled away from their fellow countrymen.

5. *Following a creeping line in scientific and technical fields.*
The "creeping line" or passive approach to development is most emphatically perceived as an attitude that is at best non-Chinese and at worst anti-Chinese. To passively wait for others to make technical progress is an admission that foreign techniques are superior to Chinese techniques.

China's Khrushchev prostrated himself before the foreigners, and put forward a creeping line in the technical field.[102]

The complete smashing of China's Khrushchev's creeping line and the eradication of the foreign slave mentality peculiar to the Chinese bourgeois intellectuals will quickly raise China's agriculture mechanization to a new level.[103]

The self-reliant and independent road to development is based, in part, on the belief in the innate capacity of the masses to forge ahead and create new technology:

Apart from this, the design sector should take the initiative to promote, organize, and demand that scientific research institutes, schools, production units, and sectors study and develop new technology, instead of passively waiting for others to make progress.[104]

6. *Refusing to place Mao's thought in command of science and technology.*
Those who oppose or question the Maoist approach to development are undoubtedly associated with Soviet methods and attitudes. Mao postulates that an independent and self-reliant policy should be pursued and that all remnants of Soviet aid and influence should be purged from Chinese society. Those who advocate that

China should accept Soviet assistance and follow the Soviet method of development for a socialist society reveal their dependence upon the Soviet Union.

> This line of learning, buying, and stealing from foreigners is entirely opposed to the policy of "relying on one's own efforts and rising in great vigor" which Chairman Mao has consistently advocated.[105]

> Chairman Mao's "independent and self-reliant" policy illuminates the forward road of our industrial development and lays bare the features of Liu Shao-ch'i who wants our industry to be dependent on imperialism and modern revisionism forever.[106]

The key question, which has yet to be empirically answered, is whether those who actually expressed a pro-Soviet orientation and/or rejected the Maoist approach to independent and self-reliant development were the Chinese who had been trained in the Soviet Union or had been in contact with Soviet technicians in China. What has been established is that Maoist criticisms of scientists and technicians make a symbolic connection between advocacy of certain policies and co-optation of strategic scientific elites.

C. Assessment of the Reasons for the Chinese Disenchantment

The propositions presented in this fourth section of the paper have attempted to explain why the Chinese rejected reliance on Soviet aid and assistance. The amount of space given to each proposition, by way of a first approximation, represents my rank ordering of the explanatory power of the eight propositions. The criticisms of "China's Khrushchev" and scientific and technical personnel who did not adhere to the Maoist precepts of development strongly suggest that much of the intensity which has motivated Chinese criticism of social imperialism was caused not by objective economic dependency, but by the co-optation of strategic elites within China.

At the systemic level, with the possible exception of selected countries in Eastern Europe, social imperialism lacks the penetrative power of capitalist imperialism, primarily because Soviet state trading corporations have yet to engage in direct foreign investment. An effective tool of imperialism is the subtle co-optation of the goal structure and behavior of the strategic elites within a client state, especially when the country being co-opted seeks to maintain a high level of revolutionary integrity and consciousness. A country which lacked the cultural ethnocentrism or the unique revolutionary dynamism of China probably would not be conscious of co-optation. But revolutionary development, like democracy, is a fragile political process which can be perverted and destroyed in a multitude of ways, not the least of which is ideological contamination. It is Mao's recognition of this fact that has been so important in shaping Chinese attitudes towards the Soviet Union since the late 1950's.

Chinese perceptions of dependence, however, may not be entirely a product of domestic factors. To what extent did the Chinese sense—with good reason—the growing reluctance of the Soviet Union to support Chinese economic or military development? By the time that the Soviet aid program to Eastern Europe, the Middle East, and South Asia really got under way in the late 1950's, the Chinese must have become painfully aware of the low priority accorded them in Soviet thinking on the question of international assistance. Indeed, Oleg Hoeffding notes that by 1958 China's export surplus to the U.S.S.R., some $250 million, was about the same as Soviet economic aid deliveries to non-bloc, less-developed countries.[107] These harsh realities would hardly have been lost on the Chinese. China's perceptions were thus not simply an assertive expression of domestic interests, but a response to external factors largely beyond their control. Figure 2 (below) attempts to design a conceptual matrix of the factors operating on Chinese perceptions and decisions in the late 1950's. Table VII attempts to delineate the different phases of Chinese calculations of the utility of Soviet aid and assistance.

TABLE VII. CHINESE UTILITY MATRIX

TIME PERIOD	INTERNAL INPUTS (Costs/benefits)	NEED FOR FOREIGN TECHNOLOGY	EXTERNAL INPUTS (Options)
1949-1954	Low consciousness of costs	Foreign technology desperately needed.	No viable alternative to "leaning to one side."
1955-1957	Industrial and agricultural base still too small to sustain independent development. Trade flow gives Chinese a consciousness of economic costs of reliance on the Soviet Union.	Foreign technology still required for an optimal rate of development.	American hostility continues to negate most foreign options although an Asian agricultural and textiles market opens up to the Chinese.

TABLE VII. (Continued)

TIME PERIOD	INTERNAL INPUTS (Costs/benefits)	NEED FOR FOREIGN TECHNOLOGY	EXTERNAL INPUTS (Options)
1958-1960	Growing consciousness of the organizational, economic, cultural, political, and revolutionary costs of reliance on Russians.	Foreign technology needed and accepted but no longer required.	Soviet Union becomes less interested in supporting Chinese development.
1961-1965	Both the costs and benefits of Soviet aid become clarified by its loss. Benefits: it supported technical and economic development. Cost: revolutionary goal and methods.	Foreign technology desired but on very restricted terms.	Soviet aid no longer a viable option. American hostility continues although allies become increasingly reluctant to be dominated by Cold War rhetoric. Trade doors begin to open.
1966-1969	The costs of foreign aid are recognized with clarity in terms of the reaction to revisionism, elitism, and in light of the heightened class consciousness of the period.	Foreign technology seems irrelevant.	All external options are closed by the Chinese themselves.
1970-1974	Costs of aid are now zero due to the self-purgative struggle of the Cultural Revolution. The polity has been cleansed of sordid foreign spirits.	The need for foreign technology and goods is greatly diminished.	The U.S. and Europe move to open the trade and technological doors to China.

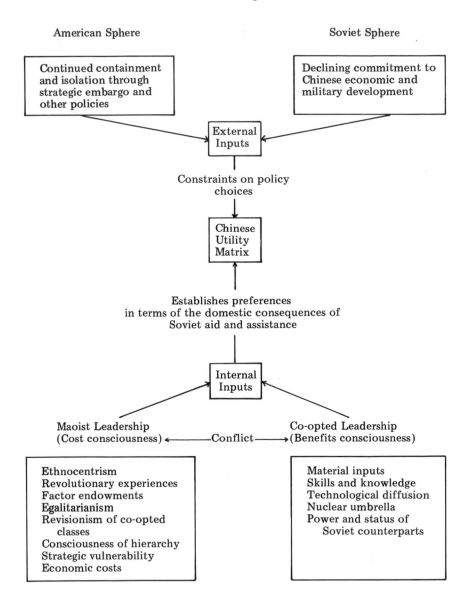

Figure 2. Conceptual Matrix of Chinese Utility Calculations Concerning Reliance on the Soviet Union.

V. CONCLUSIONS

In reviewing the contents of this paper, it seems as though four major periods in China's economic interactions with the world can be identified. From 1949 through 1957, the Chinese had no viable option but reliance on the Soviet Union. The economic and technological base of China after twenty years of civil and international warfare was so weak that China desperately needed international assistance. The situation was later described by the Chinese in these terms:

When socialist construction began, the shortage or inadequate supply of some resources was felt. It was not that these resources were unavailable in China, but rather that, limited by our scientific and technical knowledge and other conditions, we did not have a clear idea about our natural resources and some resources had not yet been discovered. Limited by our scientific, technical and other conditions, although some resources had been discovered, we had not the means to produce them on a large scale to meet the needs of construction.[108]

The American response to the Communist Revolution in China was such that the Soviet Union was the only place to which the Chinese could turn. The Chinese, however, did not simply lean to one side; they sought to get whatever they could from the Soviet Union. After the Chinese Communists had brought a degree of order to the Chinese economy and by the time that the First Five-Year Plan was supposed to begin in 1953, the Chinese economic position began to improve. The end of the Korean War and the subsequent promulgation of the Bandung Line in 1955 gave China an opportunity for marginal economic interactions with countries outside the Soviet bloc. Still, reliance on the Soviet Union remained the optimal policy for the Chinese leadership.

By 1958 the utility calculations of the Chinese leadership began to change. As the range of China's foreign economic options began to increase, the Chinese leadership became more aware of the constraints and costs of reliance on the Soviet Union. The Maoist segment of the leadership became increasingly conscious of the progressive corruption of the revolutionary spirit. In the years before 1949, the isolation of the Party elite had created a high level of integration and autonomy. When the Chinese Communists came to power in 1949, they were a relatively homogeneous elite. However, once they assumed governmental responsibility, they came into contact with preexisting and irreplaceable strategic elites, such as the intelligentsia and bourgeoisie. The carrot and stick policy used with these strategic elites necessarily implied the possibility that a portion of the Chinese Communist revolutionary movement would come into close and cooperative contact with non-revolutionary social classes. At this point, the possibility of corruption became very real. Various campaigns during this period expressed concern about the corruption of the revolutionary commitment. In addition, the size of the Party grew rapidly during the first years of the regime, implying a decline in revolutionary commitment. But most significantly (in the context of this paper) close interaction with the Soviet Union meant that many segments of the Chinese elite would be exposed to foreign interests, values, and norms. This interaction symbolized the decline in revolutionary values, commitment, and behavior in China. For these and other reasons set forth in this paper, the Maoist segment of the leadership decided to set out on a more independent path to development. This view suggests that the costs of Soviet assistance were primarily political, cultural, and ideological, not economic. The economic benefits of Soviet assistance probably outweighed the economic costs. Consequently, while the Chinese sought to escape from a growing dependency in 1958 and 1959, they continued to ask for everything they could secure from the Soviet Union.

Self-reliance is an elastic concept. While it is praised, one gets the distinct impression that the Chinese were angry at the Russians not so much for their economic imperialism as for their disinterest in subsidizing Chinese development. Self-reliance as a doctrine seems to make a virtue of necessity:

> Although Comrade Mao Tse-tung emphasizes self-reliance in revolution and construction, he also pays great attention to the important role of international support. He always holds that international support is a necessary and an important condition for winning and consolidating victories.[109]

Thus, if support is available, take advantage of it, but never depend on the continuity or enthusiasm of that support. Or, as Mao Tse-tung so aptly put it: "We hope for foreign aid . . . but we cannot depend on it."[110]

The simultaneous pursuit in 1958 of self-reliance and increased trade with the Soviet Union strongly suggests both the pragmatism and opportunism of the Chinese elite. Chinese policy in this period suggests not so much dependency as it reflects the assertion of national self-interest. This very assertion suggests a high level of autonomy and self-reliance, which, in turn, may be a prerequisite to genuine equality in international economic relationships.

The Soviet Union response to the assertion of Chinese national interest was to cut off what little assistance was being rendered to the Chinese in 1960. For the next decade, the Chinese were forced to get by with very little help from their friends and the pattern of Chinese trade shifted dramatically away from the Communist bloc. In place of an exclusive bilateral economic relationship with the Soviet Union, the Chinese developed economic relationships with a wide variety of Asian and European countries, with both Communist and capitalist countries, and with both developed and underdeveloped countries. A decade of economic development had prepared China to enter the competitive economic arena and purchase foreign technology at the best price available. In a sense, the uncomradely economic relationship between the Russians and Chinese in the 1950's had prepared the Chinese for the tough cash and carry posture assumed in the 1960's.[111] The economic terms of China's foreign trade were not really that much different in the 1960's than they were in the 1950's; the difference was in the number and variety of economic partners. The Cultural Revolution was, in part, a reaction to the progressive corruption of the revolutionary spirit, again stemming from both domestic factors and foreign interactions. During the late 1960's the Chinese retreated from virtually all forms of interaction with the rest of the world. However, after this national cataclysm of purification and cleansing had been completed, it appears the Chinese were ready once again to approach the outside world—this time on a wide variety of fronts and with a renewed sense of self-confidence, bolstered by the rekindling of both cultural and revolutionary identity. Symbolic of this new posture is the reaction of the hundreds of beneficiaries of China's new openness. Visitors to the mainland are struck, however, by the inability to fully penetrate the invisible barriers which separate the Chinese from the outside. China, in one sense, is more open to the external world than formerly, but, in another sense, is more isolated than ever. The Chinese today are able to base their approach to the outer world on the basis of self-reliance, equality, and mutual benefit.

Neither the data nor the analysis of this paper substantiate the view that China was objectively dependent on the Soviet Union. However, dependency, like any other social phenomena, may have a critical threshold; and given the degree to which segments of the Chinese Communist elite and other strategic elites were co-opted by Soviet methods and Soviet technology, it might be asserted that China was approaching a "dependency threshold" in 1958.

The emergence of a dependency relationship was reversed by the Great Leap Forward. This reversal suggests the weakness of the dependency relationship but it does not necessarily deny its growth in China. The costs of self-reliance for China were initially very high, but since China is one of the few countries in the world with the potential for national autarky, these costs were shortlived. China is now in a position to do what could not be accomplished in the decades after the Treaty of Tientsin; China can selectively borrow the technology of the outside world and integrate that technology into a dynamic and developing economy. Mao Tse-tung's strategy of national self-reliance and revolutionary transformation has finally resolved for China one of the dilemmas raised by Western power, technology, and imperialism.

NOTES

[1] *China's Principled Stand on Relations of International Economy and Trade,* 15 PEKING REV., Apr. 28, 1972, at 13.

[2] *Id.*

[3] *Id.* at 14.

[4] *Id.*

[5] *Id.* at 13.

[6] 460 SELECTIONS FROM CHINA MAINLAND MAGAZINES, Mar. 15, 1965, at 9 [hereinafter cited as SCMM].

[7] *Id.*

[8] For example, Chang Hsien-wu, China's representative to the United Nations, told the General Assembly that *"we* developing countries in Asia, Africa and Latin America have more or less the same experience and are in similar positions. We are bound closely together by our common struggle against imperialism and colonialism and by our common desire to build our respective countries." Reprinted in *Statements by PRC Delegations and Representatives to the United Nations,* 986 CURRENT BACKGROUND, Apr. 4, 1973, at 33 [hereinafter cited as CB]. China's representative at UNCTAD stated that "China is a developing country and belongs to the third world." *Id.* at 35.

[9] Editorial departments of the People's Daily, Red Flag, and Liberation Army Daily, *Leninism or Social Imperialism?—in Commemoration of the Centenary of the Birth of the Great Lenin,* NCNA, Apr. 21, 1970, in 906 CB, May 1, 1970, at 4.

[10] Editorial, *Warm Greetings to the Vietnam Workers' Party on the 40th Anniversary of Its Founding,* People's Daily, Feb. 3, 1970, 907 CB, May 14, 1970, at 94-95.

[11] *Comments on Soviet-West German Treaty,* 13 PEKING REV., Sept. 18, 1970, at 9.

[12] Lin Piao's Report to the Ninth National Congress of CPC, Apr. 1, 1969, adopted on Apr. 14, 1969, 12 PEKING REV., Apr. 30, 1969, at 32.

[13] *New Tsars Ride Roughshod Over East Europe,* 12 PEKING REV., Mar. 14, 1969, at 24.

[14] *How Soviet Revisionists Use the "CMEA" to Plunder and Exploit East European People,* 11 PEKING REV., Nov. 29, 1968, at 25.

[15] *Id.*

[16] *Id.*

[17] *Soviet Revisionists' "Economic Integration" Exposed,* 12 PEKING REV., June 20, 1969, at 17.

[18] *Id.*

19 *Theories of "Limited Sovereignty" and "International Dictatorship" are Soviet Revisionist Social-Imperialist Gangster Theories,* 12 PEKING REV., Mar. 28, 1969, at 24.

20 *Leninism or Social-Imperialism?,* 906 CB, May 1, 1970, at 8.

21 KEESING'S CONTEMPORARY ARCHIVES, 1968, at 23027.

22 *Id.*

23 *Leninism or Social-Imperialism?, supra* note 9, at 10.

24 *Id.*

25 *Id.*

26 *Id.,* at 11.

27 *Id.*

28 *Id.*

29 *Soviet Revisionist New Tsars Use "Aid" to Stretch Their Claws into Asia, Africa and Latin America,* 12 PEKING REV., Jul. 11, 1969, at 26.

30 *Id.,* at 24.

31 *Id.*

32 *Id.* at 26.

33 *Id.*

34 *See, e.g., Soviet Revisionist "Gunboat Policy": Attempt to Build Up Naval Supremacy,* PEKING REV., June 27, 1969, at 16-18.

35 Dos Santos, *The Structure of Dependence,* 60 AM. ECON. REV. 231 (May 1970).

36 Bodenheimer, *Dependency and Imperialism: The Roots of Latin American Underdevelopment,* 1 POL. & SOC'Y 332 (May 1971).

37 *See* Galtung, *A Structural Theory of Imperialism,* 9 J. PEACE RESEARCH 81-117 (1971).

38 Kronstein, *The Nationality of International Enterprises,* 52 COLUM. L. REV. 994 (1952).

39 Girling, *Dependency, Technology and Development,* STRUCTURES OF DEPENDENCY 47, 55 (F. Bonille and R. Girling eds. 1973).

40 China's dependence on the Soviet Union should not be viewed in a historical vacuum. To a great extent, China was forced to "lean to one side" because of the historical circumstances created by China's century-long confrontation with the West, the second Sino-Japanese War, and the effects and consequences of Civil War.

41 Garthoff, *Sino-Soviet Military Relations, 1945-66,* SINO-SOVIET MILITARY RELATIONS 84 (R. Garthoff ed. 1966).

42 R. RIGG, RED CHINA'S FIGHTING HORDES 302 (1952).

43 Rigg, *Red Army in Retreat,* CURRENT HISTORY, Jan. 1957, at 3.

44 Garthoff, *supra* note 41, at 86.

45 Whiting, *'Contradictions' in the Moscow-Peking Axis,* 20 J. POL. 127-61 (Feb. 1968).

46 Garthoff, *supra* note 41, at 85.

47 Rigg, *supra* note 43, at 3.

48 NCNA, June 18, 1957, cited in MacGregor, *Peiping General Criticizes Soviet [Union] on Seized Plants,* N.Y. Times, June 24, 1957, § 1, at 1, col. 8.

49 O. HOEFFDING, SINO-SOVIET ECONOMIC RELATIONS IN RECENT YEARS, 15 (RAND Memorandum P-2087, Aug. 1960, revised Dec. 1960).

50 *Id.,* at 9.

51 *Id.,* at 15.

52 Vladimirow, *The Question of Soviet Chinese Economic Relations in 1952-1966,* VOPROSY ISTORII (Problems of History) (No. 6, 1969), in 3 CHINESE ECON. STUDIES 8-9 (Fall 1969).

53 *Id.,* at 8.

54 *Id.*

55NCNA, Jul. 8, 1955, cited in L. ORLEANS, PROFESSIONAL MANPOWER AND EDUCATION IN COMMUNIST CHINA 79 (1960) [hereinafter cited as ORLEANS].

56WORLD KNOWLEDGE (No. 3, Feb. 5, 1958), cited in ORLEANS 79.

57PEOPLE'S DAILY, Oct. 4, 1959, cited in ORLEANS 79.

58It is difficult to get some comparative perspective on these figures. ORLEANS qualifies his own estimate of Chinese students abroad (which is presented in a form unusable in this study) by referring to a survey conducted by the National Tsing Hua University Research Fund and the Chinese Institute of America, A SURVEY OF CHINESE STUDENTS IN AMERICA UNIVERSITIES AND COLLEGES IN THE PAST ONE HUNDRED YEARS (1954). Between 1925 and 1953, some 9,617 Chinese students received degrees from American universities. This figure is considerably higher than Orleans' own estimate or official Kuomintang figures. The figure does suggest, however, that the Soviet Union has had a greater and more concentrated impact on Chinese education in the 1950's than any other country or group of countries in the years since World War I. According to Leo Orleans, there were 464,200 college graduates in China between 1950 and 1959. If a 20,000 figure for Chinese receiving their educations in the Soviet Union is relatively accurate, that suggests that approximately 4.3 percent of all Chinese college graduates either received some of their education in the Soviet Union, their degree in the Soviet Union, or post-graduate education in the Soviet Union.

59Suslov, *On the Struggle of the C.P.S.U. for the Solidarity of the International Communist Movement* (Report to the Central Committee, Feb. 1964), CURRENT DIGEST OF THE SOVIET PRESS, Apr. 29, 1964, at 3. A claim that 10,830 specialists in "all fields of economics, culture, and education were sent from the Soviet Union to the Chinese People's Republic" during the 1950's appears in 36 KOMMUNIST (Feb. 1960).

60PEOPLE'S DAILY, Oct. 4, 1959, cited in ORLEANS 117.

61Id., May 24, 1957, cited in ORLEANS 115.

62THE EVENING STAR (Washington, D.C.), Nov. 24, 1958, cited in ORLEANS 116.

63ORLEANS 116.

64Numerous *Peking Review* stories of model enterprises indicate that a large number of machinists, engineers and other technicians had visited the Soviet Union.

65ORLEANS 116.

66Id., at 117.

67Id.

68Suslov, *supra* note 59, at 3.

69Vladimirow, *supra* note 52, at 9.

70While not given adequate attention in this study, the impact of Soviet aid projects cannot be measured strictly in terms of location. Attention must also be given to the impact of Soviet aid on the formulation and implementation of policy in strategic economic sectors. While Soviet loans to China during the First Five-Year Plan amounted to only 11.2% of the total machinery and equipment imported during this period, Soviet industrial projects in China represented the core to industrialization program of the Plan. The Chinese emphasized during this period that the key to their industrial development were 694 "above norm" projects of which 156 were Soviet industrial projects. Not only did the importation of entire factories and machine systems tend to tie China, as recipient, to the Soviet Union, as donor, for spare parts and maintenance, but this type of assistance had considerable impact on China's organizational strategy. Roy Grow has argued that Soviet geographic and functional influence was channeled through key members of the Chinese leadership, particularly Kao Kang. Under Kao's leadership during the period of rehabilitation and reconstruction (1949-1952), Manchurian industry was not only rehabilitated more rapidly than the rest of China, it was also re-organized along Soviet lines, especially the steel and iron, coal, and railway industries. When Kao moved to the State Planning Committee in late 1952, these same industries in other parts of China began to adopt the Soviet organizational model. Professor Grow argues that the State Planning Committee may have been the mechanism through which the Chinese industrial system organized itself along Soviet lines. *See* R. Grow, The Politics of Industrial Development in China and the Soviet Union, 1973 (Doctoral Dissertation, Univ. of Michigan) and Grow, *Soviet Economic Penetration of China, 1945-1960: "Imperialism" as a Level of Analysis Problem,* PEACE SCIENCE SOCIETY (INTERNATIONAL) PAPERS GIVEN AT THE CAMBRIDGE, MASSACHUSETTS MEETING (Nov. 5-7, 1973).

[71] *See* YUAN-LI WU, THE SPATIAL ECONOMY OF COMMUNIST CHINA: A STUDY ON INDUSTRIAL LOCATION AND TRANSPORTATION (1967).

[72] *Id.* at 89.

[73] K. BUCHANAN, THE CHINESE PEOPLE AND THE CHINESE EARTH 56-7 (1966).

[74] A statement by Chou En-lai in early 1956 indicated the gradual nature of this policy of dispersion. Among other things, Chou said that "those who expect the rapid and general establishment of many industrial bases in the far reaches of western China are unrealistic in their outlook." (Quoted by YUAN-LI WU, *supra* note 71, at 18-19).

[75] There is some need to explain why 1963 figures were used when Soviet aid came to an end in 1960. Professor Wu provides data on kilometers of railway lines in operation for the years 1949, 1952, 1957, 1960, and 1963. However, it is only for 1963 that he distinguishes between trunk and branch lines. The distinction between trunk and branch lines is greater in 20 of the 25 provinces and autonomous regions included than the difference in total railway lines between 1960 and 1963. There was very little railway construction in the years of economic depression (1960-1963). Thus, in most cases, the 1963 figures are very close to the 1960 figures.

[76] For reasons of space limitations, trade data has not been given any attention in the descriptive portions of this study. A careful examination of the commodity composition of Sino-Soviet trade between 1955 and 1963 does not support an import substitution theory or a theory of unequal exchange which are fundamental theoretical foundations of dependency analysis. Tables I and II in the Appendix show that China did export primary goods (agricultural commodities and raw materials) to the Soviet Union and imported finished goods (machinery) although the finished goods were capital goods, not durable consumer goods. Indeed, until 1961 most of the imported machinery consisted of complete factories and plants. However, there is a marked reduction in Chinese exports of agricultural goods in 1961, and a gradual decrease in the export of raw materials along with a gradual increase in Chinese exports of textiles and handicrafts beginning in 1955. These three trends suggest more elasticity in the Sino-Soviet trade relationship than is generally associated with import substitution and dependency. When agricultural supplies were scarce, the Soviet Union accepted a marked increase in Chinese textiles. As China's demand for raw materials increased and as China's capacity to produce textiles increased, the pattern of Sino-Soviet trade changed accordingly.

[77] The extent and viability of China's economic alternatives during this period cannot be precisely known. Some indication could probably be found in the following types of evidence: the number and distribution of countries extending recognition during the period, and the number and distribution of

countries having more than nominal trade with China during this period.

[78] A. ECKSTEIN, COMMUNIST CHINA'S ECONOMIC GROWTH AND FOREIGN TRADE 137 (1966).

[79] C. CHIN, A STUDY OF CHINESE DEPENDENCE UPON THE SOVIET UNION FOR ECONOMIC DEVELOPMENT AS A FACTOR IN COMMUNIST CHINA'S FOREIGN POLICY 93 (Union Research Institute, Hong Kong, 1959).

[80] Chou En-lai, *The Report on the Proposals for the Second Five Year Plan*, People's Daily, Sept. 19, 1956, at 4.

[81] This paragraph is the product of an interesting conversation with Lowell Dittmar in the Spring of 1973.

[82] Chiang Chen-yun, *On Self Reliance—Notes on the Study of Chairman Mao's Works*, 1 ECON. RESEARCH, Jan. 20, 1965, in 460 SCMM, Mar. 15, 1965, at 4.

[83] W. GRIFFITH, THE SINO-SOVIET RIFT 233-34 (1964).

[84] O. HOEFFDING, SINO-SOVIET ECONOMIC RELATIONS, 1958-1962, at 3 (RAND Memorandum RM-2787-PR, Aug. 1963).

[85] *Id.* at 8.

[86] Chiang Chen-yun, *supra* note 82, at 9.

[87] *Id.* at 9-10.

[88] According to A. HSIEH, the Chinese leadership decided in 1956 to depend on a transitional military strategy that required heavy reliance on the Soviet Union. *See* her COMMUNIST CHINA'S STRATEGY IN THE NUCLEAR ERA chapter 2 (1962).

[89] W. GRIFFITH, *supra* note 83, document 7 at 351.

[90] P. SELZNICK, TVA AND THE GRASS ROOTS (1953), cited in W. GAMSON, POWER AND DISCONTENT 135 (1968).

[91] Bodenheimer, *supra* note 36, at 337.

[92] FRANTZ FANON has noted how educational and other privileged elites in almost all third world countries tend to use their former or present rulers as models for their own behavior, values, and life styles, in THE WRETCHED OF THE EARTH (1968). Stephen Andors writes that elites find in this imitation a way to affirm their own individual equality with their masters even while they accept the obvious material and psychological subordination of their nation's masses. Rather than turn to their own people for a mass mobilization, which, by its own logic, would mean the end of privilege and require a new definition of leadership, they talk in terms of "nationalism," meanwhile relying on the West for standards of success, behavior, and consumption. Andors, *Revolution and Modernization*, in Dissenting Essays on Asian-American Relations 432 (E. Friedman & M. Seldon eds. 1971).

[93] Dennis Ray, Multinational Corporations and the American Sphere of Influence 48-49 (paper presented at International Studies Association West, Portland, Oregon, Mar. 1972).

[94] *China's New Big Solar Radio Telescope*, 17 CHINA RECONSTRUCTS 25 (1968).

[95] 561 SCMM, Jan. 30, 1967, at 30.

[96] 632 SCMM, Oct. 28, 1968, at 18.

[97] Che Chih, *A Brief Discussion on the Unity of Politics, Economics and Technology in Designing Work*, 9 CHING-CHI YEN-CHIU (1965), in 4 CHINESE ECONOMIC STUDIES 86 (1968).

[98] *Id.* at 87.

[99] 632 SCMM, Oct. 28, 1968, at 12.

[100] *Id.* at 13.

[101] *China's New Big Solar Radio Telescope, supra* note 94, at 25.

[102] 632 SCMM, Oct. 28, 1968, at 18.

103*Id.* at 19.
104Che Chih, *supra* note 97, at 98.
105632 SCMM, Oct. 28, 1968, at 18.
106666 SCMM, Apr. 14, 1969, at 50.
107O. HOEFFDING, *supra* note 49, at 15.
108Chiang Chen-yun, *supra* note 82, 460 SCMM at 5.
109*Id.* at 8.
110MAO TSE-TUNG, *We Must Learn to Do Economic Work*, 3 SELECTED
WORKS 191 (2d ed. 1960).
111It might be argued that this tough business-like posture of the Soviet
Union indicates the absence of any attempt to make China dependent, for would
not dependence be maximized by long-term loans requiring perpetual debt
service and debt management? This is very true. A possible response to this
position would be that the Soviet Union simply did not understand the
relationship between the *condition* of dependency and the *mechanisms* for
creating dependency. The Kremlin simply took for granted that the Chinese
would remain subservient to Russian leadership. This explanatory hypothesis is
not entirely convincing. Another explanation of Soviet policy is that they were
much more sagacious about Chinese potential power and development than
American observers and perhaps even the Chinese themselves. They understood
that China, like Yugoslavia, would strike out on an independent path and,
consequently, under the facade of proletarian internationalism, the Russians
gave nominal assistance to the Chinese. In the meantime, they would attempt to
penetrate and "subvert" portions of the Chinese Communist leadership and
other strategic elites in China. If this failed, then the Kremlin's nominal
assistance could be withdrawn at a time most favorable to Soviet interests. This
interpretation seems to offer the best fit to the data and other material
presented in this chapter.

APPENDIX

TABLE I. COMMODITY COMPOSITION OF P.R.C.
EXPORTS TO THE SOVIET UNION, 1955-1963,
AS PERCENTAGE OF TOTAL TRADE

YEAR	AGRICULTURE	RAW MATERIALS	MANU- FACTURING	TEXTILES	OTHER
1955	49.3	34.6	1.6	9.2	3.7
1956	46.2	33.5	1.2	13.1	6.0
1957	35.9	32.9	0.9	20.0	10.5
1958	37.3	26.7	0.5	26.1	9.5
1959	30.6	24.7	1.1	36.1	7.4
1960	22.5	26.8	0.1	44.2	6.1
1961	4.7	24.9	0.1	58.1	12.3
1962	3.4	21.7	1.7	62.0	11.2
1963	5.5	19.7	1.7	65.9	7.2

TABLE II. COMMODITY COMPOSITION
OF P.R.C. IMPORTS FROM THE SOVIET UNION, 1955-1963,
AS PERCENTAGE OF TOTAL TRADE

YEAR	AGRICULTURE	RAW MATERIALS	MANU-FACTURING	TEXTILES	OTHER
1955	----	18.1	30.7	2.6	48.7
1956	0.1	22.8	41.6	1.8	33.7
1957	0.2	24.6	49.9	2.4	23.0
1958	0.2	27.2	50.2	3.0	19.7
1959	0.1	18.4	62.6	1.6	17.4
1960	----	22.7	61.7	1.9	13.8
1961	4.8	44.2	29.4	2.7	18.9
1962	8.9	49.1	11.7	6.3	23.9
1963	0.4	51.5	23.2	9.8	15.1

International Effects of China's Population Situation

I. INTRODUCTION

Upon gaining power in 1949, the new socialist government of the People's Republic of China faced one of the most difficult population situations in the world. China had within its borders more than one-fifth of the world's population, and most of its people were living at subsistence or near-starvation levels. In the succeeding 25 years, China's population has continued to increase at a rate of at least 2 percent per year and to account for over 20 percent of the earth's inhabitants; nevertheless the government is managing to feed and care for its citizens' needs. This success, in spite of a severe setback in food production in the early 1960's, makes China today a model of economic development and population planning for other less-developed nations.

The P.R.C.'s pronouncements on economic development and population problems therefore command the attention of a wide audience and inevitably have an impact on the policies of the United Nations and other international organizations. Moreover, China's population, in and of itself, has had significant effects on the policies of many nations, especially China's neighbors. Following an analysis of the P.R.C.'s current population size and growth rate, this paper will explore the effects which China's population size and population policies have had on the web of international relations, including the recently concluded United Nations Conference on World Population in Bucharest.

II. THE SIZE AND RATE OF GROWTH OF CHINA'S POPULATION

A. *Conflicting Population Estimates*

Because China's population constitutes such a large proportion of the world's inhabitants, its sheer size has a potentially significant effect on world trade patterns, power politics, and population trends. Assessing this effect requires accurate estimates of the number of people in the P.R.C. But reliable figures on China's present population size do not exist. The leadership has issued a wide range

*B.A., Swarthmore College, 1965; Ph.D. Candidate, Food Research Institute, Stanford University.

of estimates. Chou En-lai is fond of saying that he thinks the population of China today is somewhere between 700 and 800 million.[1] The 1972 Peking Atlas published population figures for China's provinces and cities totalling less than 686 million people.[2] China's Vice Premier Li Hsien-nien described the confused statistical situation in 1971:

> We have been racing against time to cope with the enormous increase in population. Some people estimate the population of China at 800 million and some at 750 million. Unfortunately, there are no accurate statistics in this connection. Nevertheless, the officials at the supply and grain department are saying confidently, "The number is 800 million people." Officials outside the grain department say the population is "750 million only" while the Ministry of Commerce affirms that "the number is 830 million." However, the planning department insists that the number is "less than 750 million."[3]

The disparity between 686 million and 830 million people is significant for agricultural and industrial planning purposes, yet this large variation in population estimates does not seem to bother the P.R.C. government. We may find it hard to believe that Chinese leaders can manage a planned economy without accurate economic and population statistics, but this is exactly what they do; most decisions on consumption, production, and internal trade are made locally and carried out locally.[4] The economy functions without accurate statistics because it is not run primarily from Peking.

China, like most less-developed countries, does not have the data systems, technology, or bureaucracy required to carry out a detailed census or maintain a reliable birth and death registration system. Moreover, the P.R.C. government apparently does not feel that knowing the present size of China's population is important. The leaders' casual attitude stems in part from China's long tradition of nonchalance toward statistical accuracy, a tradition which has persisted among those presently responsible for record keeping and data gathering.[5]

The writings of Karl Marx and other socialists have also had an important effect on the leadership's view of population issues. At the end of the eighteenth century, Malthus had written that poverty was inevitable because population tended to increase faster than the means of subsistence. Marx and Engels attacked Malthus, claiming that the means of subsistence could increase faster than population if capitalist and feudal exploitation were overcome.[6] They predicted that socialism would release the productive forces of the people, stimulating production sufficiently to overcome the natural increase in population.

Following Marx and other socialist thinkers, China's leaders in their propaganda statements have de-emphasized the world population explosion and the importance of birth control programs, while emphasizing the necessity for poor countries to throw off imperialism, colonialism, and feudalism in order to end human misery and starvation. Since the P.R.C. has carried out these radical political changes, according to Marxist and Maoist theory China's population growth should pose no problem for the welfare of the Chinese masses.

However, China's population size has continued to increase, in some years outstripping increases in food production. This is an additional reason why China's leaders are reticent about population statistics; the Chinese government seems to fear that any population statistics it publishes may be used by anti-China scholars and neo-Malthusian writers to prove that socialism is not solving the basic human welfare problems of the Chinese people. Thus, in 1954 the State Statistical Bureau slowed its program to establish a nationwide birth and death registration system because such facts would provide ammunition for scholars who were alarmed at the rapid increase in China's population.[7] This concern may also explain the failure to initiate any comprehensive census since 1953-1954.

B. *Calculating the Present Population*

1. *Extrapolating from Official Data*

Given the lack of either a recent census or a nationwide registration system for vital statistics, it is difficult to calculate the P.R.C.'s present population size. The only feasible method is to begin with the census of the early 1950's, make educated guesses about the growth rate of the population since, and calculate the present population size from these data.

According to most experts in Chinese demography, the 1953-1954 census was by far the best population count in Chinese history. The reported census total was 583 million people for the China mainland.[8] The census had certain build-in biases caused by the methods of counting, the traditional lack of concern with statistics, and the misreporting by those groups in the population who felt compelled to avoid being counted or who wished to make their families look bigger than they were. The best analysis of these biases concluded that the 1953 census was probably an undercount of the true population size by 5 percent or more.[9] This is not surprising; all censuses have biases. Although the U.S. census is one of the most thorough in the world, it regularly misses many people, causing a 2-3 percent undercount.[10] Therefore, if the 583 million population figure for 1953 is used as a starting point in population calculations, the final result will probably *under*estimate China's population size today by a substantial margin.

Estimating the annual growth rate of the population since 1953 also presents difficulties. The Chinese government has carried out occasional small-scale surveys of births and deaths, but the resulting information is not necessarily representative of the country as a whole.[11] From these surveys, the population growth rate has been consistently reported as at least 2 percent annually, and some years the P.R.C. government has reported rates of 2.5 percent or even 2.9 percent.[12] Though there are undoubtedly errors in the survey data, a yearly population growth rate of 2 percent (or slightly higher) would be reasonable for China's stage in economic development, given what we know for most other countries at a similar stage.[13]

Calculating China's present population using the 1953 census figure and assuming a 2 percent yearly increase gives a mid-1974 population size of about 885 million people. To assume that the 1953 census produced a 5 percent undercount generates a present population estimate of about 930 million people. If the population has been growing faster than 2 percent a year since 1953, the present population size would also be much larger than 885 million.

China observers remain puzzled as to the reason that the P.R.C. government would issue a wide range of total population estimates, each inconsistent with its own 1953 census results and its own survey data on population growth. A present P.R.C. population size of 700-850 million is certainly too low if the 1953 census total was correct and if population growth has been at least 2 percent in most years and 2.5 to 2.9 percent in other years as reported. Nevertheless, many observers uncritically accept the P.R.C.'s low population estimates of 750 or 800 million people and use these estimates to compute per capita consumption and production figures for comparison with other countries; this produces misleading results.

If, as P.R.C. government estimates usually suggest, China's present population is actually much less than 885 million people, there are two possible (but probably fallacious) explanations. First, the 1953 census count may have been inaccurate and much too high; but from what we know of the census procedures, this seems unlikely.[14] Second, the population may have been growing at a rate of less than 2 percent a year. Some experts on Chinese population do assume that China's population has been growing at much less than 2 percent annually.[15] I disagree with this assumption. The following analysis of the birth and death rates of the post-1949 period is an attempt to show that the P.R.C.'s population has probably been growing at around

2 percent a year, and that therefore China's population is now much bigger than the typical P.R.C. government estimates.

2. *Substantiating a Two Percent Growth Rate*

Most less-developed countries have a population increasing faster than 2 percent annually; some have reported rates of over 3 percent a year.[16] The high growth rates in less-developed countries result from a drastic reduction in death rates while the birth rates remain high. Most available evidence indicates that China experienced this phenomenon during the 1950's and 1960's. The death rate fell in the 1950's, but not until the 1960's and the 1970's did the crude birth rate fall significantly in the most developed areas of the country. In the least developed areas of China, birth rates are still high.

During the 1950's, basic preventive sanitation and epidemic disease control measures were first made available to much of the country, lowering the death rate significantly—to perhaps 20-23 per 1000 annually.[17] At the same time, birth rates probably rose slightly, to 40-45 per 1000 annually.[18] There were two major reasons for this rise. Many marriages and childbirths had been postponed during the years of foreign invasion and civil war; these occurred during the 1950's. Secondly, more adequate food supplies and disease control probably increased the population's reproductive capacity, which was previously impaired by starvation and ill health.[19] Therefore it is likely that the population grew by about 2 percent a year after the 1953 census for the rest of the 1950's.*

What about the 1960's? In 1960 and 1961, bad weather and the mistakes of the Great Leap Forward created a period of food shortages and malnutrition. The death rate probably increased, because people's resistance to disease was lower, and the birth rate may have decreased by a small amount because people tend to postpone marriages and to have fewer babies during economic depressions. Therefore the natural increase of the population may have dipped below 2 percent a year for those two years.

From 1962 until the present, China's death rate has steadily declined. A big push to provide good medical care to all city dwellers began in the early 1960's, and since 1965 Western-style modern curative medicine has become available across much of the countryside. Mobile medical teams, commune health plans, and commune clinics have provided some medical care to most rural

*To calculate the yearly percentage natural increase of the population, subtract the deaths per 1000 from the births per 1000 and divide by 10. In this case, subtract 20 per 1000 from 40 per 1000 to get a yearly natural increase of 20 per 1000 people (which equals 2 per 100, or 2%).

dwellers. And since the Cultural Revolution of the late 1960's, the "barefoot doctors" (paramedics) have provided primary health and first-aid care for the masses of people nationwide. As a result, China's overall crude death rate probably is fairly low now (maybe 10-15 per 1000 per year) and will continue to decline as medical care improves in rural and remote areas.[20]

The birth rates of the 1960's are enigmatic. In the early 1960's, a campaign promoting birth control and later marriage had some effect in lowering city birth rates but apparently had little impact on the more than 80 percent of the population which lives in the countryside.[21] The problem of population growth seems to have been ignored entirely during the Cultural Revolution, and only in 1969 when the government announced that the population had increased by an alarming 2.9 percent the previous year did the leadership decide to give top priority to birth control work.[22] Therefore government family planning programs could not have produced a significant decline in China's national birth rate during the 1960's.

My hypothesis is that the crude birth rate of the P.R.C. was steadily declining all through the 1960's, even before modern means of birth control became widely available and long before the government belatedly decided to have a real birth control program in the rural areas.* This possibility is supported by the history of declining birth rates in Western countries and, more recently, in some of the less-developed countries.

In the nineteenth century and before, there were no very effective forms of birth control, yet European and U.S. birth rates declined slowly, with only temporary deviations from the trend. Apparently many people were motivated to limit family size, and successfully did so using such means as sexual abstinence, coitus interruptus, primitive condoms, abortion, and sometimes infanticide.[23] The motivation to limit births came from economic development (with associated lower mortality rates, greater educational opportunity, increasing numbers of industrial jobs for women, and rising expectations for offspring) rather than from national family planning programs or the easy availability of good birth control devices, neither of which existed.

During recent years, a similar pattern has appeared in several of the less-developed countries for which data exist. In some countries, the birth rate began to drop and continued a steady decline both before and after a government birth control program began. In these cases, because the program began late and was slow to spread all over

*This suggestion implies that P.R.C. surveys indicating a 2.5-2.9% yearly population increase were in error, due to biased samples or incorrect data.

the country, it could not be given full credit for the birth rate decline, though it undoubtedly helped. In Taiwan and South Korea, for example, the downward trend in the birth rate began before national family planning programs were instituted.[24] In Costa Rica, the crude birth rate declined steadily from 48 per 1000 in the 1950's to 40.5 per 1000 in 1966 when the birth control program began, and continued to drop to 31.5 per 1000 in 1971.[25]

Even though there are no valid data on the P.R.C.'s national birth rate, it is possible that China has followed the pattern just elaborated. During the 1960's, economic development was proceeding over most of China. Mortality rates were decreasing, primary school education was becoming widespread, increasing numbers of women were earning full-time pay outside the home, and old-age social security was becoming a reality in the rural communes and urban factories. These factors usually coincide with a decline in the birth rate.

During that decade, the national birth control program was still minimal, and modern birth control devices were not widely available in rural areas, yet large numbers of people may have decided on their own to marry a little later and to start limiting the number of children born. A number of articles in Chinese medical journals during the 1960's indicated that there was considerable demand for abortion.[26] And some local records for suburban and rural communes, such as the following, show a birth rate decline beginning in the mid-1960's and continuing after the birth control program began to affect them:

> In the People's Commune of Tonwan, 40 kilometers southwest of Shanghai, with a population of 23,000, the birth rate had fallen from 46 per 1000 in 1963 to 13.6 in 1971. Family planning records showed that nearly 100% of married women of fertile age were practicing family planning.[27]

If in fact the P.R.C. experienced a significant birth rate decline *before* the family planning program was stressed, it would help to explain why the impact of China's birth control program seemed so impressive and so sudden in some areas of the country. In the P.R.C. as elsewhere, it would be incorrect to give the government family planning efforts full credit for recent birth rate declines.

If the scenario outlined above is correct, China's crude birth rate declined steadily in the 1960's as did the crude death rate. Their respective rates of decline may have varied slightly from one another, but their difference (the overall population growth rate) would still have remained in the neighborhood of the 2 percent a year which apparently prevailed in the late 1950's. In the period since 1970, the natural increase in the population may have dipped below 2 percent a year as the family planning program has become widespread. All this still results in a figure of about 885 million for the population of China in 1974. All the Chinese government estimates for the size of the P.R.C. population today therefore appear low, and must be adjusted upward before any meaningful per capita production or consumption figures can be calculated.

C. *Evaluating Future Trends*

An upward revision of population estimates is not meant to denigrate China's impressive successes in family planning and economic development. Whether the population of the P.R.C. today is 700 million or 1 billion is less important than whether childbearing patterns are shifting toward a small-family norm. The evidence shows that the average number of children born per couple has been declining in the 1970's. If this trend continues, the population growth rate eventually will be significantly reduced.

At present, progress throughout the country is uneven.[28] Recent local evidence indicates that birth rates in China's big cities and many of the medium and small cities, as well as in the more developed communes in the countryside, have been dropping very fast in the 1970's.[29] Anecdotal data given to visitors in China often show that city couples are now marrying in their late twenties and having two or three children on the average, while couples in the advanced countryside areas tend to marry in their early twenties and have three or four children per couple.[30] However, in the poor and backward areas of China, the family planning program does not appear to be working very well yet, probably because most people still are not strongly motivated to limit births.

With continued work on the birth control program and a steadily rising level of economic development, China's population size may stabilize sometime during the first half of the 21st century. For the 1970's and 1980's, however, the P.R.C. has the same serious problem that many poor countries face. During this whole period there will be a high proportion of the population in the childbearing ages. This bulge in the age distribution of the population is due to the lowered infant and child mortality rates of the 1950's and 1960's; most of the large numbers of children born then are living to adulthood. Therefore, even if all present and future couples in China limit family size to two children per couple, it will be difficult to lower the crude birth rate of the population much more until after these large numbers of young adults will have completed their families. Meanwhile the crude death rate will probably continue to drop, so the P.R.C. will have to work very hard just to keep the rate of population growth from increasing above its present rate during the next 15 years.

In the long run, to achieve zero population growth within China, many traditional behavior patterns must change. Extrapolating from the experience of countries which have approached zero population growth, the most important change needed is probably wide acceptance of the idea that not all people must marry or have children—that other life styles are acceptable too, such as choosing to remain single or to live as a couple without children. In the China of today, however, social pressure still strongly encourages marriage and childbearing: government social policies and birth control propaganda try to affect only *when* young people marry and *how many* children they have, and seldom mention the options of not marrying or not having children.

On a similar plane, it is usually necessary to marry in China in order to have any sexual relationships, because of the strong prohibition of sex outside marriage. If non-marital sexual relations become acceptable in the future, this should weaken the drive toward marriage and incidentally toward childbearing. Already, the available birth control and abortion technology is advanced enough to permit such social change, and the rate of premarital sexual relations is probably on the rise (surreptitiously, of course). Young adults must wait longer to marry now, while at the same time various forms of birth control can be bought anonymously in city stores. Premarital intercourse is probably not causing a rise in the rate of illegitimate births, however, because induced abortion is available to unmarried women who become pregnant. (I was told by a doctor in one rural Chinese commune I visited in 1971 that an unmarried woman would get a requested abortion after she got a good talking to.)

In order to stabilize its population size, the P.R.C. must also change the still-widespread preference for male children—a preference inherited from the Chinese past. At least in the rural areas, it still seems true that if a couple's first two children are girls, the parents are not willing to stop at two children. They continue having children until the wife bears at least one son.

Traditionally, each young woman has "married into" her husband's family, and where this custom continues, it reinforces the preference for male children. This practice is breaking down in China's cities, partly because the small apartment units encourage a nuclear family living arrangement. But in rural areas, a married woman's housework and outside income go to support both her own nuclear family and her husband's parents. Chen Pi-chao described some of the P.R.C.'s recent attempts to solve this problem:

Since a married daughter is expected to contribute to the earnings of her husband's household, the entry of the Chinese woman into the labor force tends to reinforce the age-old preference for male children. To compensate for this custom, the woman who married *out* is now increasingly obliged to maintain a financial obligation to her natural family. . . . In one hsien last year, arrangements were made for about 25 men to be married *into* girls' households where there were no brothers, or where the parents could not be supported adequately by male offspring.[31]

To lower the marital fertility rate, it must therefore become acceptable for old people to live with and be supported by their married daughters. Moreover, to encourage people not to bear children, a social security system must provide adequately for all old people whether they have children or not.

If the government of the P.R.C. works vigorously to overcome the traditional customs and attitudes favoring high fertility, it will be possible to lower the fertility rate to replacement level in the next few decades. Meanwhile, however, the population will continue to grow at a relatively rapid rate, due to the present age distribution of the population. Thus the P.R.C. must try to feed, clothe, educate, and provide jobs and medical care for increasing numbers of people in the years ahead.

III. CHINA'S FOOD SUPPLY AND THE INTERNATIONAL MARKET

The well-being of the Chinese people depends on steadily increasing food production, year after year. But because Chinese agriculture is still not fully irrigated and modernized,[32] much of the P.R.C.'s agricultural production remains subject to severe effects from drought, floods, pests, and other natural calamities. Thus in some years, agricultural output is less than the previous year's production. Under Chinese population growth conditions, such a decline can be very serious.

Beginning with the food shortages of 1960-1961, China began meeting food supply shortfalls by importing large quantities of wheat and other grains. But once that crisis had passed, the P.R.C. continued to import huge amounts of wheat, even during bumper crop years. Western observers often assert that the plentiful food supply in China is attributable to these yearly imports from Australia, Canada, the U.S., and other grain-surplus countries.* This

*China imports approximately 4-5 million metric tons (m.m.t.) of grain each year, compared to China's yearly domestic production of about 240-250 m.m.t. of grain.

assertion is similarly made about China's dependence on international fertilizer supplies; China imports more chemical fertilizer than any other country in the world.[33]

By concentrating only on food imports, such assertions ignore the variety and value of China's food exports. A comparison of food exports and imports indicates that China is actually self-sufficient in food supplies, and has used trade in foodstuffs to earn extra foreign exchange. China exports rice to southeast Asian and south Asian countries, and during the 1960's also exported soybeans, oilseeds, meats, tea, eggs, vegetables, fruits, and processed foods.[34] Whether measured by volume or by caloric value, China probably imports more food than China exports, and in that sense the level of food consumption of the Chinese people (especially urban dwellers) is partly dependent on food imports. But the foods which China sells are primarily high quality foods requiring large labor or land inputs, and bringing high prices on the world market. Thus, in value terms the P.R.C.'s food exports far exceed the value of its food imports. In 1965 the value of China's food exports rose above the value of imported foodstuffs, and by 1970 food export value was almost double the value of food imports.[35] In this sense China is a net exporter of food, and therefore is not only self-sufficient in food but has a food surplus to sell.

The exact levels of China's food imports and exports fluctuate from year to year, but the general picture is clear: almost all of the food needed in China is produced in China, even during years such as 1972 when China had disastrous weather conditions. The amount of food the P.R.C. imports and exports is small compared to the amount of domestic food production and consumption, and exports exceed imports if both are calculated in the usual way, that is, by their value. Therefore China is basically self-sufficient in food supplies.

However, China's food production is still seriously dependent on foreign sources of supply for chemical fertilizer. The high yields of the miracle strains of wheat, rice, and other grains grown throughout much of China cannot be sustained without large inputs of fertilizer. The P.R.C. does produce enormous amounts of natural and chemical fertilizers for domestic use. China is probably the world's foremost producer of natural fertilizers; most of the human feces and the animal manure is collected, treated, and put on the fields. Pigs have been bred in record numbers all over China in the last few years, both because they provide food for domestic consumption and export, and because they are a good source of fertilizer.[36]

Chemical fertilizer production has expanded rapidly in recent years also. The P.R.C. is now the world's fourth largest producer of nitrogen fertilizer (after the U.S.A., the U.S.S.R., and Japan).[37]

Small fertilizer plants have been set up all over the country, and they supply low quality but useful chemical fertilizer for nearby areas. The P.R.C. is also expanding production of high quality fertilizers. These fertilizers have great economies of scale; the only economically sensible way to produce them is in enormous factories full of specialized machinery. Therefore China imports whole capital-intensive plants—in 1973 the P.R.C. bought a huge chemical fertilizer complex from Japan.[38] In the future, the P.R.C. will probably contract to buy similar plants in order to become self-sufficient in high quality fertilizer production—and since the nation has ample supplies of the hydrocarbons (oil, coal, or natural gas) needed to produce these fertilizers, eventual self-sufficiency in chemical fertilizer is a distinct possibility.[39]

In the meantime, because modern agricultural technology is being extended to more areas of China, the use of chemical fertilizers is expanding almost as quickly as domestic production of them.[40] Imports of high quality chemical fertilizer therefore continue to be required. As of 1971-1972,* China still imported fully 35 percent of the total chemical fertilizer nutrients used in her agricultural production.[41] The international market currently (1974) cannot meet such a high percentage of China's requirements, since world chemical fertilizer production has been cut back (due to oil shortages and non-humanitarian priorities) in the major fertilizer-producing capitalist countries. China's food output in 1974 and in the next few years will be hurt by the high prices and short supply of chemical fertilizer for sale on the world market.

On balance, China's food production has so far kept up with a growing population. The Chinese people seem to be getting enough grain to eat and have steadily increased their production and consumption of other foods—eggs, fish, meat, vegetables, and fruits.[42] Recent visitors to China report that, in the areas they visited, the Chinese people no longer need their full ration of grains and do not use up all their ration coupons, because the people increasingly eat these other variety foods and thus consume smaller amounts of grain. It is clear that China has accomplished an amazing feat—wiping out starvation among almost one-fourth of the world's population, while bringing greater variety and nutritive value to the diets of most people.

But the years ahead are ominous for food supplies in China, as well as in many other developing countries. Recent bad weather in many parts of the world has caused a serious worldwide decline in reserve stocks of grain. If the P.R.C. has successive years of bad weather, and if China cannot procure or produce enough fertilizer to

*1971-1972 is the most recent crop year for which data are available.

keep up crop yields, food production gains could fall behind the population increase in the next few years. If the world grain market continues to be tight, the P.R.C. would then have to divert food from export to home consumption, causing serious dislocations in China's imports of vitally needed technology for continued economic development.[43] Famine is not imminent in China, but problems of population growth and food supply could adversely affect the P.R.C.'s steady development progress.

IV. POPULATION DISTRIBUTION AND BORDER RELATIONS

The size and rate of growth of China's population affect international trade patterns in food and agricultural inputs, but such population parameters are not the only internationally important aspects of China's population situation. The distribution pattern of the population also plays a role in the P.R.C.'s foreign affairs, especially in its relations with neighboring countries.

A sparsely distributed 5 percent of China's people live on 60 percent of the P.R.C.'s land area. These vast regions are topographically and climatically rugged, and are located mostly along China's borders; they include frigid Heilungkiang province in northern Manchuria, the grasslands and desert of Inner Mongolia, arid and mountainous Sinkiang province, the high Himalayas of Tibet, and the jungles and mountains of Yunnan and Kwangsi provinces in the south.

These lightly populated border regions are where the people of China's minority nationalities live. Although there are approximately 54 minority nationality groups, they comprise only about 6 percent of China's population; the rest of the people are of the Han ethnic group.[44] Historically the Han Chinese people spread outward, especially southward, from the Yellow River area in north-central China, displacing many of the minority peoples and pushing them into the jungles, deserts, and mountains now located along the border areas of the P.R.C. Frequently, these displaced peoples settled in such a way that members of the same nationality now live across an international border from one another; Central Asian Moslems, Mongols, Koreans, Thais, people of Tibetan stock, and many other peoples live on both sides of China's borders.[45]

Throughout history, these people of the same culture traveled and traded freely across the ill-defined borders of the Chinese empire. In the north, nomadic herders recognized no boundaries as they drove their herds across the grasslands. In the west, traders regularly moved through the mountain passes carrying their wares on the backs of animals. In the south, Han Chinese settlers in the fertile valleys slowly mixed with or displaced the minority peoples through the centuries, causing some minority group nationals to move into hilly areas in what is now the P.R.C. or to migrate southward into what are now southeast Asian countries.

Because the old Chinese empire periodically expanded and contracted, China's borders have always been vague and fluctuating. In this century, however, the Chinese, Russian, British, and French empires in Asia have been transformed into more modern nation-states with more exactly defined borders. This transformation has curtailed the free movement of people across Asia. As boundary lines are drawn or fought over, various national groups find themselves caught on the Chinese or Soviet or Indian or Burmese or Laotian side of the border, with little possibility of resettlement on the other side when they are suppressed or ignored by the political entity which currently controls them.

When border disputes arise between the P.R.C. and neighboring countries, each government uses the minority nationalities as a pawn in the struggle. During the Sino-Soviet dispute, for example, the Soviet Union and Mongolia have frequently accused China of persecuting its minority groups, and have urged the Moslems and Mongolians in the P.R.C. to flee across the border and settle permanently in the U.S.S.R. and the Mongolian People's Republic. Indeed, many minority group members have done just that—especially during the Great Leap Forward when the P.R.C. government suddenly decided to completely integrate the minority groups into the socialist economy, and again during the Cultural Revolution when minority religions and traditions were attacked. The Chinese government has met such accusations by stressing the vastly improved economic and health conditions of its minority groups, and by accusing neighboring governments of oppressing their own minority nationalities and of carrying on subversive activities in China's border provinces.[46]

Generally speaking, the governments of the Asian continent seem to care less about meeting the needs and desires of their minority groups than about controlling those groups and using the border minority peoples as instruments of the governments' national and international policies. Certainly no Asian government is willing to allow a border minority nationality to secede and form a separate state, or even to run a truly autonomous local government free of central government interference.[47]

The P.R.C. is no exception to these general rules, although China's government has genuinely tried to improve the living standards of the minority peoples. Since 1949, the P.R.C. has followed a policy of developing its enormous sparsely-populated regions economically and integrating them into the socialist economy. The government has felt that these vast areas, rich in natural resources, do not belong to the minority peoples who have historically inhabited them, but rather belong to China's people as a whole and should be developed to benefit the whole population. To this end, the government has overridden local preferences and traditional patterns of life in order to use the land in what it sees as the most productive manner. For example, many nomadic tribes of the north and northwest have been settled into communes, and some of their former grazing lands are irrigated and cultivated as large state-owned farms. In the south, slash-and-burn agriculture has been discouraged and the minority peoples have been urged to develop more productive forms of agriculture.

These economic policies have been successful in increasing the agricultural and industrial output of the minority regions. By 1956 in the minority areas of Kwangsi, agricultural output had reportedly increased 50 percent above pre-liberation levels, and these areas had become self-sufficient in food. Additionally, locally produced consumer goods had replaced those previously imported into the Kwangsi area.[48] In Sinkiang by 1966 the area of newly reclaimed land was larger than the total cultivated land area in 1949; Sinkiang had become self-sufficient in food and cotton production, and the introduction of new livestock breeds had produced a surplus of animal products in the province.[49]

Economic modernization of the border regions has required much more labor power than was originally available in these areas. For this and other reasons, such as moving people to border areas to secure the borders against hostile or potentially hostile countries, the P.R.C. has moved large numbers of people from China's densely populated areas to live and work in the hinterland. This form of internal migration may not have significantly reduced crowding in the areas these migrants have left, but it has had a major economic, social, and political impact on the places where they have settled.

The migrants have been relatively well-educated, young, and sometimes dedicated people who have helped transform the poorest and most backward areas of China into new centers of industry and agriculture. Their skill and labor power have been directed toward irrigating deserts which were otherwise unproductive, building roads and railroads which are beginning to link those remote regions with China's centers of population, and providing preventive and curative health care where there previously was none.

It is socially and politically significant that almost all of the migrants have been Han Chinese. Inner Mongolia's ratio of Han to non-Han people, for instance, rose from 4:1 in 1953 to 9:1 in the 1970's.[50] Sinkiang was only 6 percent Han in 1953, but became 40 percent Han by 1965.[51]

Whether the Han Chinese are now a majority or a minority of the population in a particular region, the Han migrants in each area have disproportionate political power, for they normally are Communist Party cadres, or members of the People's Liberation Army assigned to defend the border, or educated youth assigned to direct the transformation of the economies and societies of the border areas. The governments of all the border provinces and cities are dominated by the Han Chinese who serve in a majority of the important political positions regardless of the composition of the population. Apparently the P.R.C. government has misgivings about the loyalty of the minority peoples. These misgivings are no doubt due in part to frequent Moslem revolts against Han Chinese rule in the century before 1949 and since then as well,[52] to the Tibetan revolts in 1956-1959 and again in 1964,[53] to the recent migrations of Thai people out of China into southeast Asia whenever their Buddhist religion is attacked, and to recurrent Mongol unrest in the Inner Mongolian Autonomous Region. During the last century and the first part of this century, the minority groups of China also showed a tendency to ally with Western imperialist countries against China when Britain, France, Russia, and other countries were carving out spheres of influence and control within China; the P.R.C. government is suspicious of this particular manifestation of minority anti-Han feeling.[54]

The traditional mistrust between the Han Chinese and the minority nationalities has been exacerbated by the Han habit of looking down on the minority peoples as culturally inferior. This attitude, called Great Han chauvinism, is being combatted by China's government through various means, such as popularizing minority group dances and clothing styles and setting modern movies in minority areas. Yet thousands of years of Great Han chauvinism cannot be erased immediately; some of the Han Chinese troops and youth moving into minority areas undoubtedly display their feelings of cultural superiority and offend the minority groups.

The minority peoples have many legitimate complaints. They are not fairly represented in leadership positions, and their leaders are frequently attacked by Han cadres for identifying with their own people. Minority group customs are termed decadent where they differ from Han practices. Local languages are often pushed aside by the Chinese language in the schools. Han numerical dominance in border regions magnifies all these insults. The result is exacerbation of minority group discontent along China's borders, where their revolts strain the relations between the P.R.C. and most of the border countries.

Because of China's policy of encouraging Han migration to border areas, neighboring governments sometimes fear that China is preparing for invasions which would extend Chinese territory. These fears are typically justified on the theory that China's teeming masses of hungry people need more living space and arable land, thereby causing them to look greedily toward the rice-growing areas of southeast Asia or the vast empty spaces of Siberia for settlement and political control.[55] Scholars of China have sometimes reinforced this hypothesis,[56] and other governments have often based domestic and foreign policies on it. For instance, the Soviet Union has tried to persuade large numbers of people to populate Siberia in order to deter supposed Chinese expansionism, but the policy has met with little success because Siberia is so inhospitable to settlement.[57]

Finally, some southeast Asian governments have used predictions of Chinese aggression to oppress the resident overseas Chinese minority group. In the past, many Chinese people migrated from China to other countries. Overseas Chinese are found all over Asia, concentrated in cities, where they are shopkeepers, bankers, or small business owners, and occasionally in rural areas, where they engage in moneylending or skilled trades. Other local people often resent the overseas Chinese, whether because the Chinese seem more prosperous, because they are perceived to be cheating the local residents in money dealings, or because of existing racist and religious hatred. Consequently, it has been easy for southeast Asian governments to accuse their Chinese residents of being subversives who are the first wave of a huge influx of Chinese settlers and soldiers. Such accusations fan the racist hatreds which already exist, and allow non-Chinese citizens to dispossess and murder overseas Chinese people who live in the locale.[58]

The theory that China will inevitably try to expand its borders because of population pressure is unrealistic on two counts. First, China's population distribution is such that the less densely populated areas can accept substantially greater numbers of migrants from the denser regions than they do now. Second, fully 88 percent of China's land is not presently cultivated and some might be reclaimed; and still more of that which is now cultivated might produce higher yields with more modern techniques. These solutions would be much less costly in the long run than would any international aggression to get more agricultural land; such aggression would require China to waste vast resources on warfare and on suppressing a hostile population. Explanations of China's complex border policies based on its population size are simplistic, and obscure the real reasons for P.R.C. policies toward its neighbors. Contributing, and more realistic, reasons for any ultimate Chinese expansion might include national pride, traditional enmity between China and another country, reaction to foreign aggression, or the desire to control a strategic mountain pass on the border.

Moreover, the overseas Chinese minority groups would be

unlikely subversives on behalf of the P.R.C. Many of them are separated from China by the centuries since their ancestors left, and of the more recent emigrants, many fled China in order to avoid living in a socialist country. Generally speaking, the cultural patterns which the overseas Chinese perpetuate are Chinese rather than Burmese or Indonesian or American, but these patterns are those of old China or the Taiwan of today rather than the socialism of the P.R.C. Most overseas Chinese feel some cultural identity and pride in new China, because China is no longer a humiliated and exploited nation, but they are rarely interested in risking their own lives and economic futures by promoting P.R.C. interests in their country.[59] Therefore, if an overseas Chinese minority group is oppressed, the reason is not that its members represent the P.R.C. and its policies, but rather that the local government wishes to oppress them for other reasons.

Although there has been some migration across the borders of China since 1949 for permanent resettlement, the numbers have been very small compared to China's population size.[60] Many overseas Chinese who identified most closely with socialist China have gone to the P.R.C. to make it their home, while other people have left China legally or illegally. This population movement causes serious dislocations in one place: Hong Kong. Intermittent flows of refugees from the P.R.C. swell Hong Kong's population, increasing competition for jobs and helping to keep wages low and housing scarce. In general, however, emigration from and immigration to China are more important in terms of propaganda than they are in numbers.

China's relations with neighboring countries are thus complicated and confused by the existence of minority nationality groups straddling China's borders, by China's policy of moving large numbers of Han migrants to border regions, and by the existence of resented overseas Chinese minority groups in Asian countries. It is possible for the P.R.C. and nearby countries to ignore or overcome these barriers to understanding if their governments choose to do so, but so far many of the governments have often chosen the opposite—to aggravate racist or cultural fears and hatreds in support of their hostile policies toward each other.

V. CHINA'S INTERNATIONAL POLICY ON BIRTH CONTROL

A. *China's Position and the Population Conference*

Ultimately, one must look beyond the immediate conflict situation generated by China's population size and population movements, to the methods and philosophies, actual and declared, lying behind the P.R.C.'s control of its population increase. It is those methods and philosophies which make up the Chinese model for the less-developed nations of the world. China has both followed and contributed to international developments in family planning programs and in the technology of birth control. The P.R.C. has taken from abroad the basic knowledge needed for production of birth control pills, intrauterine devices, and other contraceptives. The process has not been one of pure imitation, however. China has tested, modified, and produced these contraceptives according to the special needs of its own population.[61] In addition, P.R.C. scientists have contributed to world progress in birth control technology by researching and developing the vacuum aspiration abortion method in the 1950's.[62] This innovation has since spread around the world, revolutionizing abortion practices and paving the way for legalized abortion in many countries, by making it clearly safer for a woman to have an abortion than to carry the pregnancy to term.

Very recently, the P.R.C. has become involved in international debate on the world "population explosion." In preparation for the World Population Conference of 1974, China for the first time attempted to formulate and enunciate a coherent statement of its ideas on world population matters. The resulting pronouncements are grounded in the belief that people are an asset and should not be regarded as a negative factor. Population growth is correspondingly regarded as a part of economic development rather than an obstacle to it. One Chinese representative expressed this philosophy as follows:

> We hold that, of all things in the world, people are the most precious. People are the decisive factor in the social productive forces. They are first of all producers and then consumers. As producers, they ceaselessly concentrate on production in breadth and depth and can produce more products than they consume.[63]

Following Marx and other socialist writers, P.R.C. leaders attribute poverty and backwardness to the imperialist aggression which destroys a country's productive forces or siphons off the country's raw materials and fruits of the people's labor. Therefore the solution to poverty is to eliminate imperialism and colonialism and develop each national economy independently. According to this theory, population problems will then resolve themselves with time. If population increases, production will increase more and living standards will rise. If people wish to limit births, they will do so, and governments can help by providing suitable birth control devices.

Chinese representatives argue that there is no *universal* world population problem calling for identical solutions; to implement a uniform world population program would interfere unduly in the domestic affairs of each country. The P.R.C. contends that some nations and localities need a family planning program and some do not; each country should develop its own population program. According to Chinese statements, variations in national programs should depend primarily on two factors. The first of these is whether the country is being exploited from outside. The P.R.C. reasons that if a country is experiencing imperialist exploitation, any population problem is likely to be more apparent than real. The second factor is population density. For example, Chinese representatives note that China encourages late marriages and birth control in its densely populated regions, but that it promotes population increase in its sparsely populated areas.

The World Population Plan of Action adopted at the Population Conference originally faced Chinese opposition because of the P.R.C.'s emphasis on differences in national and local population situations. China's opposition to the plan was also influenced by China's unwillingness to have U.N. observers meddling in China's internal population affairs and the P.R.C.'s unwillingness to gather and publish population data. Chinese policy toward the World Population Plan of Action was summarized as follows:

> The formulation of population policy and target, census and the publication of statistics are internal affairs within the sovereignty of each country and should be handled by each government in accordance with the wishes of its people. It is inappropriate and unfeasible for the United Nations World Population Conference to lay down unified regulations. International cooperation in the field of population matters must be carried out in conformity with the principles of complete voluntariness of the parties concerned, strict respect for state sovereignty and promotion of self-reliance on the part of the recipient countries.[64]

The unique character of the P.R.C.'s international population policy is based partly on China's definition of what a "population problem" is. Many population specialists and leaders of developed nations use the term in the sense of a rapid population increase which is caused by a low death rate and high birth rate, and which makes it difficult to feed and provide for the increasing population. Such observers tend to see the "problem" as a phenomenon affecting only developing nations. In contrast, P.R.C. representatives argue that unemployment, starvation, high death rates, poor health, and inequality of income are the real population problems, and that rapid population growth per se is not. Therefore, China claims that developed countries have as many population problems as have developing countries.[65]

The P.R.C. contends that there is no such thing as over-population in developing countries today, and that panic about a population explosion in those countries is unjustified:

> At present, population densities in most of the developing countries are lower than the developed countries. How can it be said that their population is too large?[66]

Moreover, China claims that talk of a population explosion is used to obscure the real issue of foreign exploitation. Population control efforts in poor countries are accordingly seen as a form of exploitation by the superpowers (the United States and the Soviet Union); and China has urged population growth in the third world as a means for fighting such foreign exploitation.[67]

The World Population Conference was dominated by socialist and developing countries which put forth arguments similar to China's. Their representatives generally denied that the world is in crisis due to its 2 percent overall yearly population increase; few of them were interested in discussing the implications of the doubling of the world's population in the next 35 years. Instead, their primary focus was on the importance of economic development. They attacked the developed capitalist nations for overconsumption, which deprives poorer countries of the basic necessities of life. These socialist and developing countries agreed that a more equitable distribution of world resources is a prerequisite to developing the poor nations' economies, and that population programs are not crucial. These countries, along with China, exhibited their determination to assess their own population situations and control their own population policies; for example, some developing countries noted that their own development programs would require larger populations.

Socialist nations as a group took a strong ideological stand against any emphasis on population control. China and the other socialist states asserted that the Western countries' concern over world population growth is an imperialist myth to keep poor countries subjugated. They maintain that to focus attention on family planning shifts attention from the need for social and economic reform.

Although most participants in the World Population Conference were not as concerned about the world's rapid rate of population growth as were the developed capitalist nations, the Conference did pass a World Population Plan of Action. The Plan reflects the strong influence of developing and socialist countries by emphasizing the importance of economic and social development as a precondition for eventually lowering fertility and listing the changes necessary to bring this about—changes in the status and role of women, the reduction of infant and child mortality, a more equitable distribution of wealth within and between countries, wider educational opportunities for girls as well as boys, and a social security system.[68] The Plan of Action encourages international assistance for family planning and for food production and supply, but it is a moderately worded and unenforceable document which emphasizes complete national sovereignty in population matters.

The most important effect of the World Population Conference was that it generated discussion, debate, and learning about world population growth, a subject previously considered taboo in international forums. The representatives of the 136 participating nations shared information and ideas at the official Conference, while these countries' unofficial representatives took part in the many concurrent meetings of nongovernmental organizations which considered the population question.

B. *A Critique*

The similarity of China's official position on population to that of a majority of governments at the Conference means that analyzing the P.R.C.'s population theory is useful for understanding the population policies of a large number of countries. What can be said about the validity or lack of validity of China's population theory as described above?

P.R.C. theorists claim that a country which is developing economically and socially can increase production faster than its population increases. This statement has strong historical support. Many now-developed countries had a steadily rising average standard of living even when their populations were increasing in size every year for more than a century. Even today, many developing countries are managing to increase production as fast as or faster than their very rapid population growth, if existing data for G.N.P. increases can be believed. But, contrary to P.R.C. theory, this process has been observed in some countries which, by the P.R.C. definition, were still being exploited from the outside. For example, Taiwan was a colony of Japan for 50 years, until 1945. Its population size has increased at a rate of 2.2 to 3 percent a year since the 1930's, but production increased faster than population during the Japanese occupation and has continued to do so during the recent period of strong U.S. and Japanese influence.[69] Therefore, while it may sometimes be necessary to get rid of imperialist exploitation in order to release the productive forces of a country, it is not always absolutely necessary. Moreover, the end of imperialism does not guarantee that national leaders will choose to develop a country for its people's benefit.

The P.R.C. asserts that each additional person in the world is an asset, because that person can produce more than she or he will consume. This observation may be true in situations where worker productivity is high, but it is questionable in very poor regions where a person consumes more for basic survival needs than that person can produce under the circumstances. In addition, the timing of consumption and production are important in a period of rapid change. At present, people spend more of their lives consuming than producing. As children and as old people, humans consume education, medical care, food, clothing, and housing, but produce very little. During a period of rapid population growth in a developing country, the ratio of dependents to workers is quite high. Each producer must support a larger number of unproductive consumers than is necessary in a developed country. Therefore the dependency burden is greatest in the countries which can least afford to deal with it.

If rapid population growth continues in the world as a whole, there is a danger that human productivity levels may eventually decline. In order to produce something, each new worker needs adequate resources with which to work. In the future, an increasing world population may strain resources to such an extent that some important and irreplaceable means of production, such as usable land, minerals, or water, may be exhausted. Under these circumstances, additional people would be primarily consumers without the means to produce very much. In the past, shortages of resources were solved through technological change which obviated the need for a particular resource or provided more efficient ways of using scarce resources. This is no guarantee, however, that all such shortages will be overcome through technological innovation in the future. As the world's population multiplies and affluence grows, we may experience simultaneous shortages of a wide range of resources, and humans may be unable to find satisfactory substitutes for some of them.

By justifying national population growth on the basis of an overly optimistic view of productivity increases, Chinese theorists minimize the very real risks of unchecked world population growth. Even if productivity could increase fast enough to overcome the limits of fixed resources and changing population patterns, important human values are threatened. The freedom from excessive crowding, the pleasure in breathing clean air and drinking clean water and experiencing open spaces, the joy of varied outdoor recreation, the serenity to be found in occasional solitude and quiet, and the enjoyment of privacy may all suffer when population expands. Work is not the only joy in life.

China's basic position, which emphasizes the production potential of increased population and stresses the exploitation of third world nations, results in a charge that family planning programs in developing countries are a form of exploitation by the superpowers. This accusation follows directly from the notion that more people can only be a benefit, *i.e.*, more people mean more power for a poor country or for the third world as a whole; birth control would therefore deprive a poor nation of its greatest strength. P.R.C. representatives support the contention that developing countries need more people for development with the observation that population densities in most developing countries are lower than in developed nations. (This observation is accurate if one compares the most densely populated Western European developed countries with most African and Latin American countries.) If in fact a country is underpopulated and needs a larger labor pool to enable it to develop its unused resources, then premature limitation of population growth might hurt the development effort. However, encouraging population growth is not the only answer in this situation; it would be better for the sparsely populated country to encourage immigration by people of working age from crowded areas of the world. Such a policy would expand the labor supply immediately available without increasing the society's dependency burden.

The Chinese position that larger population augments power is based on more than the economic rationale just considered. From the Maoist perspective, an important benefit of increased numbers is political and military strength—in the event of a guerilla "people's war" against foreign aggression, a small poor country could better defend itself against a vastly superior military machine. The Chinese argument presents a less-developed country with a dilemma. On the one hand, increased population may be necessary to support a defensive war; on the other, larger numbers may increase production for the benefit of any foreign nation which can exploit the underdeveloped economy. This dilemma may be an artifact of China's population theory, which does not consider the many other important facets of a struggle against exploitation. Population size is not the only significant variable in resisting aggression; the level of political awareness in the population, for example, could be far more important.

In general, a high birth rate in a developing country weakens the nation rather than strengthening it. Most countries with high natural population growth rates are having difficulty expanding food production, employment opportunities, and other vital services to provide for the increasing population. To supply birth control and abortion services can only help to alleviate these very real problems. That such services are provided in part by a foreign developed nation is no indication that exploitation is involved, contrary to Chinese theory.

When it comes to the facts, China might be accused of inconsistency between the theory and practice of population policy. People may be the most precious things in the world, but China is working very hard to limit the number of new people born in the P.R.C. China does not minimize the dangers of unchecked population increase in practice within its own borders—but in its statements at the U.N., China does minimize those dangers.

China's practice in population matters, coupled with its ideological commitment to equity, has led to a process of development in which distribution of income has been kept within a relatively narrow range. Inequalities still exist in China between cities and countryside, ports and interior, rich communes and poor communes, but these inequalities are small compared to those in most other nations. The magnitude of China's success is powerful evidence for the proposition that economic growth and equity are not mutually exclusive goals. This evidence reinforces the P.R.C.'s theoretical position that neither family planning nor economic development will solve poverty and misery if the programs proceed under economic systems which retain severe inequalities of income. Other evidence supports China's theory, and shows that economic development under these circumstances produces a wide distribution of income which leaves a large proportion of the people in relative (and often absolute) poverty while the middle and upper classes are wealthy by comparison.[70] P.R.C. theory and practice together offer a general solution to poverty; ending poverty means eliminating exploitation of one group of people by another, be they nations, ethnic groups, or economic classes.

C. Conclusions

Using historical analogies, it is possible to defend much of China's present international population theory. So far it has indeed been true that population growth has been an integral part of economic development in every country which is now thought of as "developed." Death rates began to decline well before birth rates did, and the population of the country multiplied in size before birth rates declined to their present levels. The P.R.C. expects, therefore, that presently developing countries will follow the same pattern if only they can rid themselves of outside control. But sometimes the lessons of history are not completely relevant to the present. The world population situation today is different from any in the past. No presently developed country ever had to cope with an annual rate of natural population increase as high as 2 to 3.5 percent, as do most developing countries today.

Providing a rising standard of living for vastly increased numbers of people and reducing the rate of increase in the world's population may require unprecedented global cooperative action. U.N. agencies are willing to coordinate such action, and nations can participate on a voluntary basis as China suggests, but the opposition of China and other developing countries to concerted worldwide action may cripple attempts to lower birth rates even in countries where people are already motivated to limit births. International family planning surveys have indicated that large numbers of couples in many poor countries are now bearing more children than they want to have, simply because contraception is unavailable and abortion is illegal.[71] Accordingly, undue emphasis on the importance of national sovereignty in population matters hampers the development of freedom of choice of women and couples around the world in matters of reproduction. The P.R.C.'s position on population encourages some of the world's most backward governments to continue ignoring their own serious population problems.

This is not to deny that China's international population policy may have some beneficial effects. It encourages developing countries to concentrate their energies on ridding themselves of foreign exploitation; in some areas of the world this is a prerequisite for the rapid economic development necessary to provide rising living standards for ever-increasing numbers of people. The population theory espoused by China and other socialist and developing countries is also a positive force for discouraging the hysterical approach which predicts inevitable disaster unless drastic measures are taken to restrict world population growth.

In the final analysis, China's international population policy has strong ideological components which help the P.R.C. to see some aspects of the world population situation more clearly, but which color the P.R.C.'s perception of reality whenever reality does not support the ideology. In order for the world to solve the population dilemmas facing it, observers of all political persuasions, including China's leaders, must take off their ideological blinders and try to see clearly the causes and effects of rapid population growth and of the other "population problems" as China defines them. Only then will the cooperation necessary to solve world population problems be forthcoming.

NOTES

[1]L. FESSLER, THE PEOPLE'S REPUBLIC OF CHINA AND POPULATION POLICY 1, 12, 14 (American Universities Field Staff, Fieldstaff Reports, East Asia Series, Vol. XX, No. 3, 1973).

[2]*Id.* at 14-15.

[3]Rida, *Days in China—An Interview with the Number 3 Man in China*, Al Jumhuriyah (Cairo), Nov. 18, 1971, at 9. Also cited in L. ORLEANS, EVERY FIFTH CHILD: THE POPULATION OF CHINA 34 (1972).

[4]Donnithorne, *China's Cellular Economy: Some Economic Trends Since the Cultural Revolution,* 52 CHINA QUARTERLY 605-619 (Oct./Dec. 1972).

[5]Orleans, *Chinese Statistics: The Impossible Dream,* 28 THE AMERICAN STATISTICIAN 47-52 (May 1974), describes the historical background of this lack of concern for correct statistics and the resulting statistical problems of the P.R.C.

[6]*Cf.* MARX AND ENGELS ON THE POPULATION BOMB (R. Meek ed. 1971).

[7]Ku Wei-lin, *Wo tui t'ing-pan sheng-ming t'ung-chi shih-pan kung-tso ti jen-shih* (My Understanding of the Suspension of Vital Statistics Experimental Work), 1 T'UNG-CHI KUNG-TSO T'UNG-HSIN (Statistical Work Bulletin), Jan. 23, 1955, at 36-37.

[8]L. ORLEANS, EVERY FIFTH CHILD, *supra* note 3, at 13-19.

[9]J. AIRD, THE SIZE, COMPOSITION, AND GROWTH OF THE POPULATION OF MAINLAND CHINA 1-24 (U.S. Bureau of the Census, International Population Statistics Reports, Series P-90, No. 15, 1961); J. AIRD, ESTIMATES AND PROJECTIONS OF THE POPULATION OF MAINLAND CHINA: 1953-1986 10-13 (U.S. Bureau of the Census, International Population Reports, Series P-91, No. 17, 1968).

[10]U.S. BUREAU OF THE CENSUS, CENSUS OF POPULATION: 1970, Vol. I: Characteristics of the Population, Part I: United States Summary, Section 2, Appendices 63-65 (1973).

[11]J. AIRD, THE SIZE, COMPOSITION, AND GROWTH OF THE POPULATION OF MAINLAND CHINA 47-51 (U.S. Bureau of the Census, International Population Statistics Reports, Series P-90, No. 15, 1961).

Snow, *Population Care and Control,* in VICTOR-BOSTROM FUND & POPULATION CRISIS COMMITTEE, POPULATION AND FAMILY PLANNING IN THE PEOPLE'S REPUBLIC OF CHINA 8 (1971).

[12]A growth rate of 2.9% was reported for 1968 during the Cultural Revolution; a 2.5% annual population increase was reported for 1969 and 1970.

See VICTOR-BOSTROM FUND AND POPULATION CRISIS COMMITTEE, *Balancing Population and Food,* in POPULATION AND FAMILY PLANNING IN THE PEOPLE'S REPUBLIC OF CHINA, *supra* note 11, at 13.

[13]*See* the reported population growth data for developing countries in the yearly WORLD POPULATION DATA SHEET compiled by the Population Reference Bureau. As can be seen from the data sheet, population growth rates of 2.0% to 2.4% exist in several other East Asian developing countries.

[14]J. AIRD, *supra* note 9 (both sources).

[15]L. ORLEANS, EVERY FIFTH CHILD, *supra* note 3, at 55.

[16]POPULATION REFERENCE BUREAU, WORLD POPULATION DATA SHEET (yearly).

[17]Orleans estimates a crude death rate of around 22 per thousand during the late 1950's. L. ORLEANS, EVERY FIFTH CHILD, *supra* note 3, at 53. Aird assumes a death rate of 22.5 for 1953, 19.5 for 1955, and 20.1 for 1960. *Aird,*

Population Policy and Demographic Prospects in the People's Republic of China, in U.S. CONGRESS JOINT ECONOMIC COMMITTEE, PEOPLE'S REPUBLIC OF CHINA: AN ECONOMIC ASSESSMENT 328 (1972) [hereinafter cited as *Joint Economic Committee Essays*].

[18]Orleans guesses a birth rate of 43 per thousand in the early 1950's, declining steadily in the late 1950's to 38 per thousand in 1960. L. ORLEANS, EVERY FIFTH CHILD, *supra* note 3, at 49. Aird estimates a crude birth rate of 45.0 in 1953, 44.0 in 1955, and 39.9 in 1960. *Joint Economic Committee Essays, supra* note 17, at 328.

[19]K.C. YEH & C. LEE, COMMUNIST CHINA'S POPULATION PROBLEM IN THE 1980s 12 (Rand Paper Series No. P-5143, 1973).

[20]Aird assumes that the crude death rate had dropped to 15.0 by 1970. Aird, *Joint Economic Committee Essays, supra* note 17, at 328. Orleans thinks that the death rate declined to 17 per thousand by 1970 and has continued to drop since then. L. ORLEANS, EVERY FIFTH CHILD, *supra* note 3, at 53-54. It is possible that the crude death rate is even below 10 per thousand, as was that for Brazil during 1965-1970. Such a low crude death rate can exist even with much ill health in the population, due to a very young age distribution—*see* U.N. POPULATION DIVISION, DEATH RATES, UN DOC. ESA/P/WP/38 (Working Paper No. 38, Feb. 22, 1971).

[21]*See* Aird, *Joint Economic Committee Essays, supra* note 17, at 304, on the negligible effects of the birth control campaign of the early 1960's.

[22]Aird, *Joint Economic Committee Essays, supra* note 17, at 311-312; *see also* Chen, *China, Population Program at the Grassroots,* in POPULATION: PERSPECTIVE 1973, 86 (American Universities Field Staff ed. 1973).

[23]Langer, *Checks on Population Growth: 1750-1850,* 226 SCIENTIFIC AMERICAN at 93-99 (Feb. 1972).

[24]Kirk, *A New Demographic Transition?,* in RAPID POPULATION GROWTH, CONSEQUENCES AND POLICY IMPLICATIONS 129 (Nat'l Academy of Sciences ed. 1971).

[25]M. GOMEZ & V. BERMUDEZ, POPULATION COUNCIL COUNTRY PROFILE: COSTA RICA 2-3 (Apr. 1974).

[26]Orleans, *Family Planning Developments in China, 1960-1966: Abstracts From Medical Journals,* 4 STUDIES IN FAMILY PLANNING at 198-202 (Aug. 1973).

[27]*IPPF Observer Reports China's Programme "Best in World",* 218 PLANNED PARENTHOOD NEWS at 1 (June 1972).

[28]This was officially admitted recently by a Chinese representative at a United Nations meeting. He stated, "Initial success has also been obtained in birth-control work in the densely populated areas, but it is not developing evenly." *See China Explains Her Views on the Population Question,* 17 PEKING REVIEW at 17 (Apr. 27, 1973).

[29]For detailed data on the recent low birth and death rates in the large cities of the P.R.C., see Faundes & Luukkainen, *Health and Family Planning Services in the Chinese People's Republic,* in 3 STUDIES IN FAMILY PLANNING 166 (Supplement, Jul. 1972).*See also* Chen, *supra* note 22, at 81.

[30]COMMITTEE OF CONCERNED ASIAN SCHOLARS, CHINA! INSIDE THE PEOPLE'S REPUBLIC 280-82, 286-87 (1972).

[31]Chen, *Panorama: People's Republic of China,* 2 POPULATION DYNAMICS QUARTERLY at 13 (Winter 1974).

[32]Erisman, *China: Agricultural Development, 1949-71,* in *Joint Economic Committee Essays, supra* note 17, at 133-143.

[33]*Id.* at 140-41.

[34]A. ECKSTEIN, COMMUNIST CHINA'S ECONOMIC GROWTH AND FOREIGN TRADE: IMPLICATIONS FOR U.S. POLICY 112, 211, 217 (1966);

Usack & Batsavage, *The International Trade of the People's Republic of China*, in *Joint Economic Committee Essays, supra* note 17, at 353.

[35]Usack & Batsavage, *The International Trade of the People's Republic of China*, in *Joint Economic Committee Essays, supra* note 17, at 336, 353.

[36]Goodstadt, *China Trade: Cut-throat Fair*, 80 F.E. ECO. REV. [FAR EASTERN ECONOMIC REVIEW] at 55 (Apr. 30, 1973).

[37]U.N. FOOD AND AGRICULTURE ORGANIZATION, REVIEW OF THE CURRENT MARKET SITUATION, TRENDS AND PROSPECTS FOR FERTILIZER SUPPLIES AND PRICES 23 (Ad Hoc Government Consultation on Fertilizers, Rome, October 22-24, 1973).

[38]*China Fertilizer Deal*, 80 F.E. ECO. REV. at 34 (Apr. 23, 1973).

[39]See the paper by Kim Woodard in this volume for details on China's present output and estimated reserves of these hydrocarbons.

[40]During 1967-1972, China's chemical fertilizer production increased by 18.5% a year, while its consumption of chemical fertilizer rose by 14.2% yearly during the same period. U.N. FOOD AND AGRICULTURE ORGANIZATION, *supra* note 37, at 12-13.

[41]U.N. FOOD AND AGRICULTURE ORGANIZATION, *supra* note 37, at 12, 13, 22.

[42]Schuman, *China: Still Eating*, 79 F.E. ECO. REV. at 25 (Feb. 5, 1973).

[43]Until recently, China had a pay-as-you-go policy for all imports, which necessitated a contraction of imports whenever exports faltered. Now, however, the P.R.C. has begun to finance some imports with medium-term loans from abroad. Such financing could be used to pay for continued imports in the event of lagging food exports, because the P.R.C. has an excellent international credit position. China would then face the problem of having to use larger amounts of foreign exchange in the future for debt repayment.

[44]Before the Ch'ing Dynasty, "Han" referred to the people in northern China who speak the Mandarin dialect; "T'ang" referred to the people of southern China who speak the Cantonese dialect. However, since the Ch'ing Dynasty (which was China's last dynasty, overthrown in 1911), the term "Han" refers to all the people of China's populous provinces, including Mandarin- and Cantonese-speaking peoples, but excluding the peoples of the frontier areas. See G. MOSELEY, THE CONSOLIDATION OF THE SOUTH CHINA FRONTIER 2 (1973).

[45]*Id.* (see index under the name of each nationality).

[46]T.S. AN, THE SINO-SOVIET TERRITORIAL DISPUTE 15 (1973).

[47]For details on the oppression of minorities in Burma, Thailand, Laos, and India, see G. MOSELEY, *supra* note 44, at 155. On page 173 he compares the treatment of minorities in China with their treatment in other Asian countries.

[48]*Id.* at 151, 153.

[49]Drew, *Sinkiang in the Modern World*, 56 ROYAL CENTRAL ASIAN JOURNAL 47 (Feb. 1969); G. MOSELEY, A SINO-SOVIET CULTURAL FRONTIER: ILI KAZAKH AUTONOMOUS CHOU 33 (1966).

[50]These ratios are only approximate, given the lack of satisfactory data. Sources differ on the exact ratio of Han to non-Han people. Watson says that Inner Mongolia went from 2:1 in 1950 to 10:1 in 1962, due partly to the incorporation of the predominantly Han province of Suiyuan into the Inner Mongolian Autonomous Region. F. WATSON, THE FRONTIERS OF CHINA 175 (1966).

[51]T.S. AN, *supra* note 46, at 71.

[52]For details on the recent century of Moslem rebellions in China, see T.S. AN, *supra* note 46, at 40-41, 53-54, 70-72; and F. WATSON, *supra* note 50, at 163. Watson also gives details of Moslem revolts on the Russian side of the

border against the Czars and Stalin, and the resulting flight of Moslems into China, *Id.* at 40-41.

[53]F. WATSON, *supra* note 50, at 88, 110, 208.

[54]G. MOSELEY, *supra* note 44, at 4, 26-30. The minorities, in an effort to avoid or to throw off Han Chinese control, sometimes called for outside assistance. For particular examples, see: A. WHITING & S.T. SHENG, SINKIANG: PAWN OR PIVOT? 7 (1958). J. FAIRBANK, E. REISCHAUER, & A. CRAIG, EAST ASIA: THE MODERN TRANSFORMATION 788-793 (A History of East Asian Civilization, Vol. 2, 1965). H. WIENS, HAN CHINESE EXPANSION IN SOUTH CHINA 254-257 (1967), G. MOSELEY, *Supra* note 49, at 12-16 (1966).

[55]*See* T.S. AN, *supra* note 46, at 89 and 117 on Siberia; and L. ORLEANS, *supra* note 3, at 154-157 on the "spillover" theory of Chinese border relations.

[56]One example is the following quotation from T. TREGEAR, A GEOGRAPHY OF CHINA 107-108 (1965): "There is a third area which invites Chinese occupation but which is outside Chinese political boundaries: the vast lowlands of the Indo-China peninsula. These lands are comparatively underdeveloped and sparsely populated.... The figures of overseas Chinese given above show that large numbers have settled here in the past. It may well be that Chinese pressure in this region today stems from socio-demographic as much as from political and ideological causes."

[57]T.S. AN, *supra* note 46, at 87; F. WATSON, *supra* note 50, at 163.

[58]The massacre of the Chinese minority in Indonesia represents only one example of the use of the overseas Chinese as scapegoats because of a supposed connection with P.R.C. expansionism.

[59]*See* F. WATSON, *supra* note 50, at 76; and L. ORLEANS, *supra* note 3, at 157-160, on the overseas Chinese.

[60]Most demographers ignore international migration in any calculation of China's population size or growth rate, because the amount of net international migration is unknown and is tiny compared to the P.R.C.'s population size and to the errors in Chinese population data. *See* L. ORLEANS, *supra* note 3, at 35, 79.

[61]*See, e.g.,* Djerassi, *Fertility Limitation Through Contraceptive Steroids in the People's Republic of China,* 5 STUDIES IN FAMILY PLANNING at 17 (January 1974), for details on China's birth control research, manufacture of contraceptives, and estimates of the extent of current birth control pill use in China today.

[62]For the original reports of this research, see K.T. Ts'ai, Y.T. Wu, and H.C. Wu, *Yung tzu chih tien tung hsi kua ch'i lai tso jen kung liu ch'an; 30 li ch'u pu fen hsi pao kao; 300 li ch'u pu fen hsi pao kao (Suction Curettage for Induced Abortion; Preliminary Report of 30 Cases; Preliminary Report of 300 Cases),* 6 CHUNG-HUA FU CH'AN K'O TSA CHIH (CHINESE JOURNAL OF OBSTETRICS AND GYNECOLOGY) 445-449 (No. 5, Oct. 1958) (with abstracts in English).

[63]*China Explains Her Views on the Population Question, supra* note 28, at 16.

[64]*China's Position on the Population Problems Expounded,* 12 PEKING REVIEW 9 (Mar. 22, 1974).

[65]*Id.* at 9.

[66]*Id.* at 8-9.

[67]New York Times, Aug. 26, 1974, at 28, col. 2.

[68]New York Times, Aug. 31, 1974, at 6, col. 4.

[69]B. Johnston and P. Kilby, *Agricultural Development in Taiwan: The*

Japanese Pattern Repeated, in AGRICULTURE AND STRUCTURAL TRANSFORMATION: ECONOMIC STRATEGIES IN LATE DEVELOPING COUNTRIES Chapter 6, 6.1-6.20 (forthcoming).

[70]Paukert, *Income Distribution at Different Levels of Development: A Survey of Evidence,* INTERNATIONAL LABOR REVIEW 97-125 (Aug.-Sept. 1973). See pages 104-105 which show the distribution of pre-tax income in the U.S. and in European developed countries. Typically, the poorest 60% of the families receive 30-35% of the income, while the richest 20% of the families get 40-50% of the income. In *non-socialist* developing countries, the distribution of income is even worse than in developing capitalist countries, in that the richest 20% of the families usually receive 50-60% of the income. (See the data on pages 114-115.) Paukert's data show that economic development in non-socialist countries tends to make income distribution worse than it was before the development began. Only after the country becomes very well-off can income distribution be expected to improve slightly. Paukert's analysis and conclusions, however, are incorrect because he includes no data for developing or developed socialist countries. If he did, he would probably find that economic development under socialism brings greater equality of income than before the country became socialist, and results in a developed country with greater equality of income than is possible under capitalist or feudal systems.

[71]For details on the results of these surveys, see Kirk, *The Effectiveness of Family Planning Programs In Less Developed Countries: The Evidence From Survey Data,* 10 FOOD RESEARCH INSTITUTE STUDIES IN AGRICULTURAL ECONOMICS, TRADE, AND DEVELOPMENT 6-8 (No. 1, 1971); and Nortman, *Population and Family Planning Programs: A Factbook,* 2 REPORTS ON POPULATION/FAMILY PLANNING 14, 67-71 (Sept. 1972).

People's China and the World Energy Crisis: The Chinese Attitude Toward Global Resource

I. INTRODUCTION

THIS ESSAY DESCRIBES the domestic and international energy policies of the People's Republic of China. "Energy" is approached here, not in strictly technical or economic language, but on the basis of societal, organizational, and governmental variables directly related to Chinese energy policies. Because such an organizational analysis of energy production, distribution, and consumption is an emerging area of inquiry, this essay remains primarily descriptive and only tentatively raises deeper explanatory theoretical questions.[1]

Data constraints further complicate an explanation at this stage. Very little aggregate data on P.R.C. domestic energy resources, commercial energy production, and public and industrial energy use are available to foreign observers. However, the data base for aggregate examination of China's domestic energy production and foreign energy trade is now very much improved over conditions existing just a few years ago. The People's Republic now makes some aggregate energy statistics available to the United Nations Economic Council for Asia and the Far East and to a publication of the U.N. Statistical Office entitled *World Energy Supplies* (WES).[2] The WES data, backdated through the last decade to 1961, are fragmentary, since solid data in the areas of refined petroleum products, bilateral energy trade, the entire natural gas sector, and installed electrical capacity are lacking. In addition, data in these areas are either inferential or calculated from bits and pieces of information and speculation in the Chinese and foreign press.[3] On the whole, foreign specialists accept the official energy statistics of the P.R.C. as reliable within five to ten percent, that is, as reliable within the knowledge of Chinese government statisticians.[4] No movitation for deliberate falsification exists, given the policy of selective data publication, nor is there evidence that Peking keeps two sets of books, one for internal use and the other for foreign consumption.[5]

Within such data constraints, the central tasks of this article consist of (a) describing the energy perspectives and policies of the Chinese government which are relevant to the current world-wide "energy crisis"; (b) comparing P.R.C. domestic energy statistics for

*B.A., Swarthmore College, 1965; M.A., Graduate School of International Studies, University of Denver, 1968; Ph.D. candidate, Department of Political Science, Stanford University.

the sixties to other countries and regions; and (c) relating China's international energy and resource policies to the organizational experience gained within the context of domestic energy development. Only the third task provides any theoretical explanation of Peking's international energy policies.

A cautionary note is necessary. The opening section of this essay describes the Chinese governmental and press reactions to the world energy crisis, highlighting salient aspects of Peking's energy policy. For that reason, the evidentiary basis of China's theoretical analysis of the energy crisis is presented with examples from the Chinese press and confirmation of the Chinese perspective from the Western press. This is not to suggest, however, that the P.R.C.'s energy policies are somehow objectively "correct" or "incorrect". So little is known about the interaction of social factors and energy variables at this stage that no such judgments are possible. A deliberate effort is made here to present a flash photograph of the present state of energy, organization, and policy at the local, societal, and international levels of analysis rather than to present a detailed historical review of any of these levels. The article includes some aggregate data for the sixties, but only to set present Chinese energy policies against a background which is in some manner comparable to energy systems in other countries.

Insofar as this essay suggests any explanatory hypothesis regarding Chinese energy policies, that hypothesis is that organizational variables intervene between domestic and international energy policies. China's international energy and resource policies are divided between policies toward the industrialized areas and policies toward the Third World. However, this bifurcation is not complete, since official Chinese statements speak of a "Second World" which lies between the large industrialized countries and the still non-industrial areas.[6] The Second World consists of small industrialized countries, principally Japan and the European countries. In any case, the hypothesis presented in the later sections of this paper is that China's energy and resource policies for Third World countries are based on organizational experience in energy production at the domestic local level and that policies toward the large industrial countries are based on organizational experience gained in production planning at the domestic societal center—*i.e.*, in Peking.

II. CHINA VIEWS THE WESTERN ENERGY CRISIS

In sharp contrast to treatment of the current energy crisis in the American press, the major press organs of the People's Republic of

China treat energy problems in terms of patterns of *distribution*, rather than patterns of *growth*.[7] That is, Western scholars and the press tend to treat energy questions in terms of the technical problems involved in maintaining high energy consumption growth rates within the context of an assumed industrial market economy.[8] There is little consideration, for example, in the pages of the *New York Times* of the underlying organizational questions raised by the failure of current energy production to keep pace with exponential increases in energy consumption. At most, the media editorialize about the high short-term profits which the oil corporations are realizing through market control and international cartel arrangements. At best, the press simply urges the capitalist countries onward toward greater technical research and development efforts.

In the Chinese press, on the other hand, the energy crisis is treated largely in terms of organizational and distributional factors. That is, energy shortages in the Western countries are treated as a matter of mismanagement and political backwardness rather than as a matter of technological difficulties. Viewed from Peking, the vast array of technological alternatives available to the industrial market economies at the present time gives the lie to arguments that the problem is primarily technological. After all, despite the fact that China's economy is still 89 percent coal-powered (1971)—uses petroleum extraction machinery—some of which dates from the fifties, has a natural gas industry that is just getting started, and has an installed hydroelectric capacity that is at present less than one percent of total hydropower potential,[9] China's per capita consumption of energy showed an annual increase of about 4.3 percent between 1961 and 1970. (The average annual percent rate of increase is surely even higher since 1970.) How can the Western countries with a developed technological infrastructure which ranges from high speed deep drilling equipment to satellite geological surveys suggest that the energy crisis is simply a matter of technological difficulties? Domestic energy problems, argues the *People's Daily*, can be traced to the capitalist management system. Trade imbalances can be traced to the failure of oil corporation imperialism.[10] To the Chinese, capitalism and imperialism are not technological matters, but rather matters of social, economic, and political organization.

A review of the history of the development of the energy crisis suggests that there is a substantial body of evidence to support the Chinese view that planning and organizational factors are prime causes of current energy shortages in the West. Take the premature decline in the Western production of coal as an example. In the Western industrialized countries, the development of coal extraction technology through the fifties and sixties revealed no serious discontinuities. Thus, although technologies are readily available today for safe mechanized extraction of subsurface coal and ecological rehabilitation of strip-mined areas, the application of these technologies lags far behind, making the extraction of coal an industry replete with a history of mine disasters, health hazards for the miners, and severe ecological damage. In using coal in power plants, electric utilities to this day resist the application of stack and effluent controls despite the obvious environmental costs of doing so. Social organization lags behind technology on both the production and consumption sides of the coal industry.[11]

A similar argument applies to the petroleum industry, despite the rapid development of petroleum and natural gas in the Western countries. The basic nature of the energy crisis in the petroleum industry (in contrast to that in the coal industry) is not a premature decline in production, but premature acceleration of consumption. For example, U.N. statistics repord a leap in the liquid fossil fuel share of energy consumption in Western Europe from 32 percent in 1961 to 56 percent in 1970.[12] The American natural gas industry shows a similar pattern of sudden growth and subsequent strain on available resources.[13]

What accounts for this pattern on petroleum and natural gas? Is the problem purely and simply the exhaustion of resources and the absence of technological remedies? Or do organizational and planning practices in the Western countries affect the boom and bust curves? The oil industry representatives currently making the rounds at energy conferences argue that price and tax structures are essentially to blame, despite the skyrocketing profit rates associated with the current price structure, and the enormous profitability of the corporate oil industry in the past.[14] But the corporations argue that the rapid depletion of crude oil reserves is due primarily to the relatively low cost of energy from petroleum during the fifties and sixties, in comparison with coal extraction and hydropower installation. Further advances in the petroleum industry are predicated (in the corporate view) on freely rising market prices of refined products, elimination of fixed prices for natural gas, retention and expansion of tax write-offs for exploration, and the lowering of ecological standards.

Yet there is an organizational factor which lies behind the screen of the pricing mechanism. Of the twelve top oil corporations, including the nine majors, each one is involved in cartel arrangements in some producing country with each of the other eleven. This cartel arrangement is so pervasive that the corporations produced more than one government upheaval in the 1950's and actually forced a decline in the well-head price of crude oil in 1960.[15]

Thus, the Chinese view that the Western energy crisis is due to corporate cartels, lack of government planning, and other features of monopoly capitalism cannot be dismissed easily. There is evidence in several branches of the contemporary Western energy production system that organizational factors are partial causes of the crisis and that a lack of government planning results in production gaps, shortages, and low levels of societal cooperation in energy consumption.

III. CHINA'S ENERGY PRODUCTION AND TRADE

The keyword in Chinese energy trade, as in the trade of most commodities, is "self-sufficiency." The story of Chinese self-sufficiency in energy production and trade revolves around the saga of the Taching oilfield. News accounts of progress at the Taching oilfield often start with a dramatic retelling of the story of the extraction of the first train load of crude oil in just one month of drilling under the most arduous of conditions in 1960. Taching is now the industrial model for the whole of Chinese industry, and symbolizes the determination to industrialize without the aid of foreign investment or foreign advisors. Considering the five- to ten-year lead time for oilfield development which is common in Western countries under optimal technological conditions, the Taching achievement is indeed quite unusual in the annals of oil history. The dramatic story tells how Chinese workers gathered on the windswept plain in northern Heilungkiang to prospect and map out the field in a single year, to haul antiquated drilling equipment by hand in freezing temperatures, and to complete the infrastructure of a modern oilfield in just three years. Within the self-sufficiency model set by Taching, the Chinese petroleum industry relies almost entirely on Chinese prospecting and analysis techniques, on a unique Chinese method of balancing water injection and oil extraction, and on a special drilling team organization which periodically sets world records in the annual number of meters drilled by a single team.[16]

The development of the Taching oilfield is, perhaps, the most dramatic chapter in the history of the Chinese energy industry, but to date the petroleum industry still occupies a rather marginal position in the domestic energy economy as a whole. For the Chinese, the maintenance of self-sufficiency in energy production implies a congruent pattern of development. That is, coal production continues to rise steadily, as the underpinning of the entire energy industry (and of industry generally), rather than giving way to replacement by oil. Foreign visitors to the People's Republic often comment on the use of coal-fired steam locomotives to drive modern passenger trains—prototype 6000 horsepower diesel locomotives are being turned out at the February 7th Rolling Stock Factory on the outskirts of Peking—while the extensive use of coal in rail transportation simply reflects the continuing dominance of coal in most energy consumption sectors. Consumption of petroleum products is still limited basically to diesel pumps, trucks, water transport, farm tractors, aircraft, and a few select modern industries. Despite an annual increase of 14.4 percent in domestic crude petroleum production from 1961 to 1971, the base consumption of solid fuels (coal and lignite) continues to move upward at an average annual increase of more than five percent.[17] (See Table I.)

Chinese energy trade during the sixties was nearly all in the form of petroleum products, from annual crude oil imports in the range of one to five million metric tons ("mmt"), to oil fuels, fuel oil, specialized lubricants, gasoline, kerosene, and jet fuel. Reliance on imports of all refined oil fuels dropped from 30.29 percent to 0.4 percent during the sixties, indicating a substantial increase in domestic refining capacity. Imports of gasoline stopped in 1968. Imports of fuel oil, kerosene, and jet fuels also dropped off markedly during the same period.[18]

During the early 1970's, however, the Chinese energy trade pattern shifted, making China in 1973 a net exporter of energy for the first time. The 1973 delivery of one million metric tons of crude oil to Japan was the first instance of substantial Chinese petroleum exports. (China is also a marginal net exporter of solid fuels, annually exporting an average of 0.867 million metric tons of coal equivalent ("mmtce")—0.3 percent of production—in solid fuels.)[19] In 1974 Japan is importing some five million tons of "sweet" low-sulfur Taching crude oil, and plans are under way for an oil pipeline from Taching to the coast to facilitate future exports as well as the domestic Chinese coastal trade. Five million metric tons of crude represents one week of current Japanese refinery capacity, but about 12 percent of China's total expected 1974 crude production of 42 million metric tons. In 1974 China is also exporting 100,000 tons of diesel fuel to Hong Kong through an intermediate sales process to oil corporation pumps (Shell and others). Thus, about one-fifth of Hong Kong's requirements are being met for the first time from Chinese sources, and for the first time in cooperation with the corporate giants. Diesel exports of 50,000 tons are going to Thailand at a low price, partly for diplomatic purposes.[20]

The principal reason for the turnabout in Chinese energy trade is that China needs foreign exchange for the purchase of entire industrial plants from Japan and several other industrial countries. The factory imports are designed to relieve bottlenecks in a few high-technology industries such as the petrochemical industry. Selective imports of oil extraction equipment are also under

TABLE I. ENERGY PRODUCTION AND CONSUMPTION BY AREA: AVERAGE 1961-1971

SECTOR	DOMESTIC ENERGY PRODUCTION (Million Metric Tons Coal Equivalent)			PER CAPITA ENERGY CONSUMPTION (Kilograms per Capita)			PETROLEUM PRODUCTION (Million Metric Tons)		
	Level	Increase	Percent	Level	Increase	Percent	Level	Increase	Percent
World	5,659	299	5.6%	1,649	54	3.4%	1,223	130	7.9%
Industrial	2,593	87	3.4%	5,474	198	4.1%	507	18.3	3.6%
Non-Industrial	1,370	125	9.7%	280	11	4.1%	919	87.8	10.2%
Africa	247	35	19.3%	288	8	3.1%	146	25	29.1%
North America	1,872	79	4.4%	9,445	321	3.5%	483	16	3.4%
Central America	319	8	2.9%	1,018	36	3.3%	217	5	2.7%
South America	56	3	6.4%	579	22	3.8%	31	2	5.9%
Middle East	655	73	11.4%	600	45	10.8%	490	53	11.3%
Asia	552	25	8.4%	n.a.	n.a.	n.a.	53	5	17.0%
(Capitalist)	203	6	3.3%	358	22	6.4%	40	3	8.6%
(Socialist)	348	19	5.4%	468	17	4.3%	13	2	16.4%
Western Europe	562	2	.4%	3,187	129	4.2%	19	.2	1.3%
Eastern Europe	1,347	68	5.3%	3,744	156	4.3%	285	21	8.2%
Oceania	68	5	9.5%	3,523	119	3.5%	2,642	2	103.3%[a]
China	324	17	6.1%	456	17	4.6%	13	1.5	14.4%
India	76	2	4.0%	176	3	2.0%	4	.7	33.4%
Japan	61	-2	-2.8%	2,156	190	9.6%	.7	.01	2.0%

Source: U.N. STATISTICAL OFFICE OF THE DEPARTMENT OF ECONOMIC AND SOCIAL AFFAIRS, WORLD ENERGY SUPPLIES 1961-70 UN DOC. ST/STAT/SER.J/15 (1972) and WORLD ENERGY SUPPLIES 1968-71 Tables 2, 8, UN DOC. ST/STAT/SER.J/16 (1973). The increases and percentage increases are averages from annual level data.
[a]Figures available for years since 1964 only.

negotiation for specialized purposes, to speed drilling, and to open new potential oilfields, particularly offshore fields under the continental shelf. The oil corporations are still reluctant to sell high technology equipment directly without strings such as crude oil sales stipulations.[21] China, of course, determinedly continues in the path of petroleum self-sufficiency, trading at increased levels, but firmly declining at each step to compromise complete domestic control of petroleum resources.[22]

The future of Chinese participation in petroleum trade is contingent on a number of factors, particularly the ultimate size of crude oil reserves. Recent Chinese statistics on known crude oil reserves are very difficult to come by. Before the opening of Taching, Western literature on the Chinese energy outlook estimated crude oil reserves as next to non-existent. Post-Taching estimates run to about 12 to 15 billion barrels of on-land reserves.[23] The greater part of likely Chinese reserves, including offshore reserves, still fall into the unknown category.[24]

IV. CONTRADICTIONS IN CHINA'S INTERNATIONAL ENERGY RESOURCES POLICY

A. *Energy Resource Distribution and International Organization:*

The Chinese policy on energy resource questions can best be understood in the context of the broader organization of the global energy system. The following section sketches the boundaries, structure, and distribution functions of that system in preparation for further exploration of the international energy policies of the P.R.C.

Virtually all energy commodities, including electricity, are movable commodities and are transported in large quantities across international boundaries. The uneven distribution of energy resources in, on, or above the earth's crust makes such transport of energy commodities to population and production centers a necessity. However, the distribution of energy resources does not presently take place in an entirely uniform manner. In fact, there are enormous differentials in per capita access to energy commodities and in per capita consumption of energy, varying from extremely low levels in slash and burn tropical agricultural economies or in arctic seal-hunting economies to extremely high levels in industrial economies. For example, per capita consumption of energy in North America is currently about 11,000 kilograms of coal equivalent per annum. The lowest per capita consumption rates are to be found in inland African countries such as Burundi and Rwanda with about 10 kilograms of coal equivalent per annum.[25] A comparison of family energy consumption in the suburbs of, say, Boston with household consumption in a remote Burundian village shows even greater differences.

The broad global range in energy distribution and energy consumption is reflected in aggregate statistics for regions and country categories. The industrial ("developed") countries currently consume energy at about 6,000 kilograms of coal equivalent per capita per annum while the non-industrial ("developing") countries consume about 350 kilograms of coal equivalent per capita per annum.[26] While this consumption ratio of 1:17 looks modest against the comparison of the Boston suburbanite and the Burundian villager, the broader statistic actually captures a world wealth differential which can be used as a rule of thumb to characterize the differences in standard of living associated with the process of industrialization. That is, industrialization means roughly a seventeenfold multiplication in standard of living.[27]

These differences in per capita consumption of energy are not simply a matter of geological energy deposits. For example, the Middle Eastern countries which are located on the richest oil deposits in the world have a per capita consumption of energy which is about half of the world average, one-fourth the per capita energy consumption of Western Europe, and one-tenth the per capita energy consumption of North America.[28] Furthermore, the distribution of wealth within the Arab producing countries is such that the actual energy consumption of the majority of Arab populations is far lower than the average statistics indicate. Therefore, natural fossil fuel deposits are not at all a guarantor of high energy use by the country's population. The human distribution system intervenes quite dramatically between the point of energy production and the point of energy consumption to determine patterns of energy allocation which are related to, but not determined by, the natural distribution of energy resources. One can hardly imagine an area with fewer energy resources (possibly excepting garbage) than New York City, yet New York City has possibly the highest per capita energy consumption level in the world. Some highly organized groups of people are engaged in creating and maintaining an energy distribution network that keeps New York in bright lights and the Arab shepherd in dried camel dung.

There are fundamentally three types of organizations involved in creating and maintaining global energy distribution patterns—governments, international organizations, and multinational corporations. In the context of Western market economy countries, the multinational corporations have been dominant throughout the first 70 years of the twentieth century. In the planned economy countries, governments are the dominant form of energy organization, at least insofar as foreign trade is concerned. Some twenty or thirty international organizations at present play an expanding role in global energy distribution, due to conditions of commodity scarcity. To a certain extent, these three types of organizations compete for influence and decision-making authority within the global energy distribution network; to a certain extent the three types of organizations coexist and even cooperate to smooth the flow of international energy transactions.[29]

Nine "major" corporations (Standard Oil of New Jersey, Shell, Texaco, Mobil, British Petroleum, Standard Oil of California, Gulf, Compagnie) now control over 80 percent of crude oil trade—although not exactly the same 80 percent that is imported by the industrial market economies. In addition to the nine majors, there are today a number of minor oil corporations with enough capital and infrastructure to equip, transport, extract, or refine some small portion of the world oil market. Several of the "minors" are government-controlled and serve primarily a single domestic market.

Facing the oil corporations and the industrial market countries are the present members of the Organization of Petroleum Exporting Countries (O.P.E.C.). O.P.E.C. members are all still non-industrial market economy countries (some with substantial government refined oil products. The interaction between the members of O.P.E.C. and the oil corporations is most intimate, since cartels among the oil corporations still "own" vast oil reserve concessions with the borders of O.P.E.C. countries.[30]

O.P.E.C. is a functionally specific multilateral organization with a regional bias toward the Arab producing countries, but with members from Latin America (Venezuela), Africa (Nigeria), and Asia (Indonesia) as well. O.P.E.C. is definitely country-dominant and functions primarily as a convenient forum for discussion and coordination of oil export policies with virtually no expectation of "task expansion" into areas other than oil policy coordination and information service. Its member countries differ widely in area, population, development policies, oil reserves, oil production growth rates, and the relative contribution of oil income to government revenues. Therefore, the area of potential agreement is sharply limited to oil export questions and consensus is difficult to achieve even in that single functional sector.[31]

The organizational structure of O.P.E.C. reflects and serves the member-government orientation. The Conference (which is member-oriented) dominates decision-making and the Board of Governors and Secretariat play interim and service roles only. The position of Secretary General rotates annually, keeping the

Secretariat firmly in the hands of the Conference.

China approaches these three types of organizations involved in global energy distribution in a manner which is puzzling and contradictory. How, for example, can Peking roundly condemn the multinational oil corporations in the press while simultaneously inviting the very same corporations to submit bids on offshore drilling equipment or while supplying these corporations with crude oil in Japan or diesel fuel in Hong Kong?[32] How can the Chinese press in the same breath praise the Arab producing countries for taking steps to conserve and protect oil reserves from foreign exploitation and praise the same countries for raising exports to the industrial countries? How can Chinese representatives in international organizations maintain both the posture of the vigorous champion of the Third World and the formal posture of structural conservatism, quiet behind-the-scenes parleys, and consciousness of the finest points of rank and protocol?

This puzzle sounds vaguely familiar as one reads back over the literature on Chinese diplomacy. Whole books by Western scholars are devoted to the proposition that China is either radical or conservative in the conduct of foreign relations, taking one side or the other of Peking's diplomatic image as projected in the Chinese press or in formal Chinese government statements, and then proceeding to show that the reality is just the opposite. According to these scholars, China either does not measure up to the "Maoist" image of foreign relations as an arena of struggle, or else the "fanatical" Chinese diplomats carry out actions deemed quite inappropriate to the conduct of such a large and prestigious country. Some scholars attempt to reconcile these two images by pointing out that there are distinct radical and conservative stages in the development of China's foreign relations since 1949—the "Bandung" era, the Cultural Revolution phase, and so on.[33]

There is considerable evidence for all of these positions in the twenty year diplomatic history of the People's Republic of China; yet these images in turn do not square with the persistence of certain press themes on foreign affairs over the course of two decades, with the general image of Chinese diplomats as paragons of integrity seldom willing to stretch a point for short term gains, and with the honesty and efficiency of Chinese trade relations.

There is some effort in the literature on China's diplomatic history to tie the foreign images of the People's Republic to the realities of the structure of domestic Chinese society. The linkages are strong, particularly in the area of attitudes toward the organization of resource distribution, between China's foreign images and the organization of the domestic Chinese resource production system.

In his essay "On the Correct Handling of Contradictions Among the People," Mao Tse-tung suggests that there are contradictions in the domestic Chinese production system which deeply affect the organization of resource distribution within China.[34] These are the contradiction between city and countryside and the contradiction between center and periphery. "Center" and "periphery" refer to the scope of decision-making authority exercised by a given component of organization. For example, decisions by the Ministry of Fuel and Chemical Industries are made at the organizational center of China's energy production system, while decisions by a drilling team at Taching are made at the organizational periphery.

The relation between these two pairs of internal contradictions is that the "center" is by and large located in the cities and the "periphery" is to be found in the rural hinterland. The organization of energy production, distribution, and consumption in China shows a marked division between the organizational patterns associated with the *societal center* (center plus cities) and the *local periphery* (periphery plus countryside). The energy planning ministries in Peking can be taken as an organizational expression of the societal center, while the model Taching oilfield can be taken as an organizational expression of the local periphery. The bifurcation of Chinese organizational patterns and the focus of Chinese organization around the societal center and local periphery is directly reflected in the formation of Chinese foreign policy, particularly in the area of Chinese diplomatic attitudes toward the organization of global resource distribution. Perhaps this domestic organizational division explains the contradictions in Chinese foreign relations noted above. And so this essay now turns to a brief description of energy organization at the local periphery.

B. *The Local Periphery*

1. *Organization of the Chinese Energy Industry in the Local Periphery*

That Taching, a remote oilfield in Heilungkiang Province, is the model for the whole of Chinese industry has organizational relevance in several respects. Taching is remote and rural; in that sense, Taching is part of the local periphery, despite the relatively high level of industrial technology which is utilized for oil extraction and on-the-spot refining. There are a number of alternative sites which do not serve as a model of development, regardless of a level of technology and efficiency which is relatively higher than that currently employed at Taching. The Shanghai machine tool industry, for example, utilizes heavier equipment, more mathematical and technological industrial analysis and instrumentation, greater energy input per worker, and so on. Some Shanghai units are considered models within a particular type of industry. And yet Shanghai industry lacks the quality of a direct and obvious relationship with the local periphery. Taching, on the other hand, combines the situational setting in the local periphery with the rapid development and high technology which characterize the movement into an industrial age.[35]

Taching represents the spirit of self-sufficiency and independence which are characteristic of most sectors of Chinese industry from the mills that produce the high tensile steel for bridges like the Nanking Yangtze River Bridge to the fledgling computer industry. The very association of the Taching experience with the withdrawal of Russian technicians and the overcoming of subsequent production difficulties in the early sixties drives home the point about self-sufficiency in industrial development.

China has the production and the life-style identity of a low per capita consumer of energy, and consequently of relatively low per capita income at the present time. The development of the Taching oilfield reflects the production necessities of a country working with low per capita energy inputs—the initial construction of simple rugged housing for the workers, the hauling of drilling equipment by hand, the utilization of equipment years and sometimes decades out of date—and yet exhibits annual production increases of 15-30 percent and higher in the face of all of these hardships.[36] Taching fits the rugged life-style which characterizes the 80 percent of the Chinese population that still work and live in the countryside. The drilling teams are quite large, numbering several hundred members each, utilizing labor-intensive methods whenever necessary. Per worker capital investment is therefore relatively low and workers maintain a constant awareness of tool maintenance and production waste recycling.[37]

Technological innovation at Taching focuses on entirely indigenous accounting and data analysis procedures which are developed on the spot to fit local conditions. "Three-in-one teams of workers, technicians, and cadres" design equipment renovation, investigate production bottlenecks, and deal with momentary crises. Inexperienced technicians are trained by the older workers. Core sampling and striation analysis are carried out through the collection and correlation of millions of bits of exact data on different parts of the oilfield, making the technological work "scientifically exact" as well as labor intensive and collective.[38]

In all of these ways, Taching is used as an industrial model to illustrate the organization of production in the local periphery. The style of organization is built up around the central concept of the self-sufficiency guideline, and differs substantially from the style of organization which is appropriate at the level of government planning in the energy industry. But the local periphery organizational style is highly relevant to the Chinese diplomatic perspective with regard to the organization of global resource distribution, particularly as that distribution affects the non-industrial or Third World countries. This perspective on the organization of resource distribution is highly contingent on a number of historical circumstances, particularly the Yenan experience and the very large size of the Chinese population relative to the primary agricultural production base. The self-sufficiency style of organization is relevant to countries with a low average per capita availability of energy to supplement human labor and with a relatively low capital margin from agriculture.

The long-term development picture is, however, not necessarily confined by these parameters, due to China's enormous potential energy and mineral resources. China has coal reserves which are among the largest in the world, and perhaps the world's largest hydropower potential. No one yet knows the full scope of Chinese petroleum reserves. The rate of *increase* in per capita energy consumption is already more than 4 percent annually, meaning a doubling time of under fifteen years. Per capita energy consumption is known to correlate very closely and linearly with monetary measures of income, indicating that the real standard of living is now doubling for the Chinese people every fourteen or fifteen years. China already ranks midway in per capita energy consumption (56th of 112 countries in 1969).[39]

2. *The Third World as Local Periphery*

There is considerable evidence that Peking applies the organizational paradigm of the local periphery to the organization of resource distribution for Third World countries. There is, of course, the direct statement by Chairperson Mao[40] that the non-industrial countries (and Europe) are a "vast intermediary zone" and that the large industrial countries constantly seek imperialist hegemony over the Third World.[41] This underlying theme is repeated in every Chinese analysis of the current situation which some Third World country faces. Africa, Asia, and Latin America are said to constitute a developing area with two-thirds of the population of the world and only a small percentage of world industrial production and consumption, but with a large contribution to world resource supplies. Thus the path to liberation for these countries is to join together, isolate the industrial "superpowers," reclaim control over indigenous resources, and throw off the yoke of capital imperialist or social imperialist control. The more chaotic and desperate the conditions in the local periphery, the more likely is the transition toward liberation, unity, and socialism. Repression breeds resistance.[42]

But beyond this rather broad theoretical view of the Third World as a vast countryside lie the demands of concrete diplomatic practice. China's diplomatic stance toward the Third World must span political systems as disparate as King Faisal's monarchy and Castro's communist party. However, this range of differences in "local" conditions is not at all unfamiliar to Peking's organizational perspective, for the enormous disparities within China in local conditions—say among the high Himalayan pastoral areas, the loess agriculture of Shansi, the industrial area in the northeast, and the alluvial plain at the mouth of the Yangtze River—require tremendous organizational flexibility at the center. Local self-sufficiency cuts two ways, liberating the locality from central control and liberating the center from local demands.

China's domestic experience in the local periphery provides lessons which are operative in the context of relations with Third World countries. The low per capita domestic consumption of primary industrial commodities, especially energy, gives China a Third World life-style identity. For example, at about 600 kilograms of coal equivalent in annual per capita energy consumption, China presently ranks with such Third World countries as Peru, Albania, Columbia, and Iran.[43] Consequently, Mao's cordial meeting with the Shah of Iran is less anomalous in the context of per capita energy consumption than by any political standard (although per capita figures are *averages* and do not reflect energy distribution within the society). China's Third World life-style identity and recent historical experience with mass poverty ensure a high degree of Chinese sensitivity to the issues of poverty and imperialist or colonial economic domination of Third World countries.

Within the context of the Third World, Chinese diplomatic practice relates to the country-government as the primary organizational unit. Virtually all Third World resource distribution questions are treated in terms of the organizational demands, needs, and control of the governments of the countries concerned. Independence is the diplomatic correlate of self-sufficiency in the domestic periphery. Indeed, the self-sufficiency guideline for domestic organization contains the same word for independence ("dulizizhu") as is used in diplomatic language.[44] All developments in the organizational control of energy resources in Third World countries are dealt with in the Chinese press in terms of whether or not such developments maximize country-government independence. At times in the context of the same article, independence means both raising petroleum production and exports to the capitalist countries and nationalizing some element of the petroleum industry. For another country, independence means restricting exports. The crucial criterion from the Chinese perspective is government control. Whatever Third World governments decide with reference to energy resources is interpreted as a visible sign of growing independence or "national sovereignty," so long as the locus of decision is at the governmental level and not dictated by oil corporation pressures or the governments of the industrial countries.[45]

In Peking's view, the same criterion of independence applies to decisions regarding energy resource distribution within the context of international organization which in any way abrogates authority over resources. For example, Peking vigorously supports the Peruvian claim to a two hundred-mile territorial limit of control over sea-bed resources, arguing that international conferences on the law of the sea have absolutely no authority to impose narrower limits in violation of coastal country sovereigntry.[46]

On the other hand, organizations which serve to maximize Third World control over domestic resources are harbingers of coming Third World influence and unity internationally. China participates very actively in international organizations and agencies which have a definite orientation toward Third World government control. Chinese representatives make strong statements on resource distribution questions on the floor of the General Assembly, in the U.N. Economic and Social Council, and in the U.N. Conference on Trade and Development.[47] These are generally considered the primary "forum" (as distinguished from "service") organizations in the U.N. system. The P.R.C. is reluctant to participate in the Food and Agricultural Organization or World Health Organization since these organizations are service-oriented, station observers and offices in member countries, collect domestic statistics in some detail, and otherwise whittle away at the organizational independence of the country-government.

Specifically with regard to energy resources, the New China News Agency regularly sends observers to and reports on the meetings of the Organization of Petroleum Exporting Countries. O.P.E.C. is oriented almost exclusively to control from the government level. Most O.P.E.C. decisions are the result of member initiatives and O.P.E.C. more often follows the general trend among the oil exporting countries than setting the trend. The Organization does, however, provide both a convenient central forum for discussion of oil-relevant issues and maneuvers vis-à-vis the corporations and the importing countries, and a vehicle for serious unified pressure in case member policies run into substantial resistance. Thus O.P.E.C. stimulates member-country unity on energy distribution questions without violating government independence, but it withdraws from any issue which seriously divides the membership, waiting until bilateral negotiations among individual members settle the issue and smooth the way for further collective action.[48]

China does not, to date, participate in the International Atomic Energy Agency, or any other organization which is concerned with nuclear power regulation. Peking in the past has a long record of vigorous opposition to "superpower hegemony" in the nuclear energy field, still to this day believing that every country has the "sovereign right" to the possession of nuclear technology and the utilization of nuclear energy, regardless of the risks to human health and organic environment. Indeed, this Chinese view corresponds rather closely to the present reality, since virtually every country large enough to have any use for nuclear technology and nuclear energy now already possesses some nuclear infrastructure—accelerators, experimental reactors, and even full scale generating reactors in some cases.

The local periphery organizational style influences Chinese diplomatic interaction with the international organizations concerned with affecting present resource distribution patterns. Decision-making by participation and the introduction of change through mass mobilization have a definite influence on Peking's formal position with regard to structural questions within the U.N. and subsidiary organizations. Chinese representatives argue that the cause of present limitations on the scope and effectiveness of international organization is the systematic structural exclusion of Third World countries from taking an active participatory role in many decisions, for Peking is unlikely soon to forget the African, Asian, and Latin American diplomats dancing in the aisles of the General Assembly on the occasion of the key representation vote in November, 1971.[49] As frequently as possible in the post-entry period, China is attempting to form and coalesce a Third World voting group, especially on structural questions.

Finally, Peking finds the emphasis on Third World government independence in resource distribution matters entirely consistent with a steady verbal attack on the role of the multinational corporations in energy and other resource trade. Every move of the oil exporting countries toward expropriation of corporate holdings and industrial infrastructure is greeted on the pages of the *People's Daily*,[50] relating such moves to the Chinese experience of winning independence first from the Western capitalists and later from the social imperialists. After all, in the Chinese view, the petroleum corporations represent no one but the owning class in industrial capitalist countries. Thus, the regular attacks on multinational oil corporations meet both the country independence criterion and the socialist emphasis on mass participation in production decisions.

There is, therefore, an evident and strong ranking of competing organizations in energy distribution from the Chinese perspective. Country-government is placed first as the primary locus of decision-making responsibility for the achievement of a more equal world balance in resource distribution. International organizations rank second insofar as each organization functions to aid in the relocation of resource control at the country-government level. Multinational corporations are at the bottom of the list and are seen as retarding the movement toward redistribution of resource control. This ranking and orientation toward the three types of organization involved in global energy distribution is largely the result of an organizational perspective gained by Chinese leaders in the context of the local periphery.

The local periphery organizational style, however, constitutes only half of the influence on Chinese diplomatic behavior with regard to energy and resource distribution questions. There is, in addition, an organizational perspective which derives from Chinese aggregate production and the domestic planning organization at the societal center.

C. The Societal Center

1. Organization of the Chinese Energy Industry in the Societal Center

Whereas the Chinese life-style identity is that of a low to medium level of per capita consumption, the aggregate energy consumption of the People's Republic of China ranks third in the world with the American and Russian "superpowers" occupying first and second place. China currently consumes about 500 million metric tons of coal equivalent annually. This amount is roughly equal to the annual energy consumption of the rest of East Asia combined, including Japan.[51]

On the production side, the aggregate Chinese energy production, again in the neighborhood of 500 million metric tons annually, also ranks high on a comparative scale, being double the energy production of the rest of East Asia, approaching the energy production of the whole of Western Europe (550 to 600 million metric tons annually), and double the annual energy production of Venezuela (about 250 mmt) and Iran (300 mmt).[52] The P.R.C. now produces about 20 percent of the world's coal, ranking second, with more than three times as much as all of the non-industrial countries combined, 100 times as much as the rest of East Asia, more than the whole of Western Europe, 65 percent of North American coal production, and 90 percent of the production of the entire Council for Mutual Economic Assistance (CMEA) group.[53] China currently produces about 9 percent of the world's crude petroleum supply, ranking 15th in the world with about the same crude oil production as Argentina, Mexico, and Western Europe.[54] With about 1 percent of China's total hydroelectric potential currently in production, the P.R.C. produces 3 percent of the world's hydroelectricity, ranking tenth, with more hydroelectricity than the whole of Africa, somewhat less than Brazil, more than India, and slightly more than Switzerland.[55]

These various consumption and production statistics demonstrate the general proposition that the People's Republic of China already has one of the world's largest energy infrastructures. Thus, in contrast to China's Third World per capita identity, the P.R.C. has the *aggregate capabilities* of a very large and growing energy producer. Given the relatively high rates of growth in domestic energy production, particularly in the petroleum sector (15 percent annually) and in hydroelectricity (10.2 percent), China is quite capable of reaching the aggregate energy consumption levels of the industrialized countries within the next four decades.[56] The development of the per capita consumption levels depends on the future of population growth and the effectiveness of present family planning programs, as well as on the growth of China's energy production.

The high aggregate energy capabilities of the P.R.C. are reflected in a number of technological developments which require energy intensive inputs. The introduction of computers, electron microscopes, diesel locomotives, and satellites, along with a host of other modern technological devices, depends on the availability of electricity and liquid fuels and the organizational and planning capability in the societal center to bring together diffuse resources and technological skills for the development of a particular device.

The main features of the organization of energy at the societal center are China's relatively high aggregate energy capabilities and the relatively centralized planning organization, just the inverse of the principal characteristics of the energy production base in the local periphery. The high aggregate capabilities at the center contrast sharply with the low per capita self-sufficiency model at the periphery, and the organizational style of tight central planning contrasts sharply with the participation and mobilization ethic in decision-making evident at Taching. That is not to assert that the center is unaware of the self-sufficiency model or that the local unit is insensitive to central planning directives. To the contrary, the societal center and local periphery planning and production organizations are highly aware of each other and seek complementary policies.

Professional Chinese diplomats are familiar with the organizational dichotomy within China and sensitive to both sides of the Chinese organizational style. Many diplomats have direct personal experience in a local industrial production unit, either as a consequence of origins and education or as a consequence of self-conscious training and re-training through participation in manual labor.

At the same time, Chinese diplomatic personnel are undoubtedly highly aware of the necessity for centrally coordinated action. Indeed, all contacts between China and the outside world, including all trade and sports contacts, are regularized through the central planning agencies of the Ministry of Foreign Affairs, the Ministry of Foreign Trade, and various sports and friendship associations. The party committees are at least as pervasive in these ministries and organizations as in the ministries which handle domestic energy production and distribution. Therefore, the organizational style center is a strong component of the experience, training, and awareness of the Chinese diplomatic community.

2. *The Industrial Countries as Societal Center*

The organizational style of the Chinese societal center spills over into China's diplomatic and trade approaches to the global energy system. There is a much quieter side to China's resource distribution policies than the strong press statements on the exploitation of Third World resources. China maintains firm diplomatic relations with most of the industrial market economy countries which are consuming the primary resource exports of the Third World. Diplomatic relations with the "superpowers" are extremely difficult for China during the present period because of the constant Russian and American tendency to seek comparative advantage in all regions of the world. From the Russian and American perspectives, China is one more area of diplomatic and economic competition. From the perspective of the People's Republic, however, there is no joining either, but simply a continual struggle to avoid domination or co-optation by both.

This point is seldom understood by American and Russian China experts who constantly predict a swing in one direction or another, as if Peking is on some sort of world trapeze. The Russian experts are nostalgic and bitter that China plays hob with the unity of the Communist bloc. The American experts are puzzled by the current political movement in China which indicates that Peking is not simply leaping into the American lap. China, on the other hand, sees a loss of world stature and independence in succumbing to either the meddling Russians or the itchy-fingered Americans. Perhaps the difficulty in both Moscow and Washington is in understanding that Peking views China, with the largest population in the world and growing per capita consumption levels, but especially with large aggregate resources and industrial capabilities, as a proud, equal, and fully capable participant in world affairs. The current Chinese verbal attacks on the Antonioni film reflect a resentment that Western commentators still view China in terms of low per capita consumption levels and ignore the achievements of China's large aggregage capabilities.[57]

China's aggregate energy capabilities also help to explain the current Chinese fascination with the European Economic Community and with Western European unity in general. Verbal support for the E.E.C. and press articles stressing European unity are more than a diplomatic flanking maneuver further to isolate the Americans and loosen the Russian grip on Eastern Europe. China's aggregate energy capabilities are roughly on par with the energy capabilities of Western Europe as a unit. Current Chinese and Western European production levels are comparable for coal, petroleum, and aggregate energy.

In the case of Western Europe, China reverses the press treatment of the role of international organizations and openly encourages regional intergration through the E.E.C.[58] Despite a high level of inter-governmental integration, China does not see the E.E.C. as violating the "national sovereignty" of member countries, or as a tool of imperialism. By contrast, the Organization of Economic Cooperation and Development (O.E.C.D.) and the Council for Mutual Economic Assistance (C.M.E.A.) are seen from Peking in precisely these terms and every breakdown of American institutional arrangements with Western Europe is greeted with a round of articles in the *People's Daily*. For example, the O.E.C.D.'s vain efforts to promote unity among oil consuming countries is taken as an indication of yet another breach in the foundations of American imperialism.[59] The difference in Chinese treatment of the E.E.C. and O.E.C.D. can be seen in part as a product of a Chinese sense of identity with the resource capabilities of Western Europe and Chinese wariness in dealing with American resource capabilities. Both responses relate to the aggregate capability side of China's organizational experience rather than to the per capita identity side.

The Council for Mutual Economic Assistance is viewed in much the same light as the O.E.C.D., being a vehicle for social imperialist domination of Eastern Europe. Again, China's present aggregate production capabilities are roughly equivalent to Eastern Europe (excluding the production statistics of the Soviet Union). China is very close to Eastern Europe in petroleum production and aggregate energy production, and produces about twice as much coal and hydropower as Eastern Europe (at 1970 levels). Rumania is China's largest petroleum extraction technology trading partner, each year exporting about thirty on-land drilling rigs and other equipment to China.[60] Here again, the sense of aggregate capability identity is a stimulus to close ties and a basis for equal trading relations.

The trade relationship between the People's Republic of China and Japan can also be viewed in terms of the relative aggregate energy capabilities of the two countries. Japan's aggregate energy consumption is about three-fourths that of the P.R.C., putting the two countries on a relatively equivalent aggregate capabilities base in energy consumption and making Japan a relatively safe trading partner, especially in high-technology manufactured commodities such as drilling equipment. On the other hand, Japan has a very narrow primary energy production base. There is little likelihood of Japan being able seriously to manipulate the export of manufactured equipment to China politically or even economically, since the reliance on Chinese primary products such as crude oil is at least as great as Chinese reliance on Japanese finished products and parts. Japan produces only 14 percent as much energy as China from domestic resources, creating an enormous Japanese thirst for Chinese crude petroleum, especially in a period of rising world crude petroleum prices. The transportation advantage of Chinese oil for the Japanese market is overwhelming and Taching produces "sweet" low-sulphur crude. These factors explain why China is willing to raise oil exports to Japan in 1974 to a substantial proportion of Chinese production, and even to build a special pipeline to the coast for future crude petroleum exports to Japan. With a tight hand on the valve, Peking can balance Tokyo's advantage in high technology equipment. China and Japan have roughly equivalent, but distinct, aggregate capabilities in the energy field.[61]

The tight central planning aspect of the Chinese organizational experience at the societal center also appears in Peking's diplomatic behavior.[62] Chinese diplomatic missions abroad are known for an extremely tight internal organizational style, for a sharp awareness and assertion of protocol, and for efficient and standardized processing of diplomatic inputs. Diplomatic representatives to the U.N. and other international organizations are carefully ranked in accordance with normal practice and speak publicly to questions at the appropriate rank regardless of more equal relations behind the closed doors of the delegation. Chinese diplomats engage in very little extracurricular socializing. Informal contacts are more frequently opened or maintained through Hai Hsin She, the Chinese press agency, than through social contacts with Chinese diplomats.

The organization of Chinese participation in international trade also reflects the tight centralized pattern which is typical of planning organizations generally at the societal center. A large proportion of regular trade business with multinational corporations flows through carefully controlled channels provided by the semi-annual Canton Trade Fair. In the Chinese view, the strict maintenance of central controls permits dealing with the capitalist corporate structure without succumbing to any form of exploitation. In the energy field, Chinese traders are very wary of oil company offers to trade extraction and offshore drilling technology for crude oil deliveries. Faced with the necessity of a choice between giving any element of control over Chinese resources to the oil corporations and not trading in oil technology (a choice which the oil corporations still insist on), China quietly refuses to trade. The 1972 purchase of the offshore drilling rig "Fugi" and the 400-ton workship "Kurushio" from Japanese corporations demonstrate a willingness to deal in used equipment rather than permit direct claims on Chinese crude petroleum. The 1974 sale of diesel fuel to Hong Kong oil subsidiaries is for cash. The 1974 sale of crude oil to Japan is on the basis of intergovernmental bargaining. China is also currently negotiating for an underseas pipeline with Mitsui, Nippon, the World Energy Development Corporation, and ENI (the state-owned Italian oil company). Here again, the most likely prospective contract winner is undoubtedly the deal with the least long-term strings.[63]

One finds, therefore, at all three levels of Chinese interaction with the organization of global energy system—the international organization, government, and multinational corporation levels—that the patterns of interaction are influenced by the Chinese organizational style of the societal center. That organizational style reflects two principal characteristics of the domestic energy production, distribution, and consumption system—China's relatively high aggregate production capabilities and China's tight central energy planning structure.[64]

V. CHINA AS THE ARBITER OF
RESOURCE DISTRIBUTION IN WORLD ORGANIZATIONS

The People's Republic of China has dual domestic energy characteristics. China ranks high in total energy production and 56th in per capita energy consumption. From a comparative perspective, therefore, the P.R.C. has the capabilities of a large aggregate producer and the life-style identity of a low per capita consumer.

China's dual domestic energy characteristics are matched by the duality of the domestic energy production system. Production of energy at the base in the local periphery relies on an organizational style of self-sufficiency. On the other hand, tight central planning and direct lines of communication comprise the societal center for energy production, distribution, and consumption.

Consequently, China's behavior with regard to global resource distribution questions within the context of international organization reflects both the dual energy characteristics and the dual organizational style of the domestic resource distribution system. China belongs both to the Third World of non-industrial countries and to the industrial world—to the former by virtue of the life-style and the quest for self-sufficiency, and to the latter by virtue of capabilities and organizational efficiency. Far from presenting an inherent and insurmountable contradiction for Chinese diplomacy, the dual energy and organizational characteristic present China with an opportunity to work with both sides of the present international system and on many sides of the resources distribution questions which capture an increasing proportion of the human energies of international organizations.

NOTES

[1] For tentative efforts to link social and energy variables, *see* H. ODUM, ENVIRONMENT, POWER, AND SOCIETY (1971); ENERGY AND POWER (Scientific Am. ed. 1971).

[2] U.N. ECONOMIC COMMISSION FOR ASIA AND THE FAR EAST, STATISTICAL YEARBOOK FOR ASIA AND THE FAR EAST: 1971, at 87-91 (1972); UNITED NATIONS, WORLD ENERGY SUPPLIES: 1961-1970 (UN Doc. ST/STAT/SER.J/15, 1972) and UNITED NATIONS, WORLD ENERGY SUPPLIES: 1968-71 (UN Doc. ST/STAT/SER.J/16, 1973) [hereinafter cited as WORLD EN'GY SUP. No. 15 or No. 16].

[3] For a patchwork statistical analysis of China's energy system,*see* YUAN LI WU & H.C. LING, ECONOMIC DEVELOPMENT AND THE USE OF ENERGY RESOURCES IN COMMUNIST CHINA (1963).

[4] B. Heenan, *China's Petroleum Industry*, 49 FAR EAST'N. ECO. REV., Sept. 23, 1965, at 565-567 [hereinafter F.E. ECO. REV]; B. Heenan, *China's Petroleum Industry (II)*, 50 F.E. ECO. REV., Oct. 14, 1965, at 93-95; Kucho Kodu, *Petroleum Industry Booms at Taching, Gijutsu Janaru* (Tokyo), Feb. 28, 1969, at 8 (trans. in JT. PUB. RES. SERV. No. 47,885, Apr. 18, 1969, at 14-21); Rawski, *Recent Trends in the Chinese Economy*, CHINA QUARTERLY, Jan.-Mar. 1973, at 25 [hereinafter CHINA Q.]; Ekstein, *Economic Growth and Change in China: A Twenty-Year Perspective*, CHINA Q., Apr.-June 1973, at 226; Chang Kuo-sin, *Situation Report on China's Oil Production*, 3 CHINESE VIEWPOINT NEWSLETTER, Feb. 3-9, 10-16, 17-23, 1974.

[5] Rawski, *supra* note 4.

[6] *Chairman of the Chinese Delegation Teng Hsiao-p'ing's Speech at Special Session of the U.N. General Assembly*, 17 PEKING REV., April 19, 1974, at 6.

[7] "Energy crisis" is used here to mean a sudden shift in global patterns of energy distribution, specifically, sudden changes in regional energy production/consumption ratios. The technical reasons for such a definition are complex and cannot be pursued in this essay. For Chinese press analysis of the energy crisis, see: *Growing Energy Crisis*, 16 PEKING REV., April 6, 1973, at

18; Chiu Pei-chiang, *"Energy Crisis" and Scramble for Energy Resources*, 16 PEKING REV., Sept. 28, 1973, at 12-14; *What is the Posted Price of Oil?*, People's Daily [in Chinese], Jan. 15, 1974, at 6; *American Monopoly Capitalists Use the "Energy Crisis Deepens, to Greatly Raise Profits*, People's Daily, Feb. 10, 1974, at 6; Chang Chian, *Behind the So-Called "Energy Crisis"*, Hong Qi [Red Flag, in Chinese], Feb. 1974, at 83-86.

[8]Analysts vary with regard to the degree of acceptance of the growth-technology-market-economy frame of analysis. *See generally* TANZER, THE POLITICAL ECONOMY OF INTERNATIONAL OIL AND THE UNDERDEVELOPED COUNTRIES (1969); Boffey, *Technology and World Trade: Is There Cause for Alarm?*, 172 SCIENCE, Apr. 2, 1971, at 37-41; R.C. North & N. Choucri, *Population, Technology, and Resources in the Future International System*, 25 INT'L. AFF. at 224-237 (1971); ENERGY AND POWER, *supra* note 1; W.D. Smith, *Energy Crisis: Shortages Amid Plenty*, N.Y. Times, Apr. 17, 1973, at 1, col. 5.

[9]WORLD EN'GY. SUP. No. 15 at 47; WORLD EN'GY. SUP. No. 16 at 27; China's total hydropower is estimated at around 500 million kilowatts, according to T. TREGEAR, AN ECONOMIC GEOGRAPHY OF CHINA 197 (1970).

[10]*The 21st OPEC Assembly Decides to Take Measures for the Prevention of Exploitation by Foreign Monopoly Capital and to Protect the Economic Interests of Member Countries, Raising the Taxes and Posted Prices of Oil for Foreign Companies*, People's Daily, Jan. 3, 1971, at 5; *The Awakening Strength of the Third World in the Struggle for Unity*, People's Daily, Jan. 23, 1974, at 6; *American Monopoly Capitalists Use the "Energy Crisis"*, *supra* note 7.

[11]J. HOLDREN & P. HERRERA, ENERGY: A CRISIS IN POWER 26-49 (1971).

[12]WORLD EN'GY. SUP. No. 15 at 9.

[13]*Charge is Denied on Gas Reserves*, N.Y. Times, July 3, 1973, at 31, col. 7; *Cutbacks Seen for Natural Gas Supply*, N.Y. Times, Aug. 16, 1973, at 52, col. 2.

[14]W.D. Smith, *Oil Concerns' Profits Rise*, N.Y. Times, July 26, 1973, at 53, col. 3; *Richfield Joining in "Gas" Price Rise*, N.Y. Times, Sept. 18, 1973, at 63, col. 1.

[15]R. ENGLER, THE POLITICS OF OIL: PRIVATE POWER AND DEMOCRATIC DIRECTIONS (1961); TANZER, *supra* note 8. The Chinese argue explicitly that monopoly arrangements lower well-head prices. See, Chang Chian, *Behind the So-Called "Energy Crisis"*, *supra* note 7. This argument is confirmed by the empirical findings of Z. MIKDASHI, THE COMMUNITY OF OIL EXPORTING COUNTRIES: A STUDY IN GOVERNMENTAL COOPERATION 111, 166 (1972). For a dissenting view, *see* G. Chandler, *The Myth of Oil Power*, 46 INT'L. AFFAIRS 710-718 (1970).

[16]For general articles on Taching oilfield, *see* C. Macdougall, *Finding the Gusher*, 43 F.E. ECO. REV., Mar. 26, 1964, at 658; Min Yu, *Taching Oilfield Developed Under the Direction of the Thought of Mao Tse-tung*, Hong Qi [Red Flag], Dec. 6, 1965, at 23-28 (trans. in JT. PUB. RES. SERV. No. 33,699, Jan. 11, 1966, at 36-54); *Production High Tide in Petroleum Stirred by Technological Innovations: The Emphasis is on Politics; the Dialectic is Being Adhered to*, Worker's Daily (Peking), Dec. 8, 1965, at 1 (trans. in JT. PUB. RES. SERV. No. 33,662, Jan. 10, 1966, at 6-8); C. Macdougall, *Taching Spirit*, 51 F.E. ECO. REV., Feb. 24, 1966, at 380-381; Ch'ing Sheng, *Taching—A New Type of Petroleum Field in China*, China News (Peking), Apr. 7, 1966, at 13-17); *Taching Oilfield Achieves High Standards*, trans. in JT. PUB. RES. SERV. No. 49,030, Oct. 10, 1969, at 33-35; *Report from Taching Oilfield: Vigorous Political and Ideological Work*, 15 PEKING REV., Jan. 14, 1972, at 11-12, 19; *Taching Oilfield's Fresh Victories*, 15 PEKING REV., Sept. 29, 1972, at 23;

Chinese Communist Party Committee of the Taching General Petrochemical Plant, Release Latent Forces and Increase Production, Hong Qi [Red Flag], Oct. 1972, at 48-51; *Twelve Glorious Years,* Hsinhua News Bulletin, Jan. 3, 1973, at 14-16; Hsinhua News Bulletin, Jan. 5, 1973, at 1-3; Hsinhua News Bulletin, Jan. 6, 1973, at 9-12; W. Burchett, *Chinese Tap Taching Potential,* 83 F.E. ECO. REV., Jan. 14, 1974, at 45-46.

[17]WORLD EN'GY. SUP. No. 15 at 108. The official P.R.C. statistics are now available on crude petroleum production only through 1971, leaving 1972 and 1973 production levels to secondary reports, rumors, and scholarly speculation, all of which put the current annual growth rates at over 75%. Chou En-lai's estimate of 1973 crude oil production at 50 million metric tons is 250% of the official production statistic (20 mmt) for 1970. See Chang Kuo-sin, *Situation Report on China's Oil Production,* 3 CHINESE VIEWPOINT NEWSLETTER, Feb. 3-9, 1974.

[18]WORLD EN'GY. SUP. No. 15 at 108, 140, 185, 211, 237.

[19]*Id.,* at 74.

[20]See N. Ludlow, *U.S. Companies and China's Oil Development,* N.Y. Times, Mar. 3, 1974, §3, at 2, col. 1, for current information on Chinese oil production and trade. Also: *China's Oil Tanker's First Voyage to Japan,* 16 PEKING REV., Sept. 28, 1973, at 21; *Port Construction,* 17 PEKING REV., Jan. 11, 1974, at 21-22; Chang Kuo-sin, *Situation Report on China's Oil Production, supra* note 4.

[21]For example, the resistance of the oil "majors" to the acquisition of domestic high technology refining capacity by the government of India. See TANZER, *supra* note 8, at 208-220, 257-274.

[22]Stewart, *Chinese Engage in Buying Spree,* N.Y. Times, Oct. 9, 1973, at 65, col. 6.

[23]175 WORLD OIL, Aug. 15, 1972 at 132.

[24]See article by Victor Li in this volume.

[25]WORLD EN'GY. SUP. No. 15 at 7.

[26]*Id.,* Table 2, N. Choucri & J.P. Bennet, *Population Resources, and Technology: Political Implications of the Environmental Crisis,* 26 INT'L. ORGAN. 175-212 (Spr. 1972).

[27]J. DARMSTADTER, P. TEITELBAUM & J.G. POLACH, ENERGY IN THE WORLD ECONOMY: A STATISTICAL REVIEW OF TRENDS IN OUTPUT, TRADE, AND CONSUMPTION SINCE 1925, at 33 (1971).

[28]WORLD EN'GY. SUP. No. 15 at 7-8.

[29]9 INT'L. REV. SERV., June 1963, at 1-91, (A. Mezerik ed.); 6 INT'L. REV. SERV. 1-66 (A. Mezerik ed. 1960); TANZER, *supra* note 8.

[30]Z. MIKDASHI, *supra* note 15.

[31]Farnsworth, *Oil Nations at Vienna Seeking More Price Increases,* N.Y. Times, Sept. 16, 1973, at 10, col. 1; *OPEC Demands Price Rise,* N.Y. Times, Sept. 28, 1973, at 49, col. 1.

[32]Chang Chian, *supra* note 7; *3,000 Ecuadorians Hold Meeting and Rally to Oppose the Exploitation by American Monopoly Capital and to Demand the Expropriation of American Corporations,* People's Daily, Jan. 6, 1971, at 5: *Opposing the Trans-National Companies,* 16 PEKING REV., Feb. 23, 1973, at 20-21.

[33]The argument is often phrased in terms of whether China's foreign policies reflect "ideology," "national interest," or some hypothetical combination brew. For examples, *see* V.P. DUTT, CHINA AND THE WORLD: AN ANALYSIS OF COMMUNIST CHINA'S FOREIGN POLICY (1964); H.C. HINTON, COMMUNIST CHINA IN WORLD POLITICS (1966).

[34]Speech by Mao Tse-tung, *On the Correct Handling of Contradictions Among the People,* Supreme State Conferenec, Feb. 27, 1957, reprinted in

TAMIMENT INSTITUTE, LET A HUNDRED FLOWERS BLOOM, Sept. 9, 1957.

[35]*Supra* note 16. For general works on the organization of Chinese industry, *see* A.D. BARNETT, CADRES, BUREAUCRACY, AND POLITICAL POWER IN COMMUNIST CHINA (1967); CHINA: MANAGEMENT OF A REVOLUTIONARY SOCIETY (J.M.H. Lindbeck ed. 1971); B.M. RICHMAN, INDUSTRIAL SOCIETY IN COMMUNIST CHINA (1966); E.L. WHEELWRIGHT and B. MC FARLANE, THE CHINESE ROAD TO SOCIALISM: ECONOMICS OF THE CULTURAL REVOLUTION (1970).

[36]For estimates of production increases at Taching, see Leary, *Mystery Matters*, 57 F.E. ECO. REV., Aug. 24, 1967, at 390; *Taching Oilfield Achieves High Standards*, *supra* note 16; *Twelve Glorious Years*, *supra* note 16; Kudo, *supra* note 4.

[37]*Twelve Glorious Years*, *supra* note 16; Burchett, *supra* note 16; Ch'ing Sheng, *supra* note 16.

[38]Ch'ing Sheng, *supra* note 16; Min Yu, *supra* note 16; *Production High Tide in Petroleum Stirred by Technological Innovations: The Emphasis is on Politics; the Dialectic is Being Adhered To*, *supra* note 16.

[39]WORLD EN'GY SUP. No. 15, at 46-47; T.R. TREGEAR, A GEOGRAPHY OF CHINA 145-56 (1965).

[40]The Chinese language term "chuhsi" is without gender, translation services (Western and Chinese) to the contrary. Thus "Chairperson Mao" is an accurate rendering of the sense of the Chinese and corresponds to modern social and legal idiom.

[41]CHAIRMAN MAO TSE-TUNG'S IMPORTANT TALKS WITH GUESTS FROM ASIA, AFRICA, AND LATIN AMERICA (Foreign Languages Press, 1960); Mao Tse-tung, *American Imperialism is Closely Surrounded by the People of the World*, trans. in THE POLITICAL THOUGHT OF MAO TSE-TUNG 383-4 (S.R. Schram ed. 1969) [hereinafter cited as POLITICAL THOUGHT]; Mao Tse-tung, *China Supports the African People's Struggle for Liberation* (trans. in POLITICAL THOUGHT, *supra* this note, at 378); Mao Tse-tung, *India's Path is Similar to that of China* (trans. in POLITICAL THOUGHT, *supra* this note, at 378-79); Mao Tse-tung, *The Chinese People Resolutely Support the Just Patriotic Struggle of the Panamanian People*, People's Daily, Jan. 13, 1964, at 1; Wen Shih-jun, *Scientific Judgment and Oversight: A Study of Chairman Mao Tse-tung's Theses on International Questions as Expounded in the Fourth Volume of Selected Works of Mao Tse-tung*, Red Flag, Nov. 16, 1960, at 7-21 (trans. in JT. PUB. RES. SERV. No. 6700, Feb. 3, 1961, at 10-30); *Mao Talks to Edgar Snow*, WASHINGTON POST, Feb. 14, 1965, pt. A, at 1, col. 3, 14, col. 1, 15, col. 1.

[42]*Hegemony Cannot Decide Destiny of World History*, 16 PEKING REV., Nov. 30, 1973, at 4-6; *How Imperialism Plunders the Developing Countries*, 15 PEKING REV., Apr. 28, 1972, at 16; *The Third World Voices Strong Demand*, 15 PEKING REV., June 2, 1972, at 16-17; *World in Great Disorder: Excellent Situation*, 17 PEKING REV., Jan. 18, 1974, at 7-11; Chung Chih-ping, *World Advances Amidst Turbulence*, 17 PEKING REV., Jan. 4, 1974, at 20; Li Chang-mao, *Awakening and Growth of the Third World*, 17 PEKING REV., Jan. 18, 1974, at 11-12; Speech by Chou En-lai, *Report to the Tenth Congress of the Communist Party of China*, August 24, 1973, adopted August 26, 1973, in Red Flag, Sept. 1973, at 12.

[43]WORLD EN'GY SUP. No. 16, at 27. The figure (560 kilograms coal equivalent per capita annual consumption in 1971) is probably a bit high due to official underestimation of the Chinese population. See article by Judith Banister in this volume.

⁴⁴For a reference to Third World Independence as "dulizizhu" see The Awakening Strength of the Third World in the Struggle for Unity, People's Daily, Jan. 23, 1974, at 6; for the use of the term "duli" alone see Speech by Chou En-lai, supra note 42; Chairman of the Chinese Delegation Teng Hsiao-p'ing's Speech at Special Session of the U.N. General Assembly, supra note 6.

⁴⁵Developing National Economies: Venezuela's Petroleum Output, 16 PEKING REV., Mar. 9, 1973, at 16; Struggle for National Economic Development, 16 PEKING REV., Feb. 16, 1973, at 6-7, 12.

⁴⁶China's Stand on Questions of Rights over Seas and Oceans, 15 PEKING REV., Mar. 10, 1972, at 14-16; Refuting Superpowers' Sophistry at the Sea-Bed and Ocean Floor Committee's Meeting, 15 PEKING REV., Mar. 31, 1972, at 17-18; Statement of the Ministry of Foreign Affairs of the People's Republic of China, 15 PEKING REV., Jan. 7, 1972, at 12; UN Conference on Law of the Sea Recommended, 16 PEKING REV., Nov. 2, 1973, at 13.

⁴⁷Chairman of Chinese Delegation Chiao Kuan-hua's Speech, 16 PEKING REV., Oct. 5, 1973, at 10-17; China at UN Economic and Social Council, 15 PEKING REV., June 9, 1972, at 16-18; China Supports Developing Countries' Demand for Improvement of Trade in Primary Products, 16 PEKING REV., Mar. 16, 1973, at 11, 18; China's Principled Stand on Relations of International Economy and Trade, 15 PEKING REV., Apr. 28, 1972, at 11-14; Hail the Successful Conclusion of the 4th Summit Conference of the Non-Aligned Countries, 16 PEKING REV., Sept. 21, 1973, at 10-11; Resolution on Permanent Sovereignty over Natural Resources, 16 PEKING REV., May 11, 1973, at 19-20; Third UNCTAD Opens in Santiago, 15 PEKING REV., Apr. 21, 1972, at 13-15; 13th Session of UN Trade and Development Board, 16 PEKING REV., Sept. 21, 1973, at 23; Chairman of the Chinese Delegation Teng Hsiao-p'ing's Speech at Special Session of U.N. General Assembly, supra note 6.

⁴⁸Mikdashi, supra note 15, at 69, 78-83, 128, 217.

⁴⁹Unite to Win Still Greater Victories, 15 PEKING REV., Jan. 7, 1972, at 8.

⁵⁰Algeria Decides to Raise the Posted Price of Oil, People's Daily, Jan. 24, 1974, at 6; The Ceylon Government Nationalizes the Shipping Infrastructure of Three Foreign Oil Companies, People's Daily, Jan. 3, 1971, at 5; 3,000 Ecuadorians Hold Meeting and Rally to Oppose the Exploitation by American Monopoly Capital and to Demand the Expropriation of American Corporations, supra note 32; Venezuela Raises the Posted Price of Oil to Protect National Sovereignty, People's Daily, Jan. 5, 1974, at 6; The Venezuelan Assembly Passes a Law Asserting the Right of the Venezuelan President to at any time Unilaterally Change the Posted Price in American Oil Agreements, People's Daily, Jan. 8, 1971, at 6.

⁵¹WORLD EN'GY SUP. No. 15, at 47, Table I.

⁵²Id., Table 2.

⁵³Id., Table 5.

⁵⁴Id., Table 8.

⁵⁵Id., Table 20.

⁵⁶Id., Tables 8 and 20.

⁵⁷Repudiating Antonioni's Anti-China Film, 17 PEKING REV., Feb. 22, 1974, at 13-16; A Vicious Motive, Despicable Tricks—A Criticism of Antonioni's Anti-China Film "China", 17 PEKING REV., Feb. 1, 1974, at 7-10.

⁵⁸Association with Developing Countries, 16 PEKING REV., Aug. 10, 1973, at 28; A Nine-Nation Summit Conference, 15 PEKING REV., Oct. 27, 1972, at 17-18, 23. For other reasons for China's close relationship with Western European countries, see Wilson, China and the European Community, CHINA Q., Oct.-Dec., 1973, at 647-66.

[59] *Fruitless Trade Negotiations,* 15 PEKING REV., Jan. 21, 1972, at 21.

[60] Heenan, *supra* note 4; MacDougall, *Business in Bloc,* 40 F.E. ECO. REV., May 9, 1963, at 302-3; Tretiak, *Has China Enough Oil?,* 44 F.E. ECO. REV., June 11, 1964, at 536-37.

[61] *Supra* note 20; Ching Jan, *Trouble Ahead for Japanese Economy,* 17 PEKING REV., Jan. 25, 1974, at 15-17. Sino-Japanese discussions of trade in crude petroleum date back to 1961. See Garratt, *Oil from Japan?,* 32 F.E. ECO. REV., May 18, 1961, at 319; Heenan, *supra* note 4; MacDougall, *supra* note 16, MacDougall, *Production Records,* 53 F.E. ECO. REV., Sept. 29, 1966, at 621-24.

[62] D.W. Klein, *The Management of Foreign Affairs in Communist China,* in CHINA: MANAGEMENT OF A REVOLUTIONARY SOCIETY 305-42, *supra* note 35.

[63] G. Hudson, *Japanese Attitudes and Policies Toward China in 1973,* CHINA Q., Oct.-Dec., 1973, at 700-707; Shabad, *Soviet and China in Oil Search: Offshore Programs Seek to Enhance Export Potential,* N.Y. Times, Mar. 12, 1974, at 49, col. 1, 54, col. 4.

[64] For an analysis of China's aggregate capabilities and growth rates, see Gurley, *The New Man in the New China: Maoist Economic Development,* 3 CENTER MAG., May, 1970, at 25.

China and Off-Shore Oil:
The Tiao-yü Tai Dispute

VICTOR H. LI*

Tiao-yü Tai (called the Senkaku Islands in Japanese) is a group of eight coral islands located approximately 150 miles northeast of Taiwan, 250 miles southwest of Okinawa, and 250 miles east of the China mainland coast. The depth of the surrounding waters is about 100-150 meters, except that a deep break in the continental shelf just south and east of the islands separates them from the rest of the Ryukyu Islands[1] These islands are small (the largest is about twenty acres) uninhabited, and until recently, quite undistinguished. They were used by fishermen from the surrounding areas as bad weather shelter and as a place for drying fish. Occasionally, the American military used them as a gunnery range.

The recent discovery that the continental shelf in this area may hold vast deposits of oil changed this situation. In November 1967, the Republic of China (Taiwan), the Republic of Korea, and the Republic of the Philippines under the sponsorship of the United Nations Economic Commission for Asia and the Far East (E.C.A.F.E.) formed a Committee for Coordination of Joint Prospecting for Mineral Resources in Asian Offshore Areas. This body, assisted by the United States Naval Oceanographic Office, conducted a seismic survey of the East China Sea and the Yellow Sea in October and November of 1968, and published a report the following May. It concluded that the organic matter deposited by the Yellow River and the Yangtse River may make the continental shelf in this region one of the most prolific oil and gas reservoirs in the world. The most favorable part of the region for development was identified as a 200,000 square kilometers area just northeast of Taiwan—or almost exactly the location of Tiao-yü Tai—where the neogene sediment is more than 2000 meters thick. Three basins in the Yellow Sea, one near Korea and two near China, with sediments of about 1500 meters thickness were also favorable areas.[2]

The E.C.A.F.E. report was followed up by a more thorough survey sponsored by the Japanese Prime Minister's Office, headed by Professor Hiroshi Niino of Tokai University. From June 14 until July 13, 1969, the survey team conducted submarine topography, geologic, magnetic, and seismic surveys of the 200,000 square kilometer area northeast of Taiwan, especially the immediate area around Tiao-yü Tai. The report was digested in the *Japan Petroleum*

*Professor of Law, Stanford Law School, and Director, Center for East Asian Studies, Stanford University.

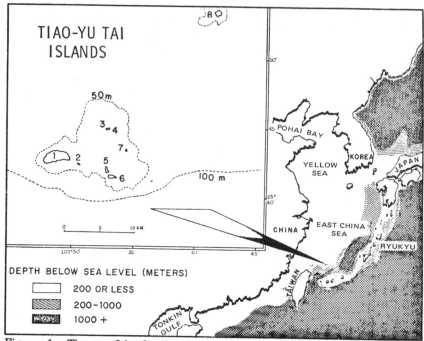

Figure 1. Tiao-yu Islands. Source: BOSTON ACTION COMMITTEE TO DEFEND TIAO-YU AS CHINESE TERRITORY, TIAO-YU ISLANDS—A LEGAL ANALYSES (Apr. 10, 1971) (On file, *Stanford Journal of International Studies*).

Weekly. This source stated (without saying whether these are the actual words of the Niino reports):

> The survey confirmed the general belief that there exists [sic] marine Neogene deposits of more than 2,000 meters thickness throughout the entire area surveyed. Existence of folding structures also have been confirmed at several locations. The E.C.A.F.E. survey which had been conducted in the fall of 1968 suggested that there existed a large scale of sediment basis and thick deposits. The recent survey by the Japanese team, taking [a] further step forward, has led us to believe the area is worth prospecting for oil resources . . . . It might be concluded from the results of the survey that there is a high possibility of natural resources in the vicinity of [the] Senkaku Islands. While this conclusion is a tentative one, because of the fact that detailed interpretation of the data still is underway, the study of the collected rocks and fossils will be able to present [a] more precise conclusion.[3]

Naturally enough, the expectations for a great oil find produced much activity. By May 1969, nearly 14,000 applications for drilling rights were filed with the Ryukyu Government, principally by the Japan Petroleum Development Public Corporation and by Kojo Omija, an amateur geologist who had been prospecting this region for some time. The number of applications approached 25,000 by September 1970.[4]

About this time, the government of Taiwan took the first steps to develop these resources. In August 1970, a statute controlling the exploration and drilling for oil and gas in Chinese territorial waters and continental shelf was passed. Various tax incentives encouraged foreign investment.[5] In a related action, the Executive Yuan created four zones for undersea oil prospecting in a 69,000-square-mile area

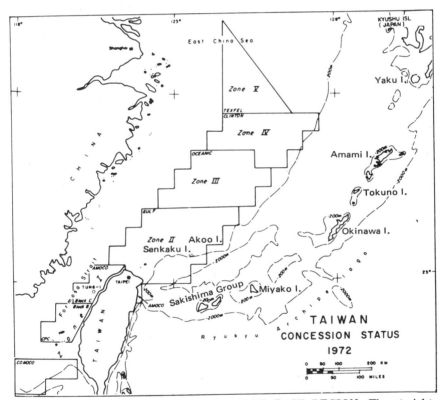

Figure 2. GENERAL STUDY SETTING OF EAST REGION. The straight dashed line separates the Yellow Sea from the Continental Shelf, and the irregular dashed line denotes the seaward edge of the shelf. Source: Wageman, Hilde, and Emery, *Structural Framework of East China Sea and Yellow Sea*, 54 AMER. ASSOC. OF PETROLEUM GEOLOGISTS BULLETIN 1612 (1970).

in the Taiwan Straits and in the sea north of Taiwan, including the Tiao-yü Tai area. Furthermore, the China Petroleum Corporation, a state-owned company, signed agreements with Amoco, Gulf Oil Company, Oceanic Exploration Company, and Clinton International Oil Company to develop these four zones jointly.[6]

On August 21, 1970, the Legislative Yuan quickly ratified the 1958 Convention of the Continental Shelf. However, two important reservations which substantially affect the meaning of the Convention were made, ostensibly with reference to Article 6.[7] The first endorsed the principle that the Continental Shelf is a natural extension of the territory of a state. The thrust of this statement appears to be that since there is a deep break in the ocean bottom, the westward "natural extension" of the Japanese and Ryukyu shelf reaches only to this trough and therefore not to Tiao-yu Tai. The second reservation asserted that peaks of the continental shelf that emerge above the sea level should be regarded as a part of the shelf. That is, non-contiguous states (such as Japan) cannot use small outcroppings (such as Tiao-yu Tai) to claim rights over the continental shelf, and also perhaps cannot even made 1, which recognizes that islands also have continental shelves, "islands" are interpreted to not include "peaks."[8]

Issue was now joined. Both sides claimed Tiao-yü Tai and the adjacent shelf, each stating the legal bases for its own claims and attacking the assertions of the other. The Japanese Foreign Minister reportedly said that "there is no question that Japan has territorial rights over (Tiao-yü Tai) and there is no need, either, to discuss their territorial status with any country."[9] Taiwan, although responding more slowly, stated that no compromise or concessions would be made with respect to these islands.[10]

The issues involved were not only economic. Many Chinese still feel strongly about the evil of imperialism, especially Japanese imperialism, and do not want to repeat the history of granting concessions to foreign states. Such feelings raised the level of rhetoric. A group of reporters from the *China Times* planted a Taiwan flag on one of the islands in September 1970; patriotic sentiments were very bruised when the flag was torn down by Ryukyu policemen and the reporters were forcibly evicted.[11] A relatively small but not unimportant "protect the Tiao-yü Tai Islands" movement developed among students and intellectuals of Chinese descent living in the United States.[12] This movement not only involved many such persons in overt political activity for the first time, but also took on international political significance as the People's Republic of China adopted a hard line on protecting the islands in late 1970, while Taiwan was moving toward compromise with Japan.

Beginning in late October 1970, the climate of controversy began to change; talks were held between officials of Japan and Taiwan to see whether the disagreements could be resolved.[13] On November 12, a "Liaison Committee" was formed in Seoul by representatives of Taiwan, the Republic of Korean, and Japan to explore jointly and exploit the underseas oil resources.

Until this time, the People's Republic of China had been strangely silent on this dispute. Perhaps it felt that its position on this issue was abundantly clear and needed no further elaboration, or perhaps it was galvanized into action through concern about extensive cooperation between Japan and Taiwan. In any case, in early December 1970 the New China News Agency denounced the formation of the "Liaison Committee" as an "act of aggression by the U.S. and Japanese reactionaries in league with the Chiang Kai-shek gang and the Pak Jung Hi clique" and as "an outright dirty deal between aggressor and traitors."[14]

The Tiao-yü Tai dispute disappeared from public view with nearly the same speed with which it had developed. The international political climate was changing in 1971; no party particularly wanted to stress points of disagreement. The United States was making approaches to the People's Republic of China by dismantling the trade embargo; ping-pong diplomacy soon followed. Throughout this period, both Japan and Taiwan moved uncertainly, waiting to see the shape of the developing Sino-U.S. rapproachement.

Nevertheless, the issue flared again in mid-1971 with the conclusion of the Okinawa Reversion Treaty. Prime Minister Sato reportedly said: "It is clearly stated in this [Treaty] that [Tiao-yü Tai] will be returned to Japan."[15] Japan included these islands in its air defense identification zone, and began to patrol the surrounding waters.[16] The statement by Sato and related activities brought forth strong attacks from the People's Republic of China on Japanese militarism and American imperialism.[17]

The dispute quieted with President Nixon's visit to China in early 1972, and with Prime Minister Kakuei Tanaka's visit later that year. While it seems likely Tiao-yü Tai was discussed during these visits, no statements were made by either side. No overt drilling is presently going on in this area.[18] Taiwan has generally been silent, possibly because it does not want to aggravate a situation over which it has so little control.

I. TO WHOM DOES TIAO-YÜ TAI BELONG?

The Tiao-yü dispute raises a host of legal and other problems. To begin with, the lack of clear rules concerning the very new subject of the continental shelf makes analysis difficult and tenuous. It is possible that at the time of the adoption of the Convention on the Continental Shelf in 1958, the magnitude and complexity of the problems in this area were not fully known. The situation of small uninhabited islands sitting atop large deposits of oil may not have been contemplated. Article 1 of the Convention states that islands have continental shelves, but debate during the Conference and commentaries written afterwards show considerable uncertainty as to whether this article applies to small islands, particularly uninhabited ones.[19] In addition, Article 6, which deals with how to divide the shelf between two states whose coasts are adjacent or opposite, is somewhat vague. The "equidistant" principle is applied unless the parties can reach agreement by themselves and there are no "special circumstances"—whatever these include. Moreover, in the *North Sea Continental Shelf Cases*,[20] the International Court of Justice said that this principle is not sufficiently accepted by all countries to constitute an international custom, and therefore it applies only to signatories to the Convention. Neither the People's Republic of China nor Japan is party to the Convention; Taiwan ratified the Convention, but with reservations that undercut Articles 1 and 6.

Based on present international practice, several solutions to this dispute are possible. First, if small uninhabited islands do not have continental shelves, Japan is cut off almost entirely from shelf resources regardless of which country owns Tiao-yü Tai. That is, in the East China Sea the deep trough, which runs roughly from the northern part of the island of Taiwan to the western part of the island of Kyushu, is a clear break in the shelf coming off the China mainland, thus precluding Japan from claiming any portion of the shelf west and north of the Trough. In the Yellow Sea and in the Tsushima Strait between Japan and Korea, Japan could claim only a very small area bounded by the median line drawn between Kyushu and the Korean island of Chefu and between the Japanese island of Tsushima and the Korean mainland.

A very different problem arises if all islands have continental shelves. In case Tiao-yü Tai belongs to China, the deep trough remains a barrier to Japanese claims. If these islands belong to Japan, however, Japan could exploit the resources in the surrounding shelf. Japan might also gain access to substantial portions of the East China Sea by arguing for a median line between Tiao-yü Tai and the China mainland. Thus the crucial issue remains: to which country does Tiao-yü Tai belong?

The complex legal issues of this case are further beclouded by uncertainties about what the situation actually was in this area a century ago and before. As might be expected, knowledge about the history of several obscure uninhabited islands is not very great. The initial claim of the Ryukyu Government was that the Tiao-yü Tai

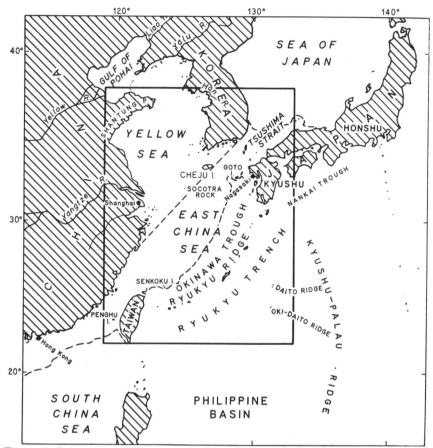

Figure 3. Taiwan Concessions, 1972. Source: Kenneth, *Petroleum Developments in the Far East in 1972*, 57 AMER. ASSOC. OF PETROLEUM GEOLOGISTS BULLETIN 2103 (1973).

Islands were "discovered" in 1884 by a Japanese fisherman, Tatsushiro Koga.[21] However, the Chinese produced historical records going back to 1403 A.D. that refer to Tiao-yü Tai.[22]

The situation is also confused by allegations which have never been proved and which may be nothing more than rumor. Nevertheless, a single allegation may be subsequently cited by many different sources, and in due course a body of literature builds up around this "fact". For example, several articles repeated that in 1941 (when Taiwan was still under Japanese rule) some Taiwan fishermen filed a suit with the "Japanese Supreme Court" claiming that Ryukyuan fishermen were trespassing on the Tiao-yü Tai fishing grounds.[23] The court supposedly ruled that these islands belonged to

the Taipei (Taiwan) prefecture, rather than the Okinawa prefecture, apparently on the grounds that they historically belonged to Taiwan rather than to the Ryukyus. This case would have shed much light on the actual status of Tiao-yü Tai. Unfortunately, a careful search of Japanese court records has not produced, as far as I know, any record of such a case, although conceivably the records were destroyed during the war.
hearings of the Senate Foreign Relations Committee on the Okinawa Reversion Treaty in October 1971, Grace Hsu, a naturalized American citizen, produced an apparently genuine document in which the Empress Dowager in 1893 awarded three of the islands in the Tiao-yü Tai group to Hsu's grandfather "as his property for the purpose of collecting medicinal herbs."[24]

A. *The Japanese Position*

As mentioned earlier, the original Japanese claim was that Tiao-yü Tai belonged to the Ryukyu Government (and hence to Japan after the Okinawa Reversion Treaty) by virtue of "discovery" by Tatsushiro Koga in 1884. This position has proved untenable in the face of Chinese historical records.

A more viable variation of this position is that while China did sight these islands several centuries earlier and thereby acquire some "inchoate title," this title was not perfected through subsequent "effective occupation and control."[25] Alternatively, China had discovered these islands some time earlier, but had essentially abandoned them through neglect and disuse by the late 19th century. In either case, Japan did establish "effective occupation and control" over the abandoned islands after 1884. Tatsushiro Koga regularly visited and used these islands for many years. The Japanese Government considered annexing Tiao-yü Tai in 1885, but ultimately declined for fear that others would accuse Japan of territorial expansionism.[26] However, in early 1895, after the Sino-Japanese war but *prior* to the signing of the Treaty of Shimonoseki, the islands were formally annexed to the Ryukyus, and subsequently were clearly treated as Japanese territory.[27] Consequently, these islands now belong to Japan since "an inchoate title . . . cannot prevail over a definite title founded on a continuous and peaceful display of sovereignty by another state; for such display may prevail even over a prior, definitive title put forward by another state."[28]

Thus, the Treaty of Shimonoseki which ceded "Taiwan, together with all islands appertaining to Taiwan" to Japan did not, in the Japanese view, concern Tiao-yü Tai at all, since it was *already* a part of Japanese territory. After the Second World War in the Statement of Surrender, the 1951 San Francisco Peace Treaty, and the 1952

Sino-Japanese Peace Treaty, Japan renounced all claims to "Taiwan and the Pescadores."[29] Again, Japan may assert that these actions do not affect Tiao-yü Tai since it was a part of the Ryukyus and not a part of Taiwan.

The United States government appears to agree with this position although it is careful to point out that the dispute should be settled by Japan and China alone. In 1971, Howard McElroy, Country Officer for Japan in the Department of State wrote:

> Under Article 3 of the Treaty of Peace with Japan, the U.S. has full administrative rights over "Nansei Shoto",[30] including the Ryukyus, south of 29 degrees north latitude. The term "Nansei Shoto" was understood to mean all islands under Japanese administration at the end of the war which were not otherwise specifically referred to in the Peace Treaty. The term, as used in the treaty, was intended to include the Senkaku Islands. . . .

> The U.S. has consistently maintained that any dispute over sovereignty over the Senkaku Islands should be settled by the parties themselves (or, if they wish, by third party adjudication). Neither the Peace Treaty nor the Reversion Agreement will dispose of such a dispute.[31]

Ordinance No. 27, promulgated on December 27, 1953, and demarcating the "geographical border of the Ryukyu Islands," includes Tiao-yü Tai within the Ryukyu group.[32] A large map clearly indicating this fact is included in every report of the Civil Administration. In 25 years, no other government has objected to the Ordinance or the map.

B. *The Chinese Position*

The positions of the People's Republic of China and Taiwan are essentially the same since both base their claims on events occurring before 1949. However, they differ in that Taiwan has signed a peace treaty with Japan in which Japan renounced all claims to Taiwan and the Pescadores, but makes no reference to "Nansei Shoto" or to Tiao-yü Tai.[33] The People's Republic of China, on the other hand, has consistently denounced both the San Francisco Peace Treaty and the treaty between Japan and Taiwan.

The fundamental Chinese claim is that discovery alone or discovery coupled with some formal act of taking is sufficient to establish sovereignty over Tiao-yü Tai.[34] Even if there is a require-ment of demonstrating effective occupation and control, "the manifestations of sovereignty over a small and distant island . . . cannot be expected to be frequent."[35] Among the manifestations of sovereignty, China can cite the use of Tiao-yü Tai by Chinese fishermen for many centuries, the including of these islands in a Chinese coastal defense system in 1556,[36] or even the alleged grant of part of these islands to Grace Hsu's grandfather in 1893. China can also point out that in the 1879 negotiations with Japan concerning title to the Ryukyu Islands both sides agreed that the Ryukyus consisted of 36 islands; the Tiao-yü Tai islands were not listed among the 36.[37]

China's position is that during the earlier centuries Tiao-yü Tai was a part of Fukien province and later of Taiwan province when it was formed in 1887. The attaching of Tiao-yü Tai to Taiwan province has important ramifications if Taiwan tries to become an independent state or if Taiwan rejoins China with some provisions for local autonomy, including a degree of control over provincial economic development. The attempted annexation of Tiao-yü Tai by Japan in early 1895 can have no legal effect since one state cannot unilaterally proclaim sovereignty over the territory of another. Instead, the Treaty of Shimonoseki ceded Taiwan province, together with Tiao-yü Tai, to Japan. During World War II, the Cairo Declaration stated "that all the territories Japan has stolen from the Chinese, such as Manchuria, Formosa, and the Pescadores, shall be restored to the Republic of China." The Potsdam Declaration, the Statement of Surrender, and the Peace Treaties similarly provided for the return of Taiwan to China.[38] Tiao-yü Tai, being a part of Taiwan, was also returned to China. In 1949 the People's Republic of China became the successor state to the Republic of China.

The lack of explicit objection to the 1953 Ordinance issued by the Civil Administration of the Ryukyu Islands does not present a particularly serious problem. The People's Republic of China has consistently denied the legality of the Peace Treaty and the actions taken under that document. Taiwan can argue that silence in the face of an adverse claim cannot, in and of itself, result in a loss of territory. In the *Island of Palmas Case*, for example, the United States had communicated to the Netherlands the contents of a treaty between the United States and Spain whereby Palmas was transferred to the United States. No objections were made by the Netherlands at the time, although seven years later the United States learned that the Netherlands also claimed Palmas. With respect to the silence of the Netherlands, arbitrator Max Huber said that "it would be entirely contrary to the principles laid down above as to territorial sovereignty to suppose that such sovereignty could be affected by the mere silence of the territorial sovereign as regards to a treaty which has been notified to him and which seems to dispose of a part of his territory."[39]

The Japanese claim to title on the basis of having occupied these islands (as part of the Ryukyus) without objection from other states since 1945 is also hard to maintain. Prescription is not clearly recognized under international law as a means of acquiring territory. Besides, 25 years may not be a sufficiently long period of time, especially when the territory in question consists of eight small, un-inhabited, and distant islands.

C. Tiao-yü Tai and International Law

To whom, then, do the islands belong? At one level, the conclusion depends on one's biases as to what the "facts" of the case are. But at another level, the answer is that international law may not provide an answer. This statement goes well beyond the usual complaints citing the procedural difficulties in getting cases before international tribunals or the lack of mechanisms for enforcing judgments. Instead, international law may lack the substantive rules for dealing with this case, and may even lack the means of developing appropriate rules.

The Clipperton Island and the *Island of Palmas* cases typify the standard international law approach. "New" lands are regarded as *terra nullius* which may be claimed by whoever first discovers them; discovery, however, sometimes must be accompanied by a ceremonial taking of possession, and followed by effective occupation and control.

On the basis of these rules, China's case is strong. (We ought to keep in mind, however, the fact that we are not certain about the actual situation in earlier times, and the present Chinese legal advantage may merely reflect the earlier development of adequate historical record-keeping.) Given the available facts, China first sighted these islands more than five centuries ago, and thereafter periodically acted in ways that manifested state authority over them. The Grace Hsu document, if genuine, gives concrete proof that China had not abandoned these islands as of 1893. Japan, on the other hand, did not manifest state authority over Tiao-yü Tai until 1895. The earlier abortive effort to annex these islands seems to show that at least in 1885 Japan did not assert a territorial claim to them. The overall result is that these islands were Chinese territory that was ceded to Japan in 1895 as part of Taiwan province. They should have been returned to China in 1945, but were erroneously grouped with the Ryukyu Islands by the United States.

Japan's greatest advantage is that the entire legal and factual situation is cloudy. First, China may have first sighted these islands, but "sighting" may not be the same as "discovery." There may have been some acts displaying Chinese sovereignty in the past, but it is unclear whether these acts were sufficiently frequent and of adequate magnitude to constitute effective occupation and control.

Furthermore, visits to and use of these islands by Japanese fishermen serve to weaken Chinese claims of absolute sovereignty. The general uncertainty is reflected by the absence of objection in 1945 and 1953 when Tiao-yü Tai was included as part of the Ryukyus. Perhaps at that time no one really knew, or even cared, what their legal status was.

The entire foregoing analysis has a fundamental weakness: it may be legal, but it is not necessarily sensible. The international law rules cited were formulated to deal with a particular situation. In the 16th and 17th centuries a number of Mediterranean and North Atlantic states were searching for new lands that would provide new wealth and power, and to a lesser extent, new opportunities for religious propagation.[40] Since all these states were sovereign equals, all were equally entitled to search and claim. To reduce the possibility of future conflict, the original discoverer was granted title or inchoate title to newly found land. There may also have been a religious consideration in these rules—that the discoverer was thought to have been directed to his find by the will of God.

The additional requirement of effective occupation and control ensured that the original purpose for granting title would be carried out: that the new land would be properly exploited and developed. If the discovering state chose not to or was unable to carry out the original objective, then the new land should go to another state which could and would do so.

The situation in East Asia was entirely different. There was no doctrine of the sovereign equality.[41] The Chinese emperor, for example, was the Son of Heaven ruling everything under heaven. As such, it was not necessary for a flag to be planted or a ceremony performed in order to show that newly discovered land belonged to him. There was little effort to discover and colonize new lands. Indeed, China prohibited emigration until the 19th century. Since China was the center of civilization, Chinese should be loathe to move away to far off lands. If "barbarians" wished to partake of Chinese culture, they could travel to China. With these traditions, China would not be expected to satisfy Western-originated rules.

In addition, the legal rules contemplate a situation involving the discovery of valuable territory. Until just a few years ago, Tiao-yü Tai was essentially worthless. It is quite possible that neither China nor Japan really cared about the islands. Certainly, neither country acted in the way it would have if it had known of their value. It is not sensible now to assign this vast wealth on the basis of actions taken a century or more ago when Tiao-yü Tai appeared to be eight small rocks in the ocean rather than a potentially huge deposit of oil.

Even if the rules of international law are appropriate for the facts of this case, there still exists another major obstacle. When speaking of international law, particularly customary international law, we basically are referring to rules developed by Mediterranean and North Atlantic states during the past several centuries. All "new" states were then bound to obey these rules. Indeed, in years past the willingness to adhere to international law was an important criterion for judging whether a "new" state was sufficiently "civilized" to join the family of nations.

The "new" states (including China and Japan) may regard this process of adherence quite differently. Many of the concepts and rules of international law were formulated without the participation of these states. Earlier, they were forced to accept these rules of the game or else they were not allowed to play. Now, with the growth in the power and importance of the Third World, many of the "new" states are reexamining and deciding afresh whether they should adhere to the substantive rules of international law. Some rules, such as those defining the status of diplomats or the concept of sovereignty, may be found to be in accord with the national interest and retained. Others, such as the requirement of compensation for nationalized property, may be attacked and rejected in whole or in part. Still other areas, including a great deal of the law of the sea, are being studied to see just where national interest and international comity lie. In any case, even where a clear and sensible rule of international law exists, some "new" states may not feel a moral or legal obligation to adhere to a norm created entirely by other parties at other times.

The recent Law of the Sea Conference tried to produce general agreement on a set of rules that defines more precisely rights over the continental shelf and related matters.[42] China participated in this Conference with considerable enthusiasm, seeing it as a fine opportunity for the developing countries to help establish rules that take their interests into account. The Chinese view is that traditional international law of the sea was "forced on various countries by imperialist and colonial maritime powers," and that the developing countries in the past "were deprived of the right to speak and had no way to safeguard their sovereignty."[43] However,

> . . . a fair and reasonable solution to this question [law of the sea] should be sought by all countries in accordance with the principle of mutual respect for sovereignty and territorial integrity, mutual non-aggression and non-interference in each other's internal affairs, and that the hegemony of the superpowers trying to partition and control the seas must be firmly opposed.[44]

China has not yet stated the exact extent of its claims to the adjacent continental shelf. In 1958, China declared that its territorial sea extended twelve nautical miles outward from a line connecting base points on the mainland coast to those on the coastal islands.[45] No mention was made, however, of the continental shelf or of sea-bed resources. Since that time, China has adopted the general principle that "the shallow-water areas are a natural extension of the territorial land of the coastal states,"[46] and that "all coastal countries have the right of disposal of their natural resources in their coastal seas, sea-bed and the subsoil thereof."[47] The term "shallow-water" suggests a depth criterion for determining the extent of the continental shelf, although no particular depth limit (such as the 200 meter mark in the 1958 Convention on the Continental Shelf) has been referred to. A depth criterion is beneficial to China since both the Yellow Sea and the East China Sea are less than 200 meters deep, and the China-Philippines shelf slopes gently out from the China mainland for a long distance. (While apparently adopting a depth criterion for itself, China has not precluded the use by other countries of a distance-from-the-shore criterion.)

Beyond the area claimed by coastal states, China believes that the "resources in the international sea-bed belong, in principle, to the people of all countries."[48] It supports the formation of a strong international authority to directly exploit and reap benefits from these resources.[49]

II. CONCLUSION

In the last analysis, it seems unlikely that any of the principals involved in Tiao-yü Tai would be willing to forego a part of all of its claims on this vast potential deposit of oil merely because of some rules of international law, especially rules of such uncertainty and doubtful suitability. The dispute will likely be resolved politically, or in the most extreme case militarily, even though the final solution may be phrased in legal terms. The striking silence of the concerned governments over the past two years may indicate that the political process of balancing and accommodating national interests is already underway.

The article by Professors Haley and Rood stresses that one of Japan's most critical national concerns is the need to ensure an adequate supply of energy resources. In recent years, Japan has tried to maintain good relations with Middle Eastern countries, while at the same time vigorously seeking new sources in Southeast Asia and on its own continental shelf.

One aspect of this search for fuel has been the effort to develop oil resources in west Siberia and gas resources in the Yakutsk and Sakhalin area jointly with the Soviet Union.[50] Progress has been slow on this front, in part because of China's opposition to any activity that increases the Soviet presence along the Chinese border. China is particularly concerned about the military significance of a proposed second Siberian railroad to transport oil from west Siberia to the coast.

For strategic, economic, and internal political reasons, Japan is anxious to maintain good relations with China. In addition, Japan hopes that in the future China will become a major supplier of oil. In 1973 China for the first time exported one million tons of oil to Japan; this will increase to three million in 1974, and possibly five million by 1975.[51] More generally, many foreign observers have pointed out that China's foreign trade has nearly doubled over the past three years, and that for the first time in over twenty years China is running a trade deficit of about $500 million.[52] Substantially increasing the export of oil could eliminate the deficit, and also provide the foreign exchange needed for further purchases and development.

One especially attractive prospect for Japan (as well as for countries such as the United States) is the possibility of supplying technology, equipment, and capital in a massive effort to help develop China's oil production capacity—and thereby increase the quantity available for export.[53] This is a sensitive area, since China would firmly oppose any form of foreign aid and probably even foreign investment. Nevertheless, Japanese and Western oil companies seem to believe that they can formulate arrangements which would be acceptable to China and still involve major participation by foreign companies. For example, China might select sites to explore and drill, hire a foreign contractor to do the job, and ostensibly control the manner in which the work is done. The foreign company would pay a fee for the right to drill and supply all equipment and capital. If oil were found, first all expenses would be repaid; thereafter China and the foreign company would share the oil output according to some equitable formula or else the foreign company would be permitted to purchase oil at a reduced price. Some foreign companies feel that such an arrangement is particularly suitable for the development of off-shore oil. Technology and cost require high investment in this area, and the physical separation of the off-shore operations would enable China to make extensive use of foreign resources, at the same time minimizing the direct effects of foreign influences on Chinese society.

China, of course, may not regard with equal enthusiasm the prospect of massive foreign participation in the development of Chinese resources. The article by Professor Ray convincingly argues that the establishing of extensive foreign economic ties also results in considerable indirect social and political costs. Self-reliance need not lead to autarky, but it does suggest that foreign involvement in Chinese economic affairs is likely to be fairly limited in the future. In addition, there is some doubt whether the kind of compensation sought by the foreign oil companies for their participation would be viewed by China as "an exchange of equal economic value."[54]

The current trade deficit does not seem to require the taking of drastic new steps, i.e., bringing in foreign oil companies. Present Chinese oil production is estimated at 45-50 million tons a year, and exceeds refining capacity by 10-20 million tons.[55] This excess, if sold instead of stockpiled, would yield about $750 million to $1.5 billion annually—enough to take care of existing and anticipated currency requirements. Moreover, production will grow at a more rapid rate than refining capacity in the foreseeable future.

Thus, China is likely to develop its oil resources slowly, using essentially its own capital to finance, on a step by step basis, additional efforts. At present, purchase of foreign equipment has been largely limited to items used for exploiting the Pohai Bay, a relatively shallow and accessible body of water.[56] As resources in this area are developed, the income generated could be used to develop other areas, both on-shore and further off-shore.

NOTES

[1] See Professor Niino's Report on Submarine Geology Near Senaku Islands, JAPAN PETROLEUM WEEKLY, Sept. 29, 1969 (outline); Oct. 6, 1969 (topography); Oct. 13 and 20, 1969 (geology); Oct. 27, 1969 (magnetic survey); Nov. 10, 1969 (seismic survey); Dec. 1, 1969 (summary.) for a detailed description of these islands and the adjacent continental shelf.

[2] Id. See also J. Wageman, T. Hilde, K. Emery, Structural Framework of East China Sea and Yellow Sea, 54 AM. ASS'N PETROLEUM GEOLOGISTS BULLETIN 1611 (1970); Choon-Ho Park, Continental Shelf Issues in the Yellow Sea and the East China Sea, Occasional Paper No. 15, (Law of the Sea Inst., Univ. of Rhode Is.) (1972); Hungdah Chiu, Tiao-yü Tai lieh-hsü wen-ti yen-chiu (Research on the Tiao-yu Tai Islets Problem), CHENG-TA FA-HSUEH PING-LUN, No. 6 (June, 1972).

[3] Professor Niino's Report on Submarine Geology Near Senaku Islands, JAPAN PETROLEUM WEEKLY, Sept. 29 and Dec. 1, 1969, supra at note 1. Further surveys were planned after the signature of the Okinawa Reversion Treaty. See JAPAN PETROLEUM WEEKLY, Apr. 26, 1971.

[4] Asahi Shimbun Analysis, Asahi Evening News, Sept. 11, 1970.

[5] Cabinet Approves Draft Statute on Drilling Oil and Gas, News From China (Chinese Information Service), Jul. 31, 1970; Legislative Yuan Adopts Statute on Oil Prospecting, News From China, Aug. 25, 1970. (These news releases are issued by a Taiwanese government information service.)

[6] Cabinet Designates Oil Prospecting Area, News from China, Aug. 18, 1970; Cabinet Marks Out Oil Areas on Continental Shelf, News From China, Oct. 16, 1970.

[7] *Taipei Ratifies Continental Shelf Pact,* News From China, Aug. 21, 1970. Article 6 says: "Where the same continental shelf is adjacent to the territories of two or more States whose coasts are opposite each other, the boundary of the continental shelf appertaining to such States shall be determined by agreement between them. In the absence of agreement, and unless another boundary line is justified by special circumstances, the boundary is the median line, every point of which is equidistant from the nearest points of baselines from which the breadth of the territorial sea of each State is measured."

[8] Article 1 of the Convention says: "For the purpose of these articles, the term "continental shelf" is used as referring (a) to the seabed and subsoil of the submarine areas adjacent to the coast but outside the area of the territorial sea, to a depth of 200 meters or, beyond that limit, to where the depth of the superadjacent waters admits of the exploitation of the natural resources of the said areas; (b) to the seabed and subsoil of similar areas adjacent to the coast of islands."

[9] Japan Times, Dec. 5, 1970, at 1, Col. 2; Protect Tiao-yü Tai Committee, *Pao-wei Tiao-yü Tai* at 7 (pamphlet, 1971).

[10] *Taipei is Firm on Tiao-yü Tai Islands Issue,* News From China, Sept. 25, 1970; *Shen Reiterates China's Firm Stand on Tiao-yü Islets,* Oct. 6, 1970. *See also Tiao-yü Tai ti shih-chien* (The Matter of Tiao-yü Tai), LIEN HO (Special Edition, New York, 1971).

[11] New York Times, Sept. 6, 1970, § 1, at 9, col. 1. The Ryukyu Government also sent a patrol ship into this area. *Tiaoyu and Other Islands Have Been China's Territory Since Ancient Times,* 15 PEKING REV., Jan. 7, 1972, at 14. *See also Formal Incorporation of Tiao-yü Tai Isles Urged,* News from China, Aug. 28, 1970.

[12] *See, e.g.,* the full page advertisement in the New York Times, May 23, 1971, § E, at 7.

[13] *See Japan to Meet with China over Tiao-yü Tai Isles,* News From China, Sept. 3, 1970; *Sino-Japanese Talks to be Held on Senkaku Islands,* News From China, Oct. 2, 1970; *Taipei, Tokyo Hold First Confab on Tiao-yü Tai Islets,* News From China, Oct. 24, 1970.

[14] *U.S. and Japanese Reactionaries Out to Plunder Chinese and Korean Seabed Resources,* 13 PEKING REV., Dec. 11, 1970, at 15, 16; *see also* Japan Times, Dec. 7, 1970, at 1, col. 2; New York Times, Dec. 6, 1970, § 1, at 32, col. 3.

[15] *Tiaoyu and Other Islands Have Been China's Territory Since Ancient Times,* 15 PEKING REV., Jan. 7, 1972, at 13; *see also* PAO-WEI TIAO-YÜ TAI, *supra* note 9, at 5-7.

[16] *Tiaoyu and Other Islands Have Been China's Territory Since Ancient Times,* 15 PEKING REV., Jan. 7, 1972, at 13, 14; *see also,* PAO-WEI TIAO-YÜ TAI, *supra* note 9, at 5-7.

[17] *Tiaoyu and Other Islands Have Been China's Territory Since Ancient Times,* 15 PEKING REV., Jan. 7, 1972, at 13, *Statement of the Ministry of Foreign Affairs of the People's Republic of China, id.* at 12.

[18] However, there has been some seismic exploration by Taiwan in other areas of the East China Sea, and Amoco has drilled the first off-shore well eight miles from the coast of Taiwan. Kennett, *Petroleum Developments in the Far East,* 57 AM. ASS'N OF PETROLEUM GEOLOGISTS BULL. 2095 (1973).

[19] A range of commentary is given in C. PARK, CONTINENTAL SHELF ISSUES IN THE YELLOW SEA AND THE EAST CHINA SEA 30-32 (Law of the Sea Institute Occasional Paper No. 15, 1972).

[20] The North Sea Continental Shelf Cases, [1969] I.C.J. 3.

[21] *Ryukyu Government Announces Ownership of Senkaku Islands,* Asahi

Evening News, Sept. 11, 1970. For further discussions, see the excellent paper by Park, *supra* note 19.

[22] *Statement of the Ministry of Foreign Affairs of the People's Republic of China, supra* note 17; *Tiaoyü and Other Islands Have Been China's Since Ancient Times, supra* note 17.

[23] *Japan to Meet with China Over Tiao-yü Isles, supra* note 13.

[24] *Hearings on the Okinawa Reversion Treaty Before the Senate Comm. on Foreign Relations,* 92nd Cong., 1st Sess., at 88-92 (1971).

[25] *See, e.g.,* the requirements for acquiring new territory discussed in The Island of Palmas Case (Netherlands v. United States), 2 U.N. Rep. Int'l. Arb. Awards 829 (1949).

[26] *Pao-wei Tiao-yü Tai, supra* note 9, at 3.

[27] *Ryukyu Government Announces Ownership of Senkaku Islands, supra* note 21.

[28] The Island of Palmas Case, *supra* note 25, at 869.

[29] Article 2 (b) of the 1951 San Francisco Peace Treaty states "Japan renounces all right, title, and claim to Formosa and the Pescadores." 136 U.N.T.S. 48.

[30] Article 3 of the 1951 San Francisco Peace Treaty states: "Japan will concur in any proposal of the United States . . . to place under its trusteeship system, with the United States as the sole administering authority, Nansei Shoto south of 29° north latitude (including the Ryukyu Islands and the Daito Islands) . . . ." 136 U.N.T.S. 50.

[31] Letter to Mrs. K. Woo quoted in PAO-WEI TIAO-YU TAI, *supra* note 9, at 4, 14. *See also Ryukyu Government Announces Ownership of Senkaku Islands, supra* note 21, which quotes Department of State Press Officer Charles Bray as saying "The term used in the treaty was intended to include the Senkaku Islands."

[32] *Ryuku Government Announces Ownership of Senkaku Islands, supra* note 21, at 14.

[33] Article II of this treaty provides: "It is recognized that under Article 2 [of the San Francisco Peace Treaty], Japan has renounced all right, title and claim to Taiwan (Formosa) and Penghu (the Pescadores) as well as the Spratly Islands and the Paracel Islands." 138 U.N.T.S. 38.

[34] The Clipperton Islands Case (France v. Mexico), 2 U.N. Rep. Int'l. Arb. Awards 1105 (1949); see also Eastern Greenland Case (Denmark v. Norway), 3 World Court Reports (Hudson 1938) 148.

[35] The Island of Palmas Case, *supra* note 25, at 867.

[36] *Tiao-yü and Other Islands Have Been China's Since Ancient Times,* 15 PEKING REV., Jan. 7, 1972, at 13.

[37] *Id.*

[38] In earlier years, there was some disagreement about the legal effect of these documents. One argument was that the Cairo and Potsdam Declarations were only non-self-executing statements of intent, which, in and of themselves, did not reconvey Taiwan to China. Moreover, in the Peace Treaties Japan renounced all rights to Taiwan, but nothing was said about to whom title should be given. Under this reasoning, Taiwan may have belonged to no one; *i.e.,* Japan gave it up, but no legal conveyance was made to China. This position has been abandoned at least since the joint United States-People's Republic of China Shanghai Communique in 1972, and perhaps earlier.

[39] The Island of Palmas Case, *supra* note 25, at 843.

[40] *See generally* 1 OPPENHEIM'S INTERNATIONAL LAW 554-561 (H. Lauterpacht ed. 1955).

[41] *See e.g.,* Mancall, *The Persistence of Tradition in Chinese Foreign Policy,*

THE ANNALS OF THE AMERICAN ACADEMY OF POLITICAL AND SOCIAL SCIENCES 14-26 (Sept. 1963); J.K. FAIRBANK, CHINESE THOUGHT AND INSTITUTIONS (1957).

[42]It should be noted that Tiao-yü Tai is only one of a number of similar disputes concerning small islands all over the world. These include Rockall (Great Britain and the Republic of Ireland), Danjo Gunto, Torishima, and Takeshima (Republic of Korea and Japan), the Kuriles (Japan and the U.S.S.R.), the Paracel Islands (China and the Republic of Viet Nam), the Spratley Islands (China, the Republic of Viet Nam, and the Republic of the Philippines), and in due course presumably other islands in the South China Sea such as the Pratas Islands and the Macclesfield Bank. Other cases may arise as more states see the strategic, fishing, continental shelf, and other advantages that might be gained through claiming nearby islands as their territory. Continental shelf disputes are likely to increase since about 20 percent of the world's oil production now comes from the sea-bed, a figure that may double by the end of this century. In addition both China and Japan must come to agreement with Korea on how to divide the continental shelf in Yellow Sea area. *Soviet-U. Contention for Sea Power: Seeking World Domination*, 29 PEKING REV., Jul. 19, 1974, at 16. See also *Doubts About Japan-ROK Continental Shelf Agreement*, ASAHI SHIMBUN, Mar. 15, 1974, translated in DAILY SUMMARY OF THE JAPANESE PRESS (DSJP), Mar. 19, 1974, at 3.

[43]Yang Ying, *Maritime Overlord's Alibi*, 49 PEKING REV., Nov. 30, 1973, at 21.

[44]*No Superpowers' Control of the Seas Is Allowed*, 33 PEKING REV., Aug. 18, 1972, at 15; see also *China's Stand on Question of Rights Over Seas and Oceans*, 10 PEKING REV., March 10, 1972, at 14, *U.N. Sea-Bed Committee Ends Session*, 34 PEKING REV., Aug. 25, 1972, at 10.

[45]*Declaration on China's Territorial Seas*, 28 PEKING REV., Sept. 9, 1958, at 21; see also a thorough article on this subject by Tao Cheng, *Communist China and the Law of the Sea*, 63 AM. J. INTERNAT'L L. 47 (1969); Liu Tse-yung, *A Major Step to Protect China's Sovereign Rights*, 29 PEKING REV., Sept. 16, 1958, at 11.

[46]*Struggle in Defense of 200-Nautical-Mile Maritime Rights*, 25 PEKING REV., June 21, 1974, at 5.

[47]*China's Stand on Question of Rights Over Seas and Oceans*, 10 PEKING REV., Mar. 10, 1972, at 16.

[48]*Struggle Against Hegemony Over Maritime Rights*, 26 PEKING REV., June 28, 1974, at 14; *On Governing International Sea-Bed Area*, 34 PEKING REV., Aug. 25, 1972, at 10.

[49]*Debate on the Regime and Machinery Governing International Sea-Bed Area*, 31 PEKING REV., Aug. 2, 1974, at 11.

[50]Gruliow, *Soviet-Japan Tie for Siberian Oil?*, Christian Science Monitor, Apr. 22, 1974, at 4; *Tanaka's Letter to Soviet Communist Party General Secretary; Cooperation on Development of Siberia*, NIHON KEIZAI, Mar. 20, 1974, translated in DSJP, Mar. 23-25, 1974, at 9.

[51]Chriss, *Offshore Oil—China Has Plenty for Lamps and Maybe for World*, Los Angeles Times, Apr. 27, 1974, § 1 at 10; *Oil—China Has Plenty, Sells Little*, Christian Science Monitor, Jul. 12, 1974, at 4.

[52]Elegant, *China Must Hustle to Pay For Imports*, Los Angeles Times, June 2, 1974, § 8 at 1; Gelb, *Trade with China Surges Ahead of U.S.-Soviet Level*, New York Times, June 4, 1974, at 1.

[53]See, e.g., *China Sounds Out Our Shipbuilding Industry on Order For Oil Field Drilling Equipment; Largest Half-Submerged Type in World*, NIHON KEIZAI, Mar. 29, 1974, translated in DSJP, Apr. 2, 1974, at 37; *China Makes*

Forward-Looking Statement on Japan's Participation in Oil Development; Deputy Premier Li to Inayama Now Visiting China, YOMIURI SHIMBUN, June 6, 1974, translated in DSJP, June 8-10, 1974, at 5. *See also* Ludlow, *China's Oil,* 1 U.S.-CHINA BUSINESS REV. 21 (No. 1, 1974).

[54] On foreign economic involvement in developing countries, *see generally Militant Call by Third World Countries,* 19 PEKING REV., May 10, 1974, at 8.

[55] Weintraub, *China's Oil Production & Consumption,* 1 U.S.-CHINA BUSINESS REV. 29 (No. 1, 1974); *supra* note 57.

[56] *Oil Technology and Equipment to China,* 1 U.S.-CHINA BUSINESS REV. 31 (No. 1, 1974).

Recent Developments in the International Financial Policies of the People's Republic of China

DAVID L. DENNY*†

In the waning days of the Great Proletarian Cultural Revolution only a few people had the insight to call attention to China's "turn outward" or to those policies that have since led the People's Republic of China to give its economic and political relations with foreign countries an emphasis that had been lacking for the decade of the 1960's.[1] This paper examines the ramifications of these new policies and the constantly changing international economic environment on one key aspect of P.R.C. international economic policy—its banking and financial relationships with its non-Communist trading partners.[2]

Western observers have recently taken up the theme that the Bank of China (B.O.C.) is playing a more aggressive role in international financial circles than heretofore.[3] Indeed, this theme has been strengthened by Chinese officials:

> The renminbi enjoys increasing prestige abroad. China in the past used foreign currencies in quoting prices and settling accounts in its foreign trade and in other economic dealings with other countries. This began to change in 1968. Now more than 60 countries and regions use the renminbi in their economic accountings with China.[4]

There are many signs that China's financial practices have changed significantly in recent years. For example, unlike other socialist countries, the Chinese began in 1968 to use their own currency to denominate and settle trade contracts with non-Communist countries. Second, the exchange rate between Western currencies and the Renminbi (R.M.B.) is changed often—sometimes as frequently as several times a week. Finally, the Chinese have recently become

*International Trade Specialist, People's Republic of China Division, Bureau of East-West Trade, U.S. Department of Commerce.

†The views expressed here do not necessarily reflect those of the agency with which the author is presently associated. While solely responsible for the conclusions, the author greatly appreciates extensive advice from colleagues, businessmen and bankers.

increasingly willing to finance the purchase of agricultural and non-agricultural products by utilizing short- and medium-term credits. These changes are important, and their source and scope must be examined closely. Despite this importance, however, these changes do not at this point signal a basic change of Chinese financial institutions and policies. As will be shown in this paper, China's policy toward foreign indebtedness, while moderated, is still essentially conservative, and the R.M.B. remains for the most part inconvertible despite its increased use in P.R.C. trade with the West.

I. REASONS FOR SHIFT IN FINANCIAL POLICIES

There are three main reasons for P.R.C. shifts in international financial practices. The first is a more aggressive solicitation of foreign trade partners and the consequent rapid growth of foreign trade levels. Second, in late 1972, the P.R.C. reverted to sizable importation of complete plants, modern equipment, and technology. A similar policy was a key aspect of the rapid industrial growth of the 1950's. Complete plant imports were resumed on a much smaller scale in the 1960's but the program was cut short by the Cultural Revolution. Finally, since the late 1960's, P.R.C. planners have been faced with increased instability of the major world currencies.

A. *The P.R.C.'s Increasing Foreign Trade*

As Table I shows, P.R.C. total foreign trade has grown 156 percent in the last four years (1969-1973). The annual rates of growth of approximately 20 percent are expected to continue through 1974. Thus, total P.R.C. foreign trade in 1974 will be about three times as large as it was in 1969. Much of this growth, of course, is not "real" and simply reflects successive devaluations of the U.S. dollar and world price inflation. It is very difficult to measure the impact of these effects, but U.S. Government analysts have suggested that at least 50 percent of the growth in 1972 and 1973 are due to inflation and currency changes.[5] This estimate is consistent with that of a Japanese research report which concluded that "these price hikes together with the currency fluctuation are estimated to account for half of the 83% Japan-China trade growth in 1973."[6] The most comprehensive study of this problem has been made by Professors Eckstein and Reynolds, who have devised price indices for Chinese imports and exports. According to their calculations, China's total foreign trade in real terms fell sharply between 1959 and 1963 and not until 1971 did it rise to the level it had reached in the late 1950's.[7] In 1972-1974 total trade reached record levels. But in real

TABLE I. CHINA'S FOREIGN TRADE

| | *Millions of U.S. Dollars* | | | | | |
| | CURRENT PRICES | | | CONSTANT PRICES *(1963 = 100)* | | |
YEAR	TOTAL	EXPORTS	IMPORTS	TOTAL	EXPORTS	IMPORTS
1952	1,890	875	1,015	1,900	794.7	1,009.0
1953	2,295	1,040	1,255	2,291	997.1	1,293.8
1954	2,350	1,060	1,290	2,278	931.5	1,346.6
1955	3,035	1,375	1,660	3,013	1,295.9	1,7616.6
1956	3,120	1,635	1,485	3,039	1,560.1	1,479.1
1957	3,055	1,615	1,440	2,911	1,530.8	1,380.6
1958	3,765	1,940	1,825	3,765	1,940.0	1,825.0
1959	4,290	2,230	2,060	4,398	2,313.3	2,085.0
1960	3,990	1,960	2,030	3,989	1,917.8	2,071.4
1961	3,020	1,530	1,495	3,069	1,542.3	1,527.1
1962	2,675	1,525	1,150	2,766	1,586.9	1,179.5
1963	2,770	1,570	1,200	2,770	1,570.0	1,200.0
1964	3,220	1,750	1,470	3,116	1,682.7	1,434.1
1965	3,880	2,035	1,845	3,789	2,003.0	1,786.1
1966	4,245	2,210	2,035	4,068	2,154.0	1,914.4
1967	3,895	1,945	1,950	3,769	1,929.6	1,839.6
1968	3,765	1,945	1,820	3,656	1,921.0	1,735.0
1969	3,860	2,030	1,830	3,611	1,920.5	1,691.3
1970	4,290	2,050	2,240	3,757	1,865.3	1,891.1
1971	4,720	2,415	2,305	4,062	2,181.6	1,880.1
1972	5,920	3,085	2,835	4,687	2,570.8	2,115.7
1973	9.870	4,895	4,975	5,813	2,943.5	2,869.1
1974	13,000	6,000	7,000	———	———	———

Source: Columns 1-3, CENTRAL INTELLIGENCE AGENCY, PEOPLE'S REPUBLIC OF CHINA: INTERNATIONAL TRADE HANDBOOK 9 (U.S. Government Doc. A (ER 74-63), Library of Congress, Sept. 1974).

Columns 4-6, Columns 1-3 deflated by price indices in Eckstein, *China's Economic Growth and Foreign Trade*, 1 U.S.-CHINA BUSINESS REVIEW 16, (No. 4, 1974).

terms it was only 30 percent or so higher than the level reached 15 years earlier.

In relation to domestic economic activity, China's foreign trade sector appears to occupy about the same position it did at the end of the First Five-Year Plan Period. Between 1957 and 1973, Western estimates infer annual rates of growth (in real terms) of 4.3 percent for gross national product and 4.4 percent for foreign trade turnover respectively. Thus, in the early 1970's P.R.C. total foreign trade turnover still accounted for less than 5 percent of domestic activity—a proportion that is low even by standards of large, continental economies.[8] However, in the past five years, China's foreign trade has clearly acquired much greater significance in relation to its domestic economy. Most observers expect this trend to continue—especially since the Chinese are already committed to substantial importation of agricultural and industrial commodities for the remainder of the 1970's.[9]

This recent trend toward an increasing emphasis on foreign trade is supported by a number of other indicators. The P.R.C. has signed several trade agreements with new trading partners, greatly increased its participation in international trade fairs, and hosted an increasing number of trade fairs.[10] Finally, it has recently resumed publication of *China Foreign Trade*, the first issue of which carried a lead article by Foreign Trade Minister Li Chiang which stated:

> Over the last two decades and more, acting upon this teaching of Chairman Mao on foreign trade, China has opened up trade with other countries on the basis of equality and mutual benefit ... Facts prove that foreign trade is necessary to the development of our national economy. At the same time, however, through foreign trade, we can increase mutual support and cooperation in the economic sphere with fraternal socialist countries and friendly countries of the third world, thus benefitting each other's economic construction and economic independence.[11]

There are, of course, ample indications that this new policy direction has opponents inside China. There have been explicit attacks against over-reliance on foreign goods and technology.[12] Some observers even see indications of deep-seated attacks on the P.R.C.'s leading advocates of foreign trade. While no definitive statement is possible at this time, it is reasonable to conclude that the current campaign inside China may moderate and slow the growth of foreign trade, but it is doubtful that opponents of foreign trade have the strength to change the present policy.[13]

In addition to significantly increasing its international economic activity in the past few years, China appears to have increased its export prices and brought them more in line with world levels. The combination of these two factors would have the effect of making China's foreign trade somewhat less competitive than it has been in past years. We might formulate a hypothesis that the institutions which service China's foreign trade have compensated for this by slowly and cautiously adopting practices that are more appealing to international traders. For example, China has apparently increased flexibility in styling exports to meet Western buyers' specifications. Similarly, the Bank of China appears to be somewhat more willing to modify its conventional practices—depending, of course, on the P.R.C.'s desire to make the deal and (not unimportantly) on the persistence of the Western businessmen.

B. *China's Purchases of Complete Plant, Technology and Modern Equipment*

From late 1972 to mid-1974 the Chinese purchased more than $2 billion worth of "complete plants." The P.R.C. will pay for these purchases on a repayment schedule that extends into the early 1980's. In the summer of 1974 few new complete plant purchases were announced, although some negotiations continued. Whether the negotiations are successful or not, the value of complete plants purchased in the last two years already greatly exceeds that of plants purchased in the mid-1960's. In addition to complete plant purchases, the Chinese have accelerated their purchase of a wide range of modern machinery including airplanes, ships, trucks, and mining and petroleum equipment.[14]

From the standpoint of finance such purchases are important since the plants have long "start up" times and since they will be utilized over extended periods of time. Despite the well known Chinese aversion to being in debt to foreign countries, such considerations have prompted the Chinese to go beyond immediate cash payment by committing themselves to "progress payments" and to five year deferred payments. These will be discussed in Part II *infra*.

C. *The Impact of International Monetary Instability*

Before 1968, China used primarily the pound sterling to denominate trade contracts and to make and receive payment. Furthermore, many of P.R.C. foreign reserve holdings were probably in sterling. Consequently, the Chinese suffered losses when the pound was devalued in the late 1960's. The Chinese then experimented with several European currencies, but general instability in the world monetary markets led the B.O.C. to make the series of changes that will be discussed below.

The Chinese sensitivity to the instability of the world monetary system is an interesting phenomenon in its own right. There are at least three ways to explain it. First, while P.R.C. foreign exchange holdings are adequate in relation to its trade levels, they are small in an absolute sense. It may not have been convenient for the P.R.C. to spread its risks among many different currencies and gold. Second, the P.R.C. is extremely sensitive to inflationary pressures for well-documented historical reasons.[15] It places a great deal of emphasis on the stability of the domestic price level and may look somewhat in askance at currencies whose values fluctuate widely. Finally, any planned economy tends to give a high priority to order and stability—even at some potential cost of economic "efficiency." Simply put, stability is vital since any failure to meet plan targets in one sector is likely to have serious repercussions throughout the economy before such effects can be discovered and the plan adjusted.

II. RECENT P.R.C. INTERNATIONAL FINANCIAL PRACTICES

This part of the paper begins with a description of the financial (or payment) clauses of Chinese trade contracts; it is followed by a section discussing the Bank of China's relationships with its correspondent banks in the West. The third section takes up the question of how the Chinese set their exchange rate, and the final section considers the financial implications of China's willingness to purchase complete plants on extended payment schedules.

A. *Payment Terms in P.R.C. Contracts*

Chinese financial practices are unusual in several ways. On the whole, however, contracts with the P.R.C. use terms and concepts that are familiar to all experienced international traders. Moreover, those variant Chinese practices that do exist are by no means rigid and unyielding. While they clearly prefer to design contracts in their own way, Chinese foreign trade corporations (F.T.C.'s) can be persuaded (sometimes after immense expenditures of time and effort) to add to or amend their normal contract procedures. Especially in the area of large, complex sales to China, the final contracts are usually long and detailed, often containing provisions that flout "normal" P.R.C. practices.[16]

Most Chinese sales and purchases are accomplished by irrevocable letters of credit.[17] Some small sales—usually samples—have been made by collection or remittance or by simply making out a check to the seller. But letters of credit predominate, even for firms having longstanding relationships with the P.R.C., despite the considerable expenditures of time, energy, and money that are necessary to amend such letters of credit in the common event of shipping delays.

In general, when the Chinese are purchasing goods, the B.O.C., like some other national banks, refuses to allow another bank to "confirm" its letters of credit. By doing so, the B.O.C. saves the F.T.C.'s "confirming charges" and also underlines the financial prestige of the B.O.C. as a bank whose credit needs no guarantee. It is possible that China has lost a few purchases because of this practice, but the B.O.C. has such an excellent reputation for financial integrity that such cases would appear to be rare occurrences. On the other hand, when the Chinese are exporting, the B.O.C. often requires "confirmed" letters of credit even when businessmen obtain letters of credit from designated correspondents of the B.O.C.

P.R.C. practice is similarly asymmetric in its insistence on transferable letters of credit when selling but not when buying. The reason for transferability when selling is that the F.T.C. is merely acting on behalf of the producing enterprise. When shipment is made, transferable letters of credit avoid bureaucratic middlemen and allow the Chinese enterprise to present drafts and documents directly to the B.O.C. When buying, the Chinese F.T.C.'s prefer to deal with producers directly, to avoid paying the costs of middlemen and trading companies. In general, this practice seems to be no great handicap for American producers who can arrange back-to-back letters of credit for the purpose of subcontracting.

Western businessmen may also encounter a problem in the P.R.C. tendency to require rather more documentation when purchasing than it proffers when selling. This may cause a number of difficulties: the Western importer may not have enough documentation for customs or other forms of inspection; and, given the B.O.C.'s scrupulous attention to detail, payment may be delayed and extra costs incurred if exports to the P.R.C. are not sufficiently documented. Consequently, the Western businessman must consider the matter of documentation a proper subject for contract negotiation.

Perhaps the most unusual aspect of trade with China is that Chinese contracts usually call for negotiation of letters of credit inside China, both when China is selling (which is normal) and when China is buying (which is not). When China is selling, the normal procedure appears to be that the enterprise brings the proper documents to the Bank of China. If everything is in order, the Bank of China reduces the R.M.B. account of a correspondent bank (usually specified in the contract). Then the Bank of China notifies the correspondent of its action so that the correspondent can, in turn, deduct the necessary amount from the account of its customer. An unusual exception to this, however, has been recently reported in which the Western buyer's bank authorized payment only after it had received the drafts and documents.[18] Reportedly one of the arguments the bank made for such a practice was that it was similar to the Chinese practice for their imports (see below).

On sales to China, contracts often specify that payment will be made after documents are received by a B.O.C. branch *in China.* This means that the seller is without goods, documents, and payment for a certain period of time. Although frequently mentioned, as a practical matter this is relatively unimportant because of the reliability of the B.O.C. A more serious problem is the fact that payment will be delayed by the time it takes documents to reach the specified branch of the B.O.C., giving the Chinese what is essentially an interest-free loan. To take account of this delay, experienced traders simply raise their asking prices.

P.R.C. export contracts are usually denominated in R.M.B., although businessmen have reported occasional successes in obtaining contracts written in other currencies. P.R.C. import contracts, on the other hand, are usually in the currency of the exporter or some mutually agreed currency. After receiving the necessary documents, the B.O.C. notifies its correspondent to pay the exporter and reimburses the correspondent from one of its hard-currency accounts. P.R.C. imports from Japan are exceptions to the general rule—they are denominated and paid in R.M.B. As a result of Japan's continuing trade surplus with the P.R.C. and its apparent reluctance to draw on its R.M.B. accounts, this has become a form of temporary interest-free loan. Presumably this is done with some reluctance on the Japanese side, and it is interesting to note that recently some Japanese sales to China have been denominated in Yen.[19]

The Chinese ordinarily prefer to open letters of credit for 95-98 percent of the invoice value and pay the remainder after the inspection of the goods. They also will frequently require Western importers to open letters of credit as much as 60-90 days in advance of an actual shipping date, while they prefer to open letters of credit only 15-30 days before the shipping date. (It should be emphasized, however, that there is a great deal of variance on the required opening dates for both P.R.C. exports and imports.) A lengthy time requirement causes a Western importer to tie up his line of credit; the problem is exacerbated by frequent P.R.C. shipping delays. Because of such difficulties, the B.O.C. has recently accommodated one importer by allowing him to open his letter of credit after the products were ready for shipment.[20]

B. *The Bank of China's Relationship with Foreign Banks*

In official statements the Chinese have emphasized the recent growth in China's foreign trade relationships, noting that the P.R.C. conducts trade with 150 different countries and regions and that it has formal trade agreements with more than 50 countries. To understand the banking and financial aspects of trade settlements, this section analyzes the various kinds of relationships the Bank of China maintains with its "correspondents" in other countries.

1. Clearing Account Agreements

As with its trading partners in socialist countries, the Bank of China conducts financial transactions with a few of its smaller trading partners in the West through clearing account agreements. Such agreements have been signed, for example, with Finland, Sweden, Denmark, and Norway.

Basically, a clearing account agreement abstracts from the problems of domestic prices and the values of the currencies in both countries. An artificial unit of account is created and officials responsible for trade in each country agree to exchange certain quantities of commodities. Values are determined by world market prices or by agreement. In some sense, the financial account is merely a device to keep track of a complicated barter arrangement. The clearing account agreement generally forces the two countries to balance any imbalance bilaterally—usually by changing their trade plan in the next period.

For example, in the P.R.C.-Finnish agreement, each country's national bank opened a noninterest bearing account with its foreign counterpart. The unit of account in this case was defined to be a "RUBLE" which was stipulated to have a gold value of 0.987412 grams. The agreement provides that debts may be accumulated to the level of 1.8 million rubles, after which "the debtor country is requested to make the utmost efforts to bring the amount within the framework of 1.8 million rubles as soon as possible."[21]

2. B.O.C. Relationship with Correspondent Banks in the West

The great bulk of China's trade with nonsocialist countries is not handled through clearing account agreements. For these countries, the B.O.C. typically establishes a correspondent relationship with one or more banks in each country. Since China has trade relations with 150 countries and at least 60 of these have agreed to use the R.M.B., it is safe to say that the B.O.C. has well over 100 correspondents. In Japan, for example, a figure of 26 correspondents was given for 1975. In the United States about 30 branches of foreign banks have been designated by the B.O.C. as banks that can open letters of credit. In general, these branches appear to have their own R.M.B. accounts at the B.O.C.

In the typical case, the B.O.C. opens an account at the correspondent bank and the correspondent bank opens an R.M.B.

account at the B.O.C. These accounts are considered noninterest bearing "working balances" that "shall not exceed specified limits." The agreements between the B.O.C. and its correspondents include regulations concerning purchases and sales of R.M.B. Examples of such agreements, hereinafter referred to as "opening agreements" and "exchange agreements" respectively, have been published and are reprinted in Appendices 1 and 2. The exchange rates for purchases and sales of R.M.B. are fixed unilaterally by the B.O.C. At the present time, the B.O.C. publishes buying and selling rates for the R.M.B. against 15 currencies.

Activity in R.M.B. accounts appears to be limited only to the bank that actually holds the account (opening agreement, Article 3). However, it is possible that, as in the Japanese case discussed below, R.M.B. accounts can be transferred among the B.O.C.'s correspondents within a country.

The most important aspect of the exchange agreement is the tight control of the B.O.C. over purchases and sales of R.M.B. For instance, Article 1 of the exchange agreement states that "a purchase of spot or forward R.M.B. by the second party [a Western bank] from the first party [B.O.C.] must be made against [foreign currency] and is limited to payment of Chinese exports and relative charges on the basis of a Chinese export control." Furthermore, the cable affecting purchase "must show a test number, the amount of R.M.B. to be bought and its equivalent in [foreign currency] and the date of delivery" (exchange agreement, Article 2). If rigorously enforced, the B.O.C. could monitor the R.M.B. accounts to ensure that every activity reflected a predetermined foreign trade activity. Not only do all R.M.B. remain in a B.O.C. account, but every use of that account is theoretically constrained by a contract that presumably reflects the P.R.C. foreign trade plan. It is in this sense that the R.M.B. is accurately known for its nonconvertibility. Although it is difficult to make any generalizations about this matter, it appears that businessmen and bankers generally perceive the B.O.C.'s controls as rather strict.

3. The Special Case of the United States

Apparently because of the still unsettled and linked "frozen assets, fixed private claims" issues,[22] the P.R.C. has not established a full scale correspondent banking relationship with a U.S. bank and refuses to accept commercial letters of credit opened by U.S. banks. It has agreed, however, to accept remittances, travelers' letters of credit, and travelers' checks drawn on U.S. banks. In fact, travelers in China have reported successfully cashing checks drawn on U.S. banks.

As stated before, the B.O.C. has designated about 30 American branches of foreign banks to perform most of the normal functions of a correspondent bank. Therefore, the U.S. businessman can conduct his P.R.C. banking business directly with one of these banks. Exports to China are often handled in this manner. Involving a U.S. bank would simply add to the number of middlemen handling the documents and might increase banking charges. On the other hand, letters of credit for imports from China are more normally opened by utilizing a U.S. bank, which then arranges with a B.O.C. correspondent to open the letter of credit to the Chinese F.T.C. Involving the U.S. bank does not generally increase costs since banks usually split banking charges.[23] Furthermore, the firm concerned may see some advantages in maintaining its relationship with its own bank.

The present system seems to work reasonably well and, since banking costs are split, does not increase banking charges. In the long run, however, it will be desirable for U.S. banks to increase their interest in and knowledge of U.S.-P.R.C. trade. At present this goal is somewhat constrained by the system of indirect relationships and split fees.

4. *The Special Case of Japan*

With their largest trading partner the Chinese have evolved a unique blend of the "clearing accounts" and "correspondent bank" types of agreement. The P.R.C.-Japanese agreement was originally signed in August 1972 for a one-year trial period. In 1973 it was extended indefinitely and now covers payments for "invisibles" (*e.g.*, insurance, freight) as well as payments for trade transactions.

The agreement is not an official government-to-government agreement; it operates between the Bank of China and the Bank of Tokyo and has been accepted as the framework for payment by 26 Japanese banks involved in trade with the P.R.C. Through the agreement, the B.O.C. establishes a Yen account at each Japanese bank and the Japanese bank establishes R.M.B. accounts at the B.O.C. The accounts "may not be used for payment abroad, but may be transferred among foreign exchange banks within Japan."[24] Such accounts are considered to be "working account balances." In the first agreement working accounts were noninterest bearing—but there are recent reports that the Chinese may now pay interest on such accounts.

The first agreement called for surpluses to be "converted into British pounds and [to] be drafted or transferred into a fixed deposit."[25] However, the combination of Japan's trade surplus and the weakening of the British pound (which was not fully offset by changes in the Bank of China's official R.M.B.-pound exchange rate) led to considerable losses for Japanese banks. This problem is expected to be less serious in the future because of the considerable narrowing of the imbalance in Sino-Japanese trade. Moreover, recently Japanese firms have begun to grant supplier credits to the P.R.C. In this way, the exchange risk has been shifted from the foreign exchange banks to the firms themselves.

In the original agreement both Yen and R.M.B. could be chosen (primarily at the option of the importer) as the currency in which the transaction was denominated. In fact, the R.M.B. is used for most Japanese exports and 80-90 percent of Japanese imports. The Japan External Trade Organization has rationalized this by arguing that R.M.B. quotations may be advantageous for the Japanese importer because of the stronger position of the Japanese Yen.[26]

The most unusual feature of the B.O.C.-Bank of Tokyo agreement is the existence of an "arbitrated" as well as an "official" R.M.B.-Yen exchange rate. Basically, the "official" exchange rate is used in transactions between Japanese banks and Japanese businessmen. From the P.R.C. point of view, this system has been the primary advantage of virtually eliminating exchange rate risk since the exchange rate is officially fixed and both export and import contracts are denominated in R.M.B.

The "official" exchange rate between R.M.B. and Yen is set unilaterally by the Bank of China and is changed periodically. The first rate (1 R.M.B. = 135.84 Yen) was set on the basis of the cross rates determined by the official R.M.B./Pound and the market Pound/Yen rate.

Under the new agreement, the "arbitrated rate" is determined by (a) the previous day's official B.O.C. pound-R.M.B. quotation; (b) the previous day's U.S. dollar-pound quotation on the New York market and the prevailing Yen-dollar rate on the Tokyo exchange. Under a roughly similar formula in the old agreement, the value of one R.M.B. on February 15, 1973 was reduced from 135.8 yen (the official rate) to 129.4 yen (the arbitrated rate), a five percent effective devaluation.[27]

How Japanese banks protect themselves against being squeezed by the divergent exchange rates is not clear. The problem may not have been too serious under the first agreement since 85 percent of the transactions reportedly fell within 3 percent of the official rate. However, there are some indications that Japanese banks were not entirely happy with the situation and may have pushed for some changes.[28] In this regard, it is interesting to note that the official R.M.B.-Yen exchange rates fluctuated surprisingly often (see Table II infra). In fact, recently the official R.M.B.-Yen rate has been maintained in such a way as to produce fairly consistent cross-rates with the major currencies. This would seem to sacrifice one of the main advantages sought in a clearing account type of arrangement—that of stable "official" exchange rates.

Two other aspects of the first agreement probably have been carried over to the second. These are a prohibition on conducting forward transactions and a requirement that R.M.B. be procured "only when there arises actual demand." In the latter case, as we have seen, similar clauses exist in agreements with Western banks.

C. *The R.M.B. Exchange Rate*

For most planned economies, setting the exchange rate between domestic and foreign currencies is not considered an important problem. Currencies of planned economies are ordinarily inconvertible; foreigners usually do not hold significant assets denominated in the planned economy's currency, and foreign trade contracts are denominated in foreign "hard" currencies. As we have seen, all R.M.B. held by foreigners is deposited at the B.O.C. and can be exchanged for other currencies only under strict regulations. Moreover, R.M.B. cannot be taken out of China; indeed, it is hard to see why anyone would want to do so since ultimately its value depends on P.R.C. acceptance of it as a valid claim on P.R.C. production. For those reasons, the R.M.B. qualifies unreservedly as an inconvertible currency.

The P.R.C. does, however, encourage R.M.B.-denominated savings deposits, especially in the so called "sister banks" in Hong Kong.[29] People often open such deposits because the Chinese have succeeded in achieving relative stability both in domestic price level and in the value of the R.M.B. vis-à-vis other currencies. To the extent that the B.O.C. desires to encourage such deposits, it has an interest in maintaining a stable or appreciating exchange rate.

Most of the Western businessman's interest in the exchange rate derives from the fact that P.R.C. export contracts are denominated in R.M.B. Thus, the businessman does not know the dollar cost of his purchases until his products are ready for shipment. The B.O.C. offers forward contracts for sales of R.M.B. for many European countries but the costs in most cases seem rather high.[30] The U.S. businessman is in an even poorer position since the B.O.C. has generally been unwilling to sell R.M.B. forward to American businessmen even if they have foreign trade contracts. Some U.S. businessmen have persuaded the P.R.C. to sign dollar-denominated contracts, but such agreements have been extremely rare to date.

Finally, many residents of Hong Kong depend on P.R.C.-made products for basic necessities. Frequent and sharp fluctuations in the R.M.B.-H.K. dollar exchange rate could have a serious impact on

Hong Kong's standard of living. This is probably one reason for the relative stability in the R.M.B.-H.K. dollar exchange rate.

The Bank of China, of course, has not released information on how the exchange rate is actually set, and it is quite possible that the strategy has changed from period to period. Thus far it has been impossible to understand the principle, let alone the mechanics, underlying the B.O.C.'s exchange rate policy. Some Western visitors to China, however, have gained the impression that the value of the R.M.B. is determined on the basis of some composite group of currencies (possibly including prices of important commodities). Whatever the mechanics used, the P.R.C. has responded quickly and sensitively to changes in world monetary conditions such as the weakening of the U.S. dollar in early 1973 and the weakening of the Japanese Yen in 1974.

Table II presents the value of the R.M.B. in terms of six leading Western currencies. The value of the R.M.B. shown is the value at the end of each month between January 1973 and September 1974. Although it is not possible to tell how the B.O.C. determines the value of the R.M.B., several interesting points emerge. First, the B.O.C. changes the R.M.B. exchange rate frequently and usually in rather small increments. For example, in the 21 months after January 1973, the R.M.B.-U.S. dollar exchange rate has been changed more than 75 times; in two-thirds of these cases the change was less than 1 percent. Second, it is possible that for some periods, the B.O.C. stabilized the value of the R.M.B. against the Hong Kong dollar and the German mark. Other exchange rates would then have been calculated on the basis of the "cross-rates"[31] as determined on world money markets. However, that is not the only possibility, as the R.M.B.-H.K. dollar exchange rate may have been stabilized in line with a P.R.C. desire to stabilize Hong Kong prices. In this case, the B.O.C. would have to allow the R.M.B.-H.K. dollar exchange rate to diverge somewhat from the levels implied by world money market conditions. Such a hypothesis derives some support from the observation that changes in the R.M.B.-H.K. dollar rate were less frequent than those for other currencies, and that when changes were made, they tended to be larger than for other currencies. Third, the value of the R.M.B. was occasionally appreciated or depreciated against *all* these curreicnes. However, the more general pattern has been for the R.M.B. to appreciate in terms of several currencies and to depreciate in terms of others. Finally, it should be noted that the cross-rates implied by the Chinese currencies are, in general, quite consistent with world monetary conditions. For example, at the Spring 1974 Canton Fair, only 2 out of 14 cross-rates diverged more than 2 percent from the New York quotations.[32]

TABLE II. VALUE OF THE R.M.B.
IN TERMS OF SIX CURRENCIES

One Unit of R.M.B. = X Units of:

PERIOD (END OF MONTH)	U.S. DOLLAR	U.K. POUND	H.K. DOLLAR	GERMAN MARK	FRENCH FRANC	JAPANESE YEN
Jan. '73	.4464	.1906	n.a.	1,5445	2,0056	135.83
Feb. '73	.4873	.2007	2.5648	1,4335	2,2800	130.25
Mar. '73	.4992	.2017	2,5648	1.4108	2.2599	132.35
Apr. '73	.4956	.2001	2,5648	1,4108	2,2599	132.25
May '73	.5099	.1985	2,5648	1,4108	2.2724	132.25
June '73	.5265	.2059	2.6316	1.3626	2.2381	139.222
July '73	.5336	.2131	2.6889	1.2425	2.1758	140.9051
Aug. '73	.5174	.2079	2.6518	1.2747	2.2257	137.380
Sept. '73	.5227	.2158	2.6788	1.2617	2.2085	138.687
Oct. '73	.5225	.2158	2.6483	1.2617	2.1867	140.087
Nov. '73	.5005	.2139	2.5336	1.3084	2.1867	139.449
Dec. '73	.4985	.2160	2.5336	1.3182	2.2983	139.449
Jan. '74	.4901	.2229	2.5336	1.3646	2.4474	147.015
Feb. '74	.4975	.2171	2.5336	1.3346	2.4474	142.1183
Mar. '74	.5122	.2132	2.5336	1.3214	2.4278	140.335
Apr. '74	.5197	.2156	2.5846	1.3214	2.5316	146.767
May '74	.5151	.2159	2.6116	1.3158	2.5276	145.005
June '74	.5116	.2141	2.5714	.13058	2.4710	148.251
July '74	.5162	.2167	2.6254	1.3161	2.4207	152.114
Aug. '74	.4995	.2158	2.5452	.13294	2.4096	150.646
Sept. '74	.4995	.2147	2.4366	1.3294	2.3781	148.348

D. *P.R.C. Foreign Financial Liabilities*

In the P.R.C. theoretical framework, China has no foreign debt since all potential foreign claims are either due to the initiative of the potential claimant (*e.g.*, the depositor at the B.O.C.) or due to what the Chinese regard as normal methods of financing commercial transactions. Nevertheless, China has incurred substantial future financial obligations; their size and timing is the focus of this section.

As mentioned above, the B.O.C. and its "sister banks" in Hong Kong do accept R.M.B.-denominated deposits that could result in a drain on China's foreign exchange. The magnitude of such deposits is not known, but Hong Kong "China watchers" have reported that such deposits have been more aggressively solicited in recent years.[33] Also of considerable interest are the numerous unconfirmed reports that Japanese banks have made hard-currency, interest-earning deposits in the Bank of China's London branch.[34] From China's point of view, such deposits provide people and banks secure and profitable opportunities for deposit. More importantly, the deposits raise P.R.C. foreign exchange levels today—but they also raise the level of potential future claims on P.R.C. foreign exchange holdings. Unfortunately the estimates of deposits at P.R.C. banks and P.R.C. foreign exchange levels are too speculative to be used here.

The preponderant share of P.R.C. future financial liabilities derives from products already purchased or contracted for. Repayments for these products will total more than 1 billion dollars during the rest of the 1970's and the repayment schedule will extend until at least 1982. Two major factors account for such liabilities: purchases of agricultural products on 12-18 month terms; and purchases of complete plants to be paid for through the vehicles of "progress payments" and "deferred payments."

In 1973, purchases of agricultural products totalled about 1.3 billion dollars and the total will again exceed 1.0 billion dollars in 1974.[35] This is more than double the 1972 level and is attributable both to substantially higher physical imports and to higher prices for agricultural products. In the immediate future, China may be expected to revert to the pattern of the 1960's, when the P.R.C. imported some 5-6 million tons of food grains annually. In fact, the P.R.C. has already contracted for 4.8 million tons annually through 1976. At present prices, China will have to allocate about 700 million dollars annually for grain purchases.[36] For 1975 and possibly 1976, P.R.C. financial liabilities will be substantially greater (more than 1 billion dollars) as principal and interest on the credits for the 1973 and 1974 agricultural shipments are repaid.

The most dramatic aspect of recent P.R.C. foreign trade policy is the purchase of 2.1 billion dollars worth of complete plants since December 1972. Nearly all of the purchases were financed on some kind of delayed payment basis—either "progress payments" or "deferred payment." Under the progress payments formula, the Chinese make a 10-20 percent down payment and essentially discharge the remaining debt while the plant is being installed. Under the system of "deferred payments," the P.R.C. pays a down payment (commonly 20 percent) and then pays the remainder at regular intervals over a five year period *after the plant is completed.* Since the builder of the plant does not begin to receive most of his money until after construction is completed, this amounts to granting a medium-term loan to the P.R.C. Although China insists that this is normal commercial procedure and should not be considered foreign debt, it has been willing to accept the principle of paying an additional amount as interest so long as the rate is moderate. Such rates (6 percent or slightly more) have been made possible through the Japanese Export-Import Bank and similar institutions in Europe.

Column 1 in Table III sets out an estimate of the repayment schedule on the plants for which the Chinese have already

TABLE III. P.R.C. FINANCIAL REPAYMENTS DUE TO COMPLETE PLANT PURCHASES

YEAR	Schedule for Purchases Contracted by Oct. 15, 1974	Schedule Assuming the Continued Purchase of $1 Billion Annually Through 1982
1975	247.4[a]	447[b]
1976	317.0	517
1977	341.5	669
1978	346.7	923
1979	245.0	1,057
1980	209.0	1,242
1981	150.8	1,290
1982	103.0	1,243

[a] The basic source for this column was the list of complete plant purchases provided in CENTRAL INTELLIGENCE AGENCY, PEOPLE'S REPUBLIC OF CHINA: INTERNATIONAL TRADE HANDBOOK (U.S. Government Document A(ER 74-63), Library of Congress, Sept. 1974). Two recent purchases totalling $100 million were added to that list. Information about financial terms, interest rates, and scheduled completion dates was from the same source, and was supplemented by information from several issues of U.S.-CHINA BUSINESS REVIEW (1974), and from H. HEYMANN, CHINA'S APPROACH TO TECHNOLOGY ACQUISITION: PART III (forthcoming Rand Corporation report).

[b] This column also assumes that: China makes 20% downpayments ($200 million) each year; the remainder is financed on five-year, 7% interest credits; and the projects would be completed 2-3 years after the contract was signed.

contracted. The required repayments are fairly constant from 1975 through 1979, rising to a peak of about 350 million dollars in 1977 and 1978. This represents only 7 percent of China's anticipated exports to non-Communist countries in 1974.[37] It will decrease sufficiently in the 1975-1980 period as trade grows both in real and money terms.

This level of required financial repayments is quite low by conventional standards (debt ratios are between 10 percent and 20 percent in East European countries and have ranged between 20 percent and 30 percent for Brazil). With the established financial reputation of the B.O.C., it seems unlikely that bankers will be very concerned, at least until the debt service ratio exceeds 20 percent.

The interesting question is whether the P.R.C. can continue its complete plant import program indefinitely without beginning to undermine its current high-credit status. Column 2 assumes that the P.R.C. will continue to purchase about 1 billion dollars worth of complete plants annually through 1982. It further assumes that they will be financed by medium-term credits and that construction will be completed 2-3 years from the time the contract is signed. The result is a steady rise in the P.R.C. repayment schedule (down payments plus repayment of principal and interest) to about 1.2 billion dollars in 1980. To maintain a relatively conservative debt repayment ratio of 15 percent, P.R.C. exports to non-Communist countries would have to rise to $8 billion by 1980. Since such exports were already 3.9 billion dollars in 1973, this would require them to grow 10 percent annually. While a 10 percent annual rate of growth of exports may sound optimistic, it would not appear unreasonable given China's current emphasis on foreign trade and the continuing inflation in world prices.

Even if payment for contracted agricultural products were included, the repayment schedule would amount to only 2 billion dollars in most years. A 20 percent debt service ratio might be maintained by a quite reasonable export growth of about 12 percent per year. However, the inclusion of repayment for agricultural credits does point up what may be a difficult short-term liquidity problem for the P.R.C. In 1975 and 1976, repayment of agricultural and industrial credits will amount to at least 1.3 billion dollars ($300 million for industrial credits and perhaps $1 billion for agricultural credits). Depending on the exact size and timing of agricultural repayments, it may be difficult to keep the debt service ratio from rising beyond 20 percent. Conceivably the necessity of importing unexpectedly large quantities of agricultural products in 1973 and 1974 has been one factor in the noticeable slowdown in complete plant purchases since the spring of 1974.[38]

III. CONCLUSION

Chinese international financial practices since the Cultural Revolution have changed significantly both in response to the pressure of growing foreign trade and to increasingly unstable international financial conditions. As in other aspects of foreign policy, the Chinese appear to be willing to participate more actively and imaginatively in such areas of international finance as contractual procedures, acceptance of foreign deposits, and medium-term foreign quasi-loans. Moreover, despite a considerable program of complete plant purchases, China's credit still seems sound enough to continue such a program, provided P.R.C. planners have made a basic commitment to continue the moderate expansion of the P.R.C. foreign trade sector.

Despite this period of innovation, however, foreign trade remains a small, albeit important, appendage on the Chinese economy. China's conservative international financial procedures continue to emphasize that the P.R.C. is a closed, planned economy with a tightly monitored foreign trade sector. The day of the convertible R.M.B. and some form of long-term loans is not imminent.

APPENDIX I. *Opening Agreement.* *

Regulations Governing the Opening Of
Renminbi Account With The Bank Of China,
Head Office, Banking Department, Peking
By

The opening of a Renminbi account with the Bank of
China, Head Office, Banking Department, Peking
(hereinafter called "the First Party") by

(hereinafter called "the Second Party") shall be
governed by the following regulations:

(1) Credits to the Renminbi account shall be limited to:

    (a) Purchase of Renminbi against [foreign currency] to be used as working balance, but such a working balance shall not exceed RMB_____.
    (b) Proceeds of Chinese imports and relative charges.
    (c) Purchase of Renminbi against [foreign currency] to be used for payment of Chinese exports and relative charges on the basis of a contract concluded with a Chinese National Import and Export Corporation.

(2) Debits to the Renminbi account shall be limited to:

    (a) Payment of Chinese exports and relative charges.
    (b) Payment of non-commercial expenses with China.
    (c) Payment within [foreign country].
    (d) Conversion into [foreign currency].

(3) The Renimibi account may be used for passing the receipts and payments between all the domestic branches of the First Party and the domestic branches of the Second Party in

see list at foot of page

*To be published by Reghizzi in LAW AND POLITICS IN CHINA'S FOREIGN TRADE (V. Li ed., forthcoming).

(4) On receipt of a statement of account of the Renminbi account from the First Party each month, the Second Party must, within a month, inform the First Party by letter of any outstanding items and whether the balance standing at the end of the month is correct.

(5) These regulations shall enter into force on the opening of the Renminbi account and have been agreed to and confirmed by the following officials of the Second Party whose authorized signatures are affixed hereunder.

APPENDIX II. *Exchange Agreement.*

Regulations Governing Renminbi
Exchange Business Between The
Bank Of China, Head Office, Bank-
ing Department, Peking, China
And

In its purchase or sale of spot or forward Renminbi
from or to the Bank of China, Head Office, Banking
Department, Peking (hereinafter called "the First
Party"),
(hereinafter called "the Second Party") must observe
the following regulations:

(1) A purchase of spot or forward Renminbi by the Second Party from the First Party must be made against [foreign currency] and is limited to payment of Chinese exports and relative charges on the basis of a Chinese export contract concluded with a Chinese National Import and Export Corporation. Spot Renminbi bought may be used as a working balance in a Renminbi account.

(2) A purchase of spot or forward Renminbi by the Second Party from the First Party must be effected by cable. The cable must show a test number, the amount of Renminbi to be bought and its equivalent in [foreign currency] and the date or period of delivery. The date of delivery for a purchase of spot Renminbi is 2 or 3 working days after the date of the despatch [sic] of the cable. The period of delivery for a purchase of forward Renminbi is based on the period of the relative contract, but it must not exceed six months.

(3) On receipt of a cable from the Second Party for a purchase of spot or forward Renminbi, the First Party shall, if agreeable to the purchase, immediately confirm to the Second Party by cable. A deal in the purchase and sale of Renminbi is thus concluded between the two sides, and both sides must make payment to each other in accordance with the deal. If it is necessary, the First Party has the right to inquire of the Second Party by cable the purpose of the purchase, for instance, the contract concerned. On receipt of the cable of inquiry, the Second Party must immediately reply by cable, so that the First Party may ascertain whether the purchase conforms to section (1) of these regulations.

(4) A sale of spot Renminbi by the Second Party to the First Party must be effected by cable. The cable must show a test number, the amount of Renminbi to be sold and its equivalent in [foreign currency] and the date of delivery. The date of delivery shall be 2 or 3 working days after the date of the despatch [*sic*] of the cable. If, on receipt of the cable, it is found that there is sufficient balance in the Renminbi account of the Second Party, the First Party shall notify the Second Party of the amount of [foreign currency] the First Party will pay and the date on which payment will be made. A deal in the purchase and sale of Renminbi is thus concluded between the two sides and both sides must make payment to each other in accordance with the deal.

(5) A sale of forward Renminbi by the Second Party to the First Party must be based on a Chinese import contract concluded with a Chinese National Import and Export Corporation and must be effected by cable. The cable must show a test number, the amount of Renminbi to be sold and its equivalent in [foreign currency] and the period of delivery. The period of delivery is based on the period of the relative contract, but it must not exceed six months. On receipt of the cable, the First Party shall, if agreeable to the sale, confirm to the Second Party by cable. A deal in the purchase and sale of Renminbi is thus concluded between the two sides, and both sides must make payment to each other in accordance with deal. If it is found necessary, the first Party has the right to inquire of the Second Party by cable the purpose of the sale, for instance, the contract concerned. On receipt of the cable of inquiry, the Second Party must immediately reply by cable, so that the First Party may ascertain whether the sale conforms to the stipulations of this section.

(6) The exchange rate for spot Renminbi against the [foreign currency] is the same as that for forward Renminbi against the [foreign currency]. The exchange rate for forward Renminbi and forward charges shall be fixed by the First Party and shall be notified to the Second Party. When the Second Party sells or buys spot or forward Renminbi to or from merchants, it should also use the aforesaid exchange rates, but it may appropriately charge commission.

(7) The exchange rates and forward charges for the purchase and sale of spot and forward Renminbi by the Second Party form or to the First Party shall be based on those notified by the Bank of China as ruling at the time when the First Party despatches its cable of agreement to the sale or purchase following the receipt of a cable from the Second Party.

(8) In the event of an amendment to or a change in these regulations, the First Party shall notify the Second Party.

(9) These regulations shall enter into force on [date] and have been agreed to and confirmed by the following officials of the Second Party whose authorized signatures are affixed hereunder:

APPROVED

NOTES

[1] *See* Tretiak, *Is China Preparing to "Turn Out"? Changes in Chinese Levels of Attention to International Environment*, 11 ASIAN SURVEY 219 (1971); Friedman, *The Nixon-Mao Pact*, 1 BULLETIN OF CONCERNED ASIAN SCHOLARS 15 (No. 3, 1969).

[2] Financial aspects of P.R.C. trade with communist countries are covered by Frank Munzel and George Ginsbergs in LAW AND POLITICS IN CHINA'S FOREIGN TRADE (V. Li ed. forthcoming).

[3] *See* Wilson, *The Bank of China Steps Out*, 124 THE BANKER 105 (1974); Lewis, *The Communist Capitalists*, 84 F.E. ECO. REV. [FAR EASTERN ECONOMIC REVIEW] 18 (No. 13, 1974).

[4] New China News Agency, Dec. 19, 1973, reported in FOREIGN BROADCAST INFORMATION SERVICE [hereinafter cited as F.B.I.S.], Dec. 19, 1973, at B-11.

[5] *See* CENTRAL INTELLIGENCE AGENCY, PEOPLE'S REPUBLIC OF CHINA: INTERNATIONAL TRADE HANDBOOK, 1 (U.S. Government Doc. A (ER 74-63), Library of Congress Document Expediting, Sept. 1974); at 2 (Oct. 1973); at 5 (Dec. 1972).

[6] JAPAN EXTERNAL TRADE ORGANIZATION CHINA NEWSLETTER [hereinafter cited as J.E.T.R.O. NEWSLETTER], Jul. 1974, at 2.

[7] *See* Table I.

[8] CENTRAL INTELLIGENCE AGENCY, Sept. 1974, *supra* note 5, at 1.

[9] On economic grounds, Professors Eckstein and Reynolds conclude that "A 10% average annual growth rate seems more plausible between 1972 and 1980." This figure is in real terms. In current prices their estimates would undoubtedly be higher. Eckstein & Reynolds, *Sino-American Trade Prospects and Policy*, 64 AMERICAN ECONOMIC REVIEW at 298 (No. 2, 1974).

[10] Since its founding, the P.R.C. has participated in international trade fairs more than 200 times. "These fairs have been held in over 70 countries." Pu Hsuan, *Develop Foreign Trade by Maintaining Independence and Keeping the Initiative in Our Own Hands and Relying On Our Own Efforts*, Peking Radio, Oct. 15, 1974, reported in F.B.I.S., Oct. 17, 1974, at A-1. Recently, China's participation has expanded considerably. For details, *see* 1 U.S.-CHINA BUSINESS REVIEW 23 (No. 4, 1974).

[11] L. Chiang, *New Developments in China's Foreign Trade*, 1 CHINA'S FOREIGN TRADE 4 (No. 1, 1974).

[12] For analyses of the debate *see:* NAI RUENN-CHEN, CHINA'S FOREIGN POLICY: A CURRENT APPRAISAL, 74-50 (U.S. Dept. of Commerce 1974); Goodstadt, *Shadows of Ideology in Canton*, 84 F.E. ECO. REV. 38 (1974).

[13] After this paper was initially written, The People's Daily of October 15, 1974, carried an article stating, "Our country's foreign trade has developed rapidly and is playing an increasingly noticeable role in promoting socialist construction in our country and expanding international economic exchange," reported in F.B.I.S., Oct. 17, 1974, at A-1.

[14] For excellent compilations of P.R.C. purchases *see generally* 1 U.S.-CHINA BUSINESS REVIEW (1974); *see also* Part III of H. HEYMANN, CHINA'S APPROACH TO TECHNOLOGY ACQUISITION (Rand Corporation Report, forthcoming).

[15] For an excellent summary of this and other matters, consult Triplett, *The Banking Industry*, in DOING BUSINESS WITH CHINA: AMERICAN TRADE OPPORTUNITIES IN THE 1970's 190 (1974).

[16] Chiang, *supra* note 11, at 5.

[17] A letter of credit is a document in which a bank (the bank which drafts the document is known as the "opening bank") promises to pay on behalf of a

buyer. An irrevocable letter of credit cannot be changed without the agreement of all parties. The confirming bank (generally located in the seller's country) guarantees that payment will be made if the conditions on the letter of credit are met. "Negotiation" of documents occurs when the seller brings the documents (*e.g.*, bills of lading) required by the letter of credit to a bank along with his draft requesting payment. If documents are complete and in order, the actual process of payment (as defined in the contract) can begin. Transferable letters of credit can be assigned to a third party and are useful when the product involved is produced by subcontractors. For a more comprehensive and sophisticated treatment, *see* Schwering, *Financing Imports From China*, 1 U.S.-CHINA BUSINESS REVIEW 36 (No. 5, 1974).

[18]*Id.* at 39.

[19]*See* H. HEYMANN, *supra* note 14.

[20]Schwering, *supra* note 17, at 37.

[21]JAPAN EXTERNAL TRADE ORGANIZATION, HOW TO APPROACH THE CHINA MARKET 16 (1972).

[22]Assets which are owned or controlled by the P.R.C. and which are located in the United States are blocked under provisions of the Foreign Assets Control Regulations. On the other hand, United States' citizens have claims against the P.R.C. for property lost in 1949. P.R.C. assets in the United States potentially could be attached for the satisfaction of such claims. *See* Denny & Stein, *Recent Developments in Trade Between the U.S. and the P.R.C.: A Legal and Economic Perspective*, 38 LAW & CONTEMPORARY PROBLEMS 260 (1973).

[23]*See* Schwering, *supra* note 17.

[24]J.E.T.R.O. NEWSLETTER, June 1973, at 1.

[25]*Id.*

[26]*Id.* at 7. But J.E.T.R.O., possibly thinking of Japanese exports, warned: "Under the existing situation with the Japanese Yen so strong, and still subject to change, the exchange problem remains a major obstacle to the trade between Japan and China."

[27]*Id.* at 8.

[28]*See* the quotation at note 26, *supra*, and the following comment: "Unless the Chinese side recognizes the conversion of the Yuan balance into Yen on a fixed Yen-Yuan basis, risk is always liable to arise from the undulation of the currencies of third countries in the present Yen-Yuan settlement system." *Id.*

[29]For descriptions *see* the chapters authored by Christopher Lewis and Allen Smith in LAW AND POLITICS IN CHINA'S FOREIGN TRADE, *supra* note 2. *See also* Strauss, *China Boosts Lure of RMB Deposit Plan*, Journal of Commerce, Nov. 5, 1974, at 1, col. 7.

[30]1 U.S.-CHINA BUSINESS REVIEW 50 (No. 3, 1974). Six month forward R.M.B. costs 3 percent for pound sterling. Against less stable currencies the cost has reportedly run as high as 5 to 6 percent.

[31]Whenever one country (*e.g.*, P.R.C.) quotes exchange rates for two other currencies (*e.g.*, U.S. and U.K.), there is an implied exchange rate between the latter two currencies. This is the "cross rate" and can be compared with the free market rate for consistency.

[32]1 U.S.-CHINA BUSINESS REVIEW 51 (No. 3, 1974).

[33]*See, e.g.*, Awanohara, *When Japan Deposits, China Borrows*, 84 F.E. ECO. REV. 42 (1974).

[34]*See* CENTRAL INTELLIGENCE AGENCY, Sept. 1974, *supra* note 5, at 1.

[35]Lewis, *supra* note 29, says that R.M.B. accounts in H.K. account have been estimated at $150 million, but admits that this "could be off the mark." He believes that the rate of growth of such deposits fell off somewhat in 1973.

[36]The following assumptions were used to derive the $700 million figure.

Annual purchases of 5.5 million tons were assumed at $120 per ton. Half of the purchases were assumed to be paid off over a 12-month period. The remaining amount was assumed to be financed over 18 months. An annual interest rate of 8 percent was applied to all calculations.

[37] Repayment of principal and interest as a proportion of a country's exports is a crude measure of credit worthiness. It is referred to as the debt service ratio.

[38] By late 1974 it became apparent that P.R.C. exports were not expanding as rapidly as in the preceding two years. Businessmen have reported deteriorating business conditions at both 1974 Canton Trade Fairs. In part, this was due to soft world markets for P.R.C. exports (e.g., textiles). It is possible this will mark another significant turning point or it may be merely a temporary pause in the growth of foreign trade.

China's Major Trading Partner: Japan Dependent

P. EDWARD HALEY*
HAROLD W. ROOD†

Since 1945, Japan's prosperity and security and the integrity of her domestic institutions have always been hostage to a world order over which she has had little control. While that order was stable and beneficent, it was easy to forget Japan's vulnerabilities. During the last three decades, trade and wealth grew reassuringly among the industrial nations, while Japan herself enjoyed remarkable economic success. Capital and goods moved with relative freedom around the world, and aggressive traders like Japan were able to exploit comparative advantages in production and reap large profits without having to pay in kind. The prices of raw materials and petroleum products remained low. As long as these pleasant conditions lasted, forecasts of Japanese greatness, based on linear projections of established economic and political patterns, seemed convincing, or at least plausible.[1] They now seem badly and even cruelly mistaken. In fact, the developments of the last few years—severe inflation, the revaluation of dollar and yen, the explosion in the costs of primary materials, the evaporation of Japan's foreign exchange surplus—have only served to reveal vulnerabilities that were always present.

More than this, the recent and unhappy developments that plague Japan, and most of the world's nations, whether developing or "post-industrial," invite a reassessment of the approach one should use in forming an appreciation of a nation's international or domestic situation. The shocks Japan has received since 1970 counsel against basing judgment solely on projections of established economic and political patterns. To a remarkable extent, the problems now facing the Japanese government can only be marginally influenced by Japanese initiative and action, assuming that the existing constitutional order in Japan remains intact. For example, Japan, like the other major industrial nations of the world, has been able to react only feebly to the shift of wealth from consumers to producers of petroleum. To be sure, Japan's reaction has been influenced by

*Associate Professor of International Relations, Claremont Men's College and Claremont Graduate School; International Affairs Fellow of the Council on Foreign Relations.

†Professor of Political Science, Claremont Men's College and Claremont Graduate School; member of the staff of Stanford Research Institute.

established internal political and economic forces. But her ability to cope with the challenges of an increasingly hostile economic, military, and political order will depend as much on the strengths and weaknesses of her dependent role, as it will on the renowned industry and discipline of her workers, the aggressiveness of her salesmen, or the skills of her politicians, diplomats, entrepreneurs, and economists.

The purpose of this essay is to examine the nature of Japan's current international situation—whether and in what ways it is strong and weak—and to ask if such an analysis sheds any light on the future of Japan's relations with the People's Republic of China. Strength is here understood to mean the degree of economic self-sufficiency a country enjoys and its ability to take significant unilateral political and military action.[2] Using this definition, one would judge the Soviet Union to be relatively self-sufficient and capable of major unilateral action (strong/strong). China would rate high in economic self-sufficiency and low in capacity for taking unilateral military or political initiatives (strong/weak). Japan is neither self-sufficient nor capable of significant unilateral political or military action (weak/weak). It remains to describe Japan's weakness or dependence and to discover its meaning for Japanese foreign policy.

I. JAPAN'S ECONOMIC DEPENDENCE

Japan is a nation that must trade to live, but the nature of that trade is sometimes misunderstood. Japan's overseas trade runs at about ten percent of its Gross National Product, an amount much smaller than the norm in other industrial countries.[3] Moreover, raw materials account for 70 percent of imports, as against 30 percent for foreign manufactures.[4] Fortunately for Japan, many important suppliers of these crucial materials are advanced Western nations with stable political regimes and a large vested interest in both Japanese prosperity and world economic stability. For Japan's iron and steel industry, Australia supplied 43.3 percent of Japan's 1972 imports of iron ore, or about 48 million out of a total 111 million tons. India (16.1 percent), Brazil (8.4 percent), Peru, and Chile were also significant exporters to Japan. Japan produces no bauxite for its large aluminum industry and, in 1972, obtained 60.2 percent of its needs from Australia, and other large supplies from Indonesia (21.5 percent), and Malaysia (16.4 percent). About half Japan's needs in coking coal, lead, and zinc must be imported from the United States, Australia, Peru, and Canada. Nearly 73 percent of Japan's copper needs in 1972 were met by imports, chiefly from Canada (37.5 percent), the Philippines (32.9 percent), and Australia (7.5 percent).[5]

Japan's dependence on foreign supplies is even greater in regard to energy than to raw material. Saburo Okita reported that for the fiscal year 1972: ". . . three-fourths of Japan's primary energy was supplied by oil, and the rest by coal (16.6 percent), hydroelectric power (6.3 percent), natural gas (0.8 percent), atomic energy (0.7 percent), and other sources (0.8 percent). Since two-thirds of the coal is imported, the degree of dependence on imported energy was 86 percent, and the domestic supply of energy was only 14 percent."[6] Japan has no domestic supplies of uranium, and before the Arab cuts in oil production her needs for 1975 were projected to be 15,660 short tons.[7]

The movement in both raw materials and energy has often been from self-sufficiency to total reliance on foreign supplies. Japan at one time exported copper. She once took her iron ore from Korea and China, over which she exercised great political, and ultimately military, control in the 1920's and 1930's. In 1935, as Okita observed, domestic coal (62 percent), hydroelectric power (19 percent), and wood and charcoal (10 percent) supplied nearly all Japan's energy needs. Only 9 percent was supplied by imported oil, and a spare 26 million barrels were taken in 1935, as against about two billion barrels in 1973.

A similar movement away from self-sufficiency has occurred in food supplies as the Japanese diet has improved. Japanese citizens have more to eat today than they did two decades ago, and it is more nutritious food, consisting of twice as much animal protein, four times as much milk and milk products, and nearly five times as much meat. Japan imports 47 percent of the grain used to feed livestock, and of the wheat, soybean, maize, and sorghum imported in 1973 (18.1 million metric tons), 81 percent (14.7 million metric tons) came from the United States.[8]

As the figures for imports of raw materials and food suggest, Japan's trade with advanced nations has increased dramatically in importance since 1955. Table I illustrates these shifts. The large reductions in percentage shares of trade with the developing nations conceal large volume increases resulting from the ten-fold expansion of Japanese trade since 1955. They also hide what Ellingworth called East and Southeast Asian trade dependence on Japan. Table II shows the degree of dependence in 1970.

Japan is an efficient and impressive processor of imported raw materials, but these strengths are mitigated by weaknesses that arise from her dependence on foreign supplies, and the result is perplexing. Gary Saxonhouse described the Japanese economy as one with "a decidedly nineteenth-century pattern of trade." Richard Ellingworth observed that Japan has approached foreign trade as "a process whereby her industry has been fuelled and supplied, rather

TABLE I. GEOGRAPHICAL DISTRIBUTION OF JAPAN'S FOREIGN TRADE

| | Percentages of: | | | |
| | 1955 | | 1970 | |
SECTOR	EXPORTS TO	IMPORTS FROM	EXPORTS TO	IMPORTS FROM
Developed World	42.2	50.8	58.0	55.4
Developing World	55.9	45.6	36.6	39.9
Mainland China	1.4	3.3	2.9	1.3
Soviet Union	1.5	2.5	1.8	2.5

Source: INTERNATIONAL INSTITUTE OF STRATEGIC STUDIES, STRATEGIC SURVEY 1971, at 61.

TABLE II. JAPAN'S SHARE OF EAST AND SOUTHEAST ASIAN TRADE IN 1970

| | Proportion of: | |
COUNTRY	IMPORTS FROM JAPAN	EXPORTS TO JAPAN
R.O.K.	41.2%	27.4%
Taiwan	45.9%	17.6%
Thailand	35.8%	27.3%
Philippines	37.5%	50.0%
Malaysia	12.0%	24.9%
Vietnam	15.3%	25.0%

Source: ECONOMIC PLANNING AGENCY, ANNUAL REPORT FOR 1971 (Japanese language version) 113, cited in R. ELLINGWORTH, JAPANESE ECONOMIC POLICIES AND SECURITY, n. 26 at 34 (Adelphi Papers No. 90, 1972).

than one which is intrinsically desirable for the international exchange of goods. . . . The main stimulus to production has been given by domestic investment and the business opportunities within Japan created by the constantly increasing purchasing power of the Japanese people. There has been no ready disposition to share more of this market than absolutely necessary with foreigners."[9]

Obvious problems have arisen for Japan as resources have become scarcer and more expensive. Japan may find two possible external remedies in diversifying sources of supply and in building plants within other countries holding materials or energy; in the latter case Japan would import finished or processed goods.[10] China possesses large reserves of coal and oil, and the U.S.S.R. and Japan have begun negotiations for joint development of Siberian oil and mineral wealth. Whether these possibilities will be exploited in ways of benefit to Japan depends on the approach of the Soviet and Chinese governments to foreign trade in general and with Japan in particular, and depends as well on the political and economic incentives Japan can find to use in shaping Sino-Japanese and Russo-Japanese relations.

II. JAPAN'S DIPLOMATIC AND MILITARY DEPENDENCE

While the constitutional prohibitions against the use of force endure, no Japanese government can provide adequate security for the country without the help either of the United States or conceivably of the Soviet Union. The shortfall in security may be inherent and not just constitutional, for there is some doubt that a country as small and as densely populated as Japan could establish a credible nuclear deterrent, even one entirely composed of submarine-launched ballistic missiles.[11]

The improbability or irrationality of a policy has not always prevented nations from adopting it, but the arguments against Japan "going nuclear" are strong and opposition to such a course is widespread and fervent in Japan.[12] Established Japanese military doctrine apparently is designed to cope with two kinds of developments: conventional attack from the mainland and externally-sponsored insurgency at home. Should attack come from the mainland, Japan's Self-Defense Forces would try to last ten days while the government invoked the security treaty with the United States. If no response comes in time, "the doctrine calls for the Japanese army to give up before risking a slaughter of civilians."[13] In response to large-scale insurgency, the Army will strive to defeat the insurgents, recover captured territory, and reestablish transportation and supplies of food and other materials.

Japan has regularly spent less than 1 percent of Gross National

Product (GNP) for defense. This has allowed a limited military expansion because GNP has increased significantly in the last two decades. Other advanced industrial nations spend in a ratio from four to eight times greater. The Soviet Union spends nine times more as a percentage of GNP and China about six times more.[14] The Fourth Five-Year Defense Plan for Japan envisaged no important changes.[15] In 1973, Japan spent $3.84 billion for defense, or 0.8 percent of a GNP of $439.4 billion. Table III shows the military and economic strengths of Japan's neighbors and the United States. These figures make it clear why Japan is outclassed militarily even by a country like South Korea, which has only a fraction of Japan's population

TABLE III. COMPARISON OF ELEMENTS OF MILITARY STRENGTH OF EAST ASIAN ACTORS, 1973

COUNTRY	POPULA-TION (millions)	ARMED FORCES	G.N.P. ($billion)	DEFENSE EXPENDITURES ($million)	(% of G.N.P.)
China—Peoples Republic	800-900	3,000,000	140	7,000	5.0
China—Republic of (Taiwan)	16	491,000	9.4	878	9.0
Japan	104.33	233,000	439.4	3,530	0.8
Korea—D.P.R. (North)	15.51	467,000	3.5	620	17.7
Korea—Republic of (South)	33.74	625,000	12.6	476	3.8
United States	213.46	2,174,000	1,289	79,500	6.2
U.S.S.R.	252.53	3,525,000	608.6[a]	85,800[a]	12.2[a]

Source: INT'L INSTITUTE OF STRATEGIC STUDIES, MILITARY BALANCE 1973-74.

[a] For an explanation of the difficulty of establishing correct amounts for the Soviet Union, *see* INT'L INSTITUTE OF STRATEGIC STUDIES, MILITARY BALANCE 1973-74 at 8-9. A careful examination supports the view of that journal that the "equivalent dollar costs of Soviet resources devoted to defense may well be comparable to [total] American spending and perhaps well above it. It must be borne in mind that this method uses United States price weightings. The relationships could be very different if Soviet prices were used as weights instead." We have used the 1973 official exchange rate of $1 = 0.72 rubles, a Soviet G.N.P. of 441 billion rubles for 1973, and an average of high and low estimates for defense expenditures.

and economic strength. The figures also make clear why the Fourth Defense Plan stated unequivocally that Japan can meet only small-scale aggression with her own resources and must rely on the cooperation of the United States to meet larger conventional or nuclear threats. Japan's position is truly, as Saburo Okita put it, "defenseless on all sides," or *happo-yabure* in the terminology of *kendo*.

One of the important consequences of Japan's military weakness is that she is unable to defend the sea-routes over which her vital oil and raw material supplies must travel. "The Straits of Malacca," as Yoshifumi Saito observed, "have been the watershed of the postwar Asian economy."[16] Through this narrow channel and down its "eastward slope" flows the 80 percent of Japan's oil that comes from the Persian Gulf. More than one hundred ships pass the Straits every day, while the waterway itself has a relatively shallow unstable bottom and is vulnerable to changes in the political attitudes and ambitions of the states bordering it, namely Indonesia, Malaysia, and Singapore.[17] One can argue, as Masataka Kosaka does, that world sea routes probably cannot be disrupted by the military forces of one country, that military forces neither threaten nor guarantee world economic interdependence, and that a nation may possess global economic power without having to deploy large military forces.[18] One may assume, as does Kiichi Saeki, that safe trade routes will be secured for Japan more effectively through economic and diplomatic efforts than through a strong military response.[18] Another prominent Japanese commentator, Junnosuke Kishida, concluded that her geography and need for foreign resources compel Japan to refrain from ever becoming a strong military power.[20] Indeed, one must make these kinds of arguments, assumptions, and conclusions if he is to maintain the position of these spokesmen, a position widely held in Japan, that the country need not and must not acquire great military power. The point is not that exactly opposite conclusions could be reached, or even that in the past Japanese governments and most Japanese, even some as well-intentioned and eminent as those cited here, have reached exactly the opposite view. Rather, there are two crucial points. First, as Tables II and III and the discussions of raw material imports and the Straits reveal, Japan has vital interests in the Pacific and Southeast Asian regions. These are trade and open and secure waterways—both of which depend, in turn, on the stability and prosperity of the countries in the two areas.[21] Second, with a small army and a navy of some 14 submarines and 27 destroyers, Japan must rely on the goodwill of other naval powers, notably that of the United States and the Soviet Union, to maintain open sea routes and free-flowing trade.

Japan's military dependence limits her ability to take

independent diplomatic initiatives, while her growing economic importance throughout Asia frequently stirs nationalist and anti-Japanese sentiments (despite small increases in Japan's foreign aid in Asian countries). Even in an area as important as relations with China, Japan could only follow the American lead in normalizing relations.[22] The violent, anti-Japanese demonstrations in Thailand and Indonesia during Premier Kakuei Tanaka's visit to Southeast Asia in January 1974 suggest the kinds of difficulties that lie in the path of achieving Japan's commercial and political objectives by diplomatic and economic means. Trade continues to grow between Japan and the countries of Southeast Asia and the Pacific, but in addition to the problems with Jakarta and Bangkok, there is growing economic nationalism in Australia and, to a lesser extent, in the Philippines, and relations continue to be turbulent with South Korea.[23]

III. JAPAN'S ADVANTAGES

While Japan may indeed be "defenseless on all sides," she is not completely helpless as a result of her dependence on foreign markets, raw materials, and military support. There are some favorable aspects to Japan's current international position, and these, as well as the vulnerabilities, will bear on her present and future relations with China.

What few advantages Japan has exist because of the desire of others—China, the U.S.S.R., and the United States, and less powerful nations of Asia and the Pacific, as well—to have Japan take economic and political decisions and actions that serve their interests or at least do not harm them.

A. *China's Objectives Regarding Japan*

China's political goal is to prevent Japan from siding with the U.S.S.R. or from being drawn into Russian security and economic systems. She also desires to weaken but at present not to destroy Japan's ties with the United States. For now what the Chinese government terms "the menace from the bear in the North" receives greater stress than the dangers of "U.S. imperialism," or, as the New China News Agency put it on July 8, 1974: "In all this, the activities of Soviet revisionist social-imperialism are more vicious and hypocritical [than the American]."[24] Chinese propaganda aimed at Japan plays a number of themes as a round: the Soviet retention of the islands Habomai, Shikotan, Kunashiri, and Etorofu; the extreme reluctance of the

U.S.S.R. actually to allow Japan to begin receiving large amounts of oil and other resources from Siberia—the Chinese carefully point out how the Russians could use the Siberian ventures to drive a wedge between the U.S. and Japan; the dangers to Japan of membership in a Soviet-sponsored "Asian collective security system"; and the threats to Japan from the repeated violations by Soviet planes and warships of Japanese air space and territorial waters.

The Sino-Japanese communique of September 28, 1972, issued during Prime Minister Tanaka's visit to the People's Republic, reveals a number of other objectives China seeks from Japan. In addition to obtaining recognition as the sole legal government of China, and endorsement of Taiwan as an integral part of China, Peking enlisted Japan's support for the principles of peaceful coexistence (which include prohibitions of intervention and aggression) and her promise not to seek hegemony in Asia and the Pacific, and, most important of all, her agreement to a statement of opposition "to efforts by any other country or group of countries to establish such hegemony."[25] Regardless of disclaimers to the contrary in the same paragraph from which this phrase is taken, the Chinese aimed this commitment directly at the U.S.S.R. and, indirectly, at the United States.

The two countries agreed in the communique to terminate both the state of war and the "abnormal state of affairs" that had existed between them. The Japanese government interpreted this to mean that they had "terminated" their peace treaty with the Republic of China and had established normal diplomatic relations with the People's Republic. Article 8 then drew the conclusion from these two premises: having broken the old relations, it remains for both countries to elaborate the new by concluding a treaty of peace and friendship. But the actual peace negotiations—and thus the exact determination of Japan's relationship with China—were left for a future time, just as the preamble of the communique spoke only in the conditional about what "should and can" be done to establish peaceful and friendly relations between the two countries.[26] As Gene Hsiao observed, this makes the status of Sino-Japanese political relations resemble Soviet-Japanese affairs, at least in the sense that while a state of war terminated as long ago as 1956, it has not been possible to reach a fundamental, definitive settlement.[27] Nonetheless, some progress has occurred. In January 1974 a new trade agreement was signed, replacing the earlier Memorandum Trade Agreement. In April, a civil aviation agreement was signed, causing the nationalists to end their service to Japan and halt the flights by Japan Air Lines to Taiwan. "The advances made in the [Sino-Japanese] relationship," observed one commentator, "are of course not unrelated to China's fear of the Soviet Union." The Chinese feel pressure from the Russians on China's northern borders, in the Southwest as a result of strong Indian ties to the Soviet Union and a large and active Russian naval presence in the Indian Ocean, and in the Southeast as a result of Soviet overtures to the nations there and the rapid decline of American power in the region. "There are signs that Moscow is seeking contacts with South Korea, and this may extend even to Taiwan.... A pro-Moscow and anti-Peking government across the Sea of Japan would constitute a significant and formidable portion of the ring Moscow is attempting to join around China, and Peking has demonstrated its willingness to pay the price of not letting this become reality."[28] At present, of course, the price China has paid has not been costly to her. She can easily afford the increased oil exports; her tolerance of the Japan-U.S. Security Treaty helps protect her against the Russians; her trade with Japan is balanced evenly; and her flexibility during the aviation talks actually enabled her to increase the isolation of Taiwan in a small way. The greatest benefit to Japan comes from the prolongation of the Sino-Soviet dispute and the relatively pragmatic Chinese response to the dangers of isolation in the last few years. Together these two facets of the situation in north Asia increase Japan's freedom of action and augment her slender diplomatic capabilities.

Japan's refusal to make a complete break with Taiwan remains as a major obstacle in the way of further improvements in Sino-Japanese relations, although conventional relations no longer exist between Taiwan and Japan. The affairs of the Republic of China are handled in Tokyo by the association of East Asia Relations, and the Japanese embassy in Taipei has been replaced by the Japan Interchange Association. Both are staffed by members of the two diplomatic services and bureaucracies who are "temporarily on leave." The duties of both are vaguely and broadly defined and easily include all the typical consular and diplomatic functions. The arrangement apparently works well, for trade between Japan and Taiwan continues to grow, and was worth $2,261 million in 1973, with a balance in favor of Japan of $610.3 million.[28] Japanese trade with the People's Republic reached $2,015 million in 1973, an increase of 83 percent over 1972, with a balance favorable to Japan of some $67 million. Japan's obvious success in giving a new twist to "the separation of politics and economics," and the advantages of such favorable trade and commercial relations, make it attractive for Japan to try to remain its established economic links with Taiwan, while increasing trade with the mainland. There is, as well, a large number of influential members of the ruling Liberal Democratic party, especially the faction headed by former Premier Eisaku Sato, who strongly favor preserving Japan's links with Taiwan. Japan's relative freedom to choose the kind of relationship she will have with Taiwan thus becomes an additional element of strength in her relations with Peking, for the Chinese government is eager to have Japan decide in its favor and against the Nationalists.

B. *Soviet Objectives Regarding Japan*

The Soviet Union's objectives toward Japan show as a mirror-image of the Chinese: to prevent Japan from siding with China and to weaken but not to overthrow Japan's ties with the United States. For both great powers, these objectives have the attraction of being steps necessary (although not sufficient) to bring Japan to a pro-Soviet or pro-Chinese orientation inside and out.

While Japan's political strengths are real but small when she deals with China, they are even smaller when she deals with the U.S.S.R., because of the great industrial and military strength of that country. China has sought to put every weight she can find into the balance in order to cope with Russian pressure, taking care, of course, not to contradict other vital domestic and foreign objectives. The Soviets mean by threat and economic promise to keep Japan from siding with China, but there is nothing of the urgency in this that has marked China's detente with the United States and Japan. There are a number of matters in contention between Japan and the Soviet Union. Some resemble those under discussion between Japan and China, but others have no parallel in Sino-Japanese relations. There has been no Soviet-Japanese treaty of peace ending World War II, just as there has been no comparable Sino-Japanese peace treaty. But the Japanese have been unwilling to sign with the Soviet government until it returns four islands north of Honshu—Shikotan, Habomai, Etorofu, and Kunashiri—seized by the Russian armed forces at the end of World War II. The islands are undeniably Japanese, and they were recognized to be such by Russia in 1855 by the Treaty of Shimoda.[30] No similar territorial conflict divides China and Japan.

The Russians have also forced Japan, over the past eighteen years, to reduce both the areas in which her fishermen may work as well as the catches they may take. To enforce this tough position, the Soviet government has seized more than 1,300 Japanese fishing boats, of which it has released only a little more than half, and has imprisoned and held a score of Japanese fishermen. There is no comparable source of conflict and hostility between China and Japan.

A third Soviet concern is to obtain Japanese and American help in the development of Siberian natural resources. There are a number of major projects in which the Japanese desire to participate. On July 25, 1973 at a press conference, Armand Hammer, president of Occidental Petroleum, announced that two U.S. companies, El Paso Natural Gas and Occidental, and the Tokyo Gas Company had reached full agreement with the Soviet government on plans to develop natural gas reserves in Yakutsk. The tripartite agreement envisioned the movement of two billion cubic feet of gas a day through a pipeline 2,000 miles long from Yakutsk to a gas-liquefaction plant to be constructed near Vladivostok as part of the arrangement, and the shipment of equal shares of the liquid fuel to Japan and the United States over the next 30 years. Mr. Hammer set the total investment needed as $10 billion, $4 billion to come from the West and part of the rest, $2 billion, from Japan, and gave six years as the estimate of the time needed from the start of construction to the first use of the fuel in households for cooking.[31] On March 10, 1974, Japan and the Soviet Union agreed to begin a joint project to locate and mine what are thought to be vast deposits of coal in Yakutsk. Six weeks later, on April 26, the two governments signed an agreement in Tokyo confirming the earlier Russian-Japanese-American natural gas project for Yakutsk. The project is contingent on U.S. participation, which the U.S. Congress has made contingent on Soviet willingness to permit freer immigration from the U.S.S.R.[32]

The Soviets have also sought Japanese participation in the development of the Tyumen oil fields in Western Siberia. Negotiations for a Japanese credit of $2 billion for the project seem to have begun in 1971 or 1972. The Soviet government was apparently led to request such massive external support by the country's serious economic difficulties, acknowledged by General Secretary Leonid Brezhnev at a meeting of the Central Committee of the Communist Party on December 15, 1969. Exactly a month later in a joint statement the Central Committee and the Council of Ministers undertook to expand production of the Tyumen oil fields from 20 million tons to 100-120 million tons annually in 1975 and 230-260 million tons by 1980. Two years later, at the conclusion of the fifth meeting of the Japanese-Soviet Joint Economic Committee on February 24, 1972, the Soviet government asked for Japanese economic assistance in the construction of a trans-Siberian oil pipeline. The line was to run parallel to the one already joining the Tyumen oil fields and Irkutsk and to be extended to Nakhodka, a port on the Sea of Japan, 60 miles southeast of Vladivostok. Several Soviet requests were also made for Japanese aid in evaluating coal mines in Yakutsk and natural gas deposits on the continental shelf near Sakhalin.[33] On November 24, 1972, the two governments signed a memorandum in Tokyo agreeing to conduct a joint search of oil and natural gas off Sakhalin Island. At the time the Soviets were thought to have asked for $200 million in credits for the necessary machinery and equipment, an additional $30 million for the purchase of Japanese consumer goods, and were said to have been seeking $3 billion from the U.S. and Japan to finance the Sakhalin project and the development of the gas supplies in Yakutsk and the oil reserves in Tyumen.[34]

The Tyumen oil agreement encountered difficulties even before the Yom Kippur War (which itself led to a quick reversal of Japan's pro-Israel policy and highlighted Japan's weakness to the Soviets). On September 6, 1973, the Soviet government announced it was cutting from 40 to 20 million tons the amount of oil Japan could receive each year from the Tyumen fields. The Arab-Israeli war coincided with Premier Tanaka's visit to Moscow, and, understandably perhaps, the joint Soviet-Japanese communique left uncertain the future of the Tyumen pipeline and the $2 billion credit needed from Japan.[35] In November, Soviet Premier Alexei Kosygin gave part of the explanation, saying that Soviet production of oil and natural gas had not met the planned goal for 1973 and would not meet in it 1974. Petroleum experts in the West believe that unless the Soviet Union reduces oil exports, it will have to increase significantly its imports of Middle Eastern oil, which has recently quadrupled in price.[36] The choice is cruel for the Soviets, because oil exports to the West supplied about 30 percent of the hard-currency earned by the U.S.S.R. in 1972, funds desperately needed for the purchase of the advanced machinery and technology the government desires.

Finally, on May 27, 1974, the Tyumen project collapsed. The Soviet Minister of Oil Production, Valentin Shashin, announced that instead of an oil pipeline from Irkutsk to the Sea of Japan, the U.S.S.R. would build a railroad 1,960 miles long to join the Trans-Siberian net at Komsomolsk. The U.S.S.R., he added, had also changed the basis of foreign participation in the development of Soviet oil reserves, and would now accept only the exchange of technical information and the sale of oil equipment and would handle all oil projects without any other kind of assistance.

The Chinese government had objected vociferously to the development of the Tyumen fields and the construction of the pipeline and to Japanese participation in the project, since increased oil supplies in Siberia could only augment Soviet industrial and military strength in the region, a development of ominous significance for China given the hostile state of Sino-Soviet relations. While the Russian decision to cancel the pipeline and to change the basis of oil development in Siberia undoubtedly will slow the expansion of the Russian presence in the region, Minister Shashin left little reason for the Chinese to be pleased about the railroad. A train, he pointed out, would carry "anything you want," but a pipeline could move nothing but oil. A week after the cancellation announcement, the Russian and Japanese governments agreed that Japan would provide the U.S.S.R. with $450 million in credits in exchange for 104.4 million tons of coal in 1979-1980. Tass hurried to point out on May 31, three days before the agreement was signed, that there remained "great possibilities for the future" of Soviet-Japanese trade.[37]

Plainly, Japan has suffered grievous disappointments over Siberian oil and has been played along cruelly on other Soviet development plans—in part by Russian design, and in part by the political coincidence of the rise of the Jewish emigration issue in the U.S. Congress in conjunction with U.S.-Soviet trade. No doubt the reluctance of the Soviets to honor their undertakings may be partly explained by the drastic change in the world prices and World perceptions of primary materials. There are, as well, major technical problems to be solved before development may succeed in the frozen lands of Siberia. The Japanese, for their part, have been extremely sensitive to China's vehement opposition to the oil project, and the cancellation was not an unmitigated disaster for Japan. These explanations do not tell the whole story, and there is no doubt the Russians understand that the economic carrot is both more attractive to Japan and more useful politically if it cannot be eaten. A taste now and then will suffice, and can be flavored heavily with the sauce of promises and good intentions. There is no comparable difficulty with China, in large part, perhaps, because the rich oil deposits off the China coast cannot be developed until there is a settlement between China and Taiwan.[38]

The fact remains that the current state of Soviet-Japanese relations might be described as no peace treaty, no oil, no islands, and less fish. So long as Japan continues to seek to improve relations with both Russian and China, she will possess too little political clout to move the Russians on any of these issues. She has little choice: for the Japanese government to make any serious move toward China would be to endanger Japan's security, to forfeit the islands, to lose access to Siberian resources, and to suffer ever-greater reductions in fishing rights. A move toward Russia would harm and perhaps destroy Japan's lucrative trade with China and be profoundly disruptive in Japanese internal politics as well.

C. U.S. Dealings with Japan

Japan's ties to the United States differ in purpose and in scope from her dealings with China and the U.S.S.R. What gives Japan political leverage in her relations with the United States is the great American desire to keep Japan as an ally and to continue to base American military forces in that country, even if they are only naval forces. The alliance with Japan enables the United States to counter the otherwise overwhelming impact of Soviet power on Japan's security and internal politics. The Americans intend (as do the Chinese) to keep the enormous Japanese industrial and military potential from being harnessed to Soviet objectives and capacities, already threateningly great in themselves. The alliance, by guaranteeing Japan against nuclear threat and large-scale conventional attack, also removes the need for Japan to develop the huge military forces her economic capacity would support.

An implicit imbalance exists in the Japanese-American security relationship and has been a source of frustration and irritation for both sides. Japan depends on the United States to protect her, but because she is an island she can be protected by the Seventh Fleet, and deterrence can be maintained by nuclear missiles in silos in the northwestern U.S. thousands of miles away or in Polaris submarines deep in the sea. Because she lacks a land frontier with either China or the U.S.S.R., Japan has never been obligated to meet her security needs by developing large forces of her own and integrating them closely with those of the United States, as the West European states have done. For these reasons, the longing of many Japanese to be less dependent on the United States is probably as impossible to realize as American hopes that Japan will assume a more active military role in Asia and the Pacific. As Masataka Kosaka observed, however much the two partners may chafe over the dependence and the unequal burdens imposed by the Security Treaty, "Its basic characteristics have remained and will continue to do so, for larger Japanese contributions to the overall security efforts are either unnecessary or undesirable."[39] It lies outside the scope of this essay to discuss the widespread pacifist and nationalist sentiment in Japan—the two are not exclusive as Kosaka demonstrated—which oppose the American alliance.[40] This body of opinion would probably be strong enough to prevent closer military cooperation with the United States, even if that country's security needs demanded a larger Japanese role.

The problems generated between the two countries by the Security Treaty, though annoying and worrisome, have in recent years been dwarfed by serious economic difficulties between them. We do not intend to attempt to unravel these difficulties.[41] For our purpose it must suffice to point out one of Japan's economic advantages that gives her an advantage in dealing with the U.S.: Japan is a natural market for the resource-exporting countries of Southeast Asia and the Pacific. Most assuredly, these countries seek better terms of trade, and Indonesian and Australian attempts to receive more for their primary materials and petroleum offer an example of this. But trade with Japan is of mutual advantage and will continue to grow short of a worldwide collapse of purchasing power. The U.S. has long understood the relation between a strong Japanese

economy and economic stability and progress in the region to the
south and west of Japan. In fact, the need to hasten economic
recovery in the other nations of Asia was one of the strongest
arguments in favor of ending the occupation regime in Japan
and allowing Japanese economy to begin to function once again.
The price to be paid for a kind of economic development in Asia that
would be consistent with the American-run world payments system
was to get the Japanese economy started in a big way. Once Japan
was started, of course, with the nation fully independent and
harboring tender feelings about the occupation and the American
alliance, it became extremely difficult to influence Japanese
economic policy. The successful efforts to force Japan to appreciate
the yen and the less successful attempts to force her to curb exports
and to allow more imports were always bounded by the knowledge
that the Japanese economy could aid the development of other Asian
nations only if the U.S. and the other industrial nations could
purchase large amounts of Japanese manufactures.

IV. CONCLUSION

The preceding analysis of the strengths and weaknesses of Japan's
current international situation has a number of implications for
Sino-Japanese relations and for Japan's foreign policy as a whole.
Japan's dependent economic position makes it imperative for her to
maintain and expand her established trade with the nations rich in
the resources and markets which her economy must have to survive
at its present level. There seems little prospect of increasing
significantly the already huge amounts of supplies of raw materials
Japan receives from Australia, Canada, the United States, and the
nations of Southeast Asia. If Canada's elimination of oil exports to
the United States is an accurate indication of the future conduct of
other exporters of primary materials, Japan will be doing well to
maintain imports from these nations at current levels. In regard to
petroleum, Japan has no choice in the short term but to pay the
political price demanded by the Arab states while working to
discover new sources of supply, to diversify its suppliers, and to shift
to other forms of energy. Nor does Japan's export trade to the U.S.,
the E.E.C., and the countries of Southeast Asia and the Pacific
promise more than slow and steady expansion. All of this gives an
exceptional importance to the future of Japan's trade with China and
the U.S.S.R. The internal consumer markets of these two countries
are virtually undeveloped, and they both possess large reserves of
primary materials. In theory, economic relations with the two great
powers of north Asia could become the fastest growing part of
Japanese economy. The sections that follow concentrate first on the

future of Japan's trade with China and then on the political implications of Japan's weakness for Sino-Japanese relations.

A. *The Future of Sino-Japanese Trade*

China has it in her power to ease Japan's need for primary materials and markets and to benefit her own economy and people at the same time. Despite an 83 percent increase in Sino-Japanese trade in 1973, many Asia experts are extremely doubtful that China will choose to allow this to happen. Most would agree with Gene Hsiao's summary:

> Prior to the rapprochement, Japanese businessmen held out high hopes for a vast increase in trade. After that they even anticipated certain types of Japanese "aid" to the People's Republic in return for the latter's renunciation of reparation claims as specified in Article 5 of the joint statement. The fact of the matter is, however, that the basis of China's economic policy is self-reliance, with a consequent rejection of any type of foreign aid except short-term credits. . . . Equally, in the area of trade, China prefers to maintain an equilibrium as far as possible.[42]

In addition to practicing self-reliance and balancing trade accounts, after allowing foreign trade to grow rapidly for ten years, the Chinese government chose in 1959 to freeze the aggregate amount allowed for China's foreign trade and to keep it at about that level for the next decade. The first two decades of China's economic development were marked by such large fluctuations in many areas. There is consequently no justification for basing generalizations on economic performance in either decade, and for concluding that China's foreign trade will never be allowed to expand on a scale large enough to be of substantial benefit to Japan. It is clear, nonetheless, that substantial changes in Chinese economic policy will have to occur for this to happen, and that Japanese businessmen and economic planners cannot afford to count on a great expansion of trade with China to ease their shortages of raw materials and energy.[43]

This would probably not be as important as it is if there were not a widespread belief to the contrary among many Japanese businessmen. The wish for an expansion of Sino-Japanese trade is often the father to the thought that it is soon to occur.[44] This raises the question of China's ability to use economic leverage in her relations with Japan. Because Japanese businessmen continue to ignore the evidence of sharp limits to Sino-Japanese trade, because the Japanese people continue to view

China in a highly emotional way, and because Japan so badly needs trade and raw materials, the stage would seem to be perfectly set for Chinese manipulation of these hopes and needs.

In the past China has repeatedly if relatively unsuccessfully tried to use economic means for political ends, and there is no reason to believe she will stop trying. Of the various economic means of coercion China has used, the most notable have been the boycott of 1958-1959 and the ensuing trade crisis that lasted until 1963 in an unsuccessful attempt to unseat the Kishi government, and the use of the memorandum trade talks to undermine the Sato government.[45] In both cases Soviet efforts to increase trade with Japan helped convince the Chinese of a need to ease their pressure on the Japanese. China has also used trade with "friendly firms," businesses controlled by groups with ideological positions similar to the current Chinese view at a particular time, to generate political pressure favorable to Chinese objectives. There are few Japanese industries relying on imports from China that those industries could not find elsewhere with relative ease. Of these imports, Chinese silk is the largest, accounting for more than one-third of total Japanese imports of that commodity. Several segments of Japan's metal and chemical industries, however, depend fairly heavily on exports to China, especially the producers of chemicals and manufactured fertilizers. Adroit pressures on these "natural China lobbies" has produced immediate endorsement of Chinese objectives in the past.[46] Table IV compares the factors that would aid or hamper Chinese attempts to manipulate Japan by means of economic pressure and makes clear that China is unable under present circumstances to seriously injure the Japanese economy: Sino-Japanese trade is too small, too few Japanese industries depend on imports from China, and the Japanese economy is diversified and dependent only on trade with the United States. China can touch Japan's jugular—her ability to import—only indirectly by pressure on the nations of Southeast Asia, Korea, the United States and, perhaps, the U.S.S.R. Even so, prolonged worldwide economic difficulties could multiply the efficacy of Chinese means of economic coercion. As one author observed:

> The Japanese economy is not directly vulnerable to Chinese economic coercion at this time. The present weakness of the Chinese economy as compared to that of Japan are [sic] fundamental reasons for this. Nevertheless, China is able to gain a significant political advantage from the lure of increased trade, and may be able to use other more direct economic weapons in the future, primarily because of certain Japanese attituded which render [Japan] more vulnerable than would be expected from purely economic consideration.

Especially in the event of a trade war with its leading partners or a repetition of anything resembling the depression of the 1930s, China could expect to be able to inflict a heavy political price upon Japan.[47]

TABLE IV. FACTORS RELATING
TO CHINA'S ABILITY TO MANIPULATE
JAPANESE POLICY BY USING ECONOMIC PRESSURE

FAVORABLE TO MANIPULATION	UNFAVORABLE TO MANIPULATION
1. China maintains tight state control of foreign trade.	1. Most of Japan's foreign trade is conducted by a few large firms with close ties to the ruling L.D.P. and to each other; government involvement in foreign trade is greater than in Western countries.
2. Japan's need to import raw materials and energy is great, as is her need to export large amounts of manufactured goods.	2. Sino-Japanese trade accounts for only 2% of Japan's total trade and 20% of China's. China has stressed economic self-sufficiency during the last decade, and Japan has stressed integration in the world economy.
The chemical industry in Japan is fairly heavily dependent on exports to China; selective economic pressure on firms dependent on China trade could bring results.	China's reserves of raw materials and energy, while large, are not now available for export in abundance; they could be made available only by infusion of large amounts of Japanese capital, and this is not likely. Japan has well-diversified markets and sources of supply; she has avoided excessive dependence on any one country save the U.S., which accounts for 30% of Japan's total trade.

TABLE IV *(Continued)*

FAVORABLE TO MANIPULATION	UNFAVORABLE TO MANIPULATION
	Japan has sophisticated planning and buying habits that stimulate competition for her market; her good buying practices obtain goods on favorable terms.
	The experience of the 1960's suggests Japan can achieve high levels of trade without trading extensively with China.
	The recent large increases in Sino-Japanese trade have been brought about mostly by allowing Japan's share of China's total trade to grow; it is doubtful that this will be allowed to continue.
	Because of limited agricultural resources China has had to spend substantial amounts of foreign exchange on imports of food and feed grains.
3. "Ideologically . . . the Chinese leadership views economic and political relations as inseparable, and historically the use of economic means for attaining political ends in China has been very common. If the means seem meager, the intention at least is clear."[a]	3. In response to the poor state of relations with the Soviet Union, Chinese leaders have put heavy emphasis on defense spending; this has altered industrial growth and normal trade patterns: China has been stockpiling copper and rubber for the last few years, for example, to prepare for war with the U.S.S.R.
The potentially enormous Chinese market appeals strongly to many Japanese and convinces them of the need to make political concessions to China, especially at a time of uncertainty in Japan's economic relations with the E.E.C. and the U.S.	Attempts at economic coercion could backfire, as they did in 1958.
	Japan's other trading partners—notably Taiwan, the U.S.S.R., and the U.S.—would bring heavy economic pressure to bear on Japan if she began to be excessively moved by Chinese pressures.

TABLE IV *(Continued)*

FAVORABLE TO MANIPULATION	UNFAVORABLE TO MANIPULATION
Many Japanese businessmen were engaged in trade with China before World War II and in their eyes China is a natural trading partner.	
Whenever Japan's trade falters the argument is revived that a large trade with China is essential for Japan.	
An increase in Sino-Japanese trade can be seen as a way of asserting independence from the U.S.	
"The Japanese opposition and a significant fraction of the LDP itself are predisposed toward echoing the inevitable claim that hostile action [by China] must be blamed on the Japanese government."[b]	

[a]Brown, *Chinese Economic Leverage in Sino-Japanese Relations,* 9 ASIAN SURVEY, at 760 (1972), *See* Unger, *Japan: The Economic Threat,* F.E. ECO. REV. (Oct. 16, 1972), for examples of Chinese uses of economic means to attain political ends.

[b]Brown, *supra* note a (this Table), at 768.

Economically, it would seem Japan would wish to reform her imbalanced and vulnerable pattern of trade and industry before its advantages disappear. One would expect Japan to show a more sensitive and far-sighted appreciation of "the vital connection between the functioning of the global system and her own interests," and to draw some of the conclusions from this: namely, to permit more horizontal trade and to spend more on housing and welfare at home, thereby reducing the need for so great an investment in heavy industrial production.[48] Such developments, if they occur, would not necessarily bring greater trade and closer economic relations between China and Japan. Indeed, to the extent that Japan was able to move its industrial structure away from the processing of huge amounts of primary materials to a structure based on sophisticated technology and highly skilled labor, she would require fewer raw materials, and the need for the more obvious kinds of trade with China would diminish.

B. *The Future of Japan's Political Relations with China*

In regard to the implications of Japan's weakness for her political relations with China, it seems clear from the preceding discussion that any early loss or serious impairment of the Security Treaty would be dangerous not just for Japan but for China as well. Left without the nuclear and naval protection of the United States, Japan, and perhaps China too, would have to come to terms with the Soviet Union, and it is certain the terms would be more Russian than Chinese or Japanese.

A host of specific initiatives suggest themselves and of these two will be discussed here: the deepening and strengthening of Sino-Japanese and Soviet-Japanese relations and the renunciation by Japan of nuclear arms. Analogies are attractive and dangerous in international affairs, but it would, nonetheless, seem that West Germany's course in improving her relations with the U.S.S.R. is relevant for Japan as she ponders her relations with China and the Soviet Union. Germany remains a firm ally of the United States, in fact the best American ally in Europe. Germany continues to enjoy American nuclear and conventional protection, even as she pursues rapprochement with the Soviet Union and the nations of Eastern Europe. Germany has renounced the acquisition or production of nuclear weapons within a framework of supervision by the Western European Union. The bitterness of the Sino-Soviet dispute had no parallel in Europe at the time Willy Brandt launched his *Ostpolitik*, but this serves only to underline the importance of Japan finding a way to avoid being drawn into the conflict between Russia and China.

The two kinds of initiatives mentioned here cannot be pursued for their own sake or piecemeal. To have meaning they must be undertaken as part of a larger conception of the kind of structure and stability Japan would like to have established in Asia. The difficulties in the way of realizing such an order are large. China now seems to have little interest in such an arrangement, and to a certain extent the United States has aligned her policy with China's. The Soviet Union is extremely interested in a collective security system, but hers looks more like a net of bilateral security pacts than a general mutually beneficial system, and at present only the Indians have entered the bear's embrace. A search for ways to establish security cooperation among all four powers—China, U.S.S.R., Japan, U.S.—may well offer Japan the kind of general framework within which she could broaden her ties with China, as well as with the

Soviet Union, renounce nuclear arms, and achieve a decrease of tension in the Korean Peninsula.[49]

There is another reason why this political approach and the kinds of economic and social reforms mentioned earlier make sense for Japan. The long-term goals of Chinese and Russian foreign policy remain the destruction of the Japanese political order and the overthrow of the American alliance. Both nations continue to withhold and manipulate their economic relations with Japan for short-term political ends that are often harmful to Japanese security and economy, apparently in hopes of stretching Japanese society thin in a time of recession and scarcity, thus hastening the different kinds of political changes they believe to be to their advantage. It would be well in these circumstances for Japan to have constructive and overarching objectives to pursue both at home and abroad. If she acts along the lines sketched here or in other positive ways it is possible that peace and well-being will follow for all the powers concerned. No one can give a guarantee. On the other hand, unless Japan acts in a way both resolute and wise it is certain that neither peace nor well-being can be achieved in Asia, and this could only have the gravest consequences for the rest of the world.

NOTES

[1]*See* H. KAHN, THE EMERGING JAPANESE SUPER-STATE, CHALLENGE AND RESPONSE (1970).

[2]Compare this definition with the discussion in R. ARON, *Power and Force, Or On the Means of Foreign Policy*, PEACE AND WAR, A THEORY OF INTERNATIONAL RELATIONS 44*ff.* (R. Howard & A. Fox trans., abridged ed. 1973).

[3]Ellingworth pointed to ratios of 43% for the Netherlands, 38% for Belgium, about 20% for Britain and West Germany, and 14% for France. The United States' ratio is about 5%, in part as a result of an internal market even larger than Japan's. R. ELLINGWORTH, JAPANESE ECONOMIC POLICIES AND SECURITY 11, 34 (International Institute of Strategic Studies, London, Adelphi Papers No. 90, 1972) [hereinafter cited as ELLINGWORTH and the series as Adelphi Papers]. *See also* INT'L INSTITUTE OF STRATEGIC STUDIES, STRATEGIC SURVEY 1971, at 61 [hereinafter STRATEGIC SURVEY 1971]; *and* Saxonhouse, *A Review of Recent U.S.-Japanese Economic Relations*, 9 ASIAN SURVEY 926-27 (1972).

[4]ELLINGWORTH at 11.

[5]The figures for 1972 are taken from Okita, *National Resource Dependency and Japanese Foreign Policy*, 52 FOREIGN AFFAIRS 718-19 (Jul. 1974).

[6]*Id.*, at 714. Arab nations supplied 43% of this oil, and Iran alone supplied 37%.

[7]STRATEGIC SURVEY 1971, at 60.

[8]Okita, *supra* note 5, at 716-17.

[9]Saxonhouse, *supra* note 3, at 726, and ELLINGWORTH at 11.

[10]Okita, *supra* note 5, at 720-21.

[11] A large number of Western and Japanese strategists doubt the utility of a Japanese nuclear force. A typical opinion is that of a former minister of the American Embassy in Tokyo, J. EMMERSON, ARMS, YEN, & POWER: THE JAPANESE DILEMMA (1971), cited in Halloran, 20 JAPAN QUARTERLY 347-48 (1973): "Japan, with its small islands, its jammed industrial complexes, its ever-growing, crowded cities, and its gigantic, continuously extending Tokyo-Yokohama megalopolis, which is both the heart and nerve center of the country, could scarcely be more vulnerable to nuclear obliteration from Chinese or Soviet missiles within immediate range. Some argue that nuclear submarines, safe from attack, would assure a second-strike capability. However, the chance to fire a few missiles with nuclear warheads at an enemy that had already destroyed the cities and industries of the homeland would be hollow comfort for the demoralized survivors of an all-out atomic bombardment."

[12] See Wakaizumi, Japan's Role in a New World Order, 51 FOREIGN AFFAIRS 313 (Jan. 1973); Kishida, Japan's Non-Nuclear Policy, 15 SURVIVAL 15-20 (Int'l Institute of Strategic Studies, Jan.-Feb. 1973); M. KOSAKA, OPTIONS FOR JAPAN'S FOREIGN POLICY (Adelphi Papers No. 97, 1973); K. Saeki, Japan's Security in a Multipolar World, in EAST ASIA AND THE WORLD SYSTEM: THE REGIONAL POWERS (Adelphi Papers No. 92, 1972); Takeo, Future Japanese Diplomacy, 20 JAPAN QUARTERLY 20-24 (Jan.-Mar. 1973); Wilcox, Japanese and Indian National Security Strategies in the Asia of the 1970s: The Prospect for Nuclear Proliferation, in EAST ASIA AND THE WORLD SYSTEM: THE REGIONAL POWERS 30-39 (Adelphi Papers No. 92, 1972).

[13] N.Y. Times, Mar. 4, 1973, § 1, at 16, col. 1.

[14] INT'L INSTITUTE OF STRATEGIC STUDIES, THE MILITARY BALANCE 1974-1975, 50, 78-79 [hereinafter cited as MILITARY BALANCE 1974-1975]. No precise figures for Chinese defense expenditures are available. We have taken the low average of an Australian estimate of $4-5 billion and a British estimate of $10-12 billion, and compared the resulting $7 billion to an American estimate of China's 1973 G.N.P. as $140 billion.

[15] The text of the Plan and a comparison of forces under the Third and Fourth Defense Plans may be found in 15 SURVIVAL 184-87 (Jul.-Aug. 1973).

[16] Saito, THE NEW SITUATION IN ASIA, 20 JAPAN QUARTERLY 37 (Jan.-Mar. 1973).

[17] Three years ago Indonesia and Malaysia began to claim territorial jurisdiction over the Straits simply by asserting that the twelve-mile limit they claim for their territorial waters also applies to the Straits. The Straits are often less than 24 miles wide, see ELLINGWORTH at 18-20. See also the articles on the Straits and Denzil Peiris on the Indian Ocean by Pillai in F.E. ECO. REV. [FAR EASTERN ECONOMIC REVIEW] 27-28 (Nov. 19, 1973).

[18] Kosaka, supra note 12, at 12.

[19] Saeki, supra note 12, at 23.

[20] Kishida, supra note 12, at 16.

[21] Soedjatmoko, The Role of the Major Powers in the East-Asian Pacific Region, 14 SURVIVAL 28, at 30 (Jan.-Feb. 1972).

[22] See D. HELLMAN, JAPAN AND EAST ASIA: THE NEW INTERNATIONAL ORDER (1972). Hellman's argument is that factional politics, an ever more complicated bureaucracy, and the lack of national consensus on basic foreign policy questions make Japanese diplomacy reactive and ad hoc, and give external developments in East Asia far more importance in shaping Japanese policy than internal decisions.

[23] F.E. ECO. REV. 29-31 (May 14, 1973); 10-14 (Jan. 28, 1974); 33-56 (May 18, 1974).

[24]China's efforts to block Soviet-Japanese cooperation and the softening of her opposition to the expansion of Japanese military strength and the maintenance of the U.S.-Japan Security Treaty are discussed by Hsiao, *The Sino-Japanese Rapproachement: A Relationship of Ambivalance*, 57 CHINA QUARTERLY 117-18 (Jan.-Mar. 1974). Robert Scalapino gave this assessment of what the Chinese currently regard as most important in their foreign policy: "For the time being, Chinese interest in the political-military containment of Japan and in keeping Japan from becoming too intimately involved with the Soviet Union takes precedence over China's long-term interest in loosening Japanese-American ties. Indeed, China sees certain short-range advantages in an American presence in the area; her leaders recognize that the Security Treaty reduces the possibility of Japan taking the nuclear path. At a later point, of course, Chinese perspectives may be quite different." Scalapino, *China and the Balance of Power*, 52 FOREIGN AFFAIRS 376 (Jan. 1974).

[25]A copy of the communique is in 14 SURVIVAL 289-90 (Nov.-Dec. 1972). Similar objectives were expressed in a joint statement by the China-Japan Friendship Association and a Komeito delegation visiting China a week before Henry Kissinger's first secret trip in July 1971. The joint statement is quoted in Hsiao, *supra* note 24, at 103.

[26]Scalapino, *supra* note 24, at 374. A more detailed account of the Liao mission is given in Hudson, *Japanese Attitudes and Policies Toward China in 1973*, 56 CHINA QUARTERLY 700-07 (Oct.-Dec. 1973).

[27]Hsaio, *supra* note 24, at 116.

[28]Awanohara, *Japan and China, Chou: Doing It His Way*, F.E. ECO. REV. 24 (May 13, 1974). *See* Hudson, *supra* note 26, at 704-05, on the air route negotiations; and, on the close link in Japanese diplomatic strategy between negotiations with the Russians and the Chinese, *see* Nakamura, *Ideological Foes Woo Japan*, F.E. ECO. REV. 18 (Oct. 18, 1974).

[29]F.E. ECO. REV. 54 (May 13, 1974).

[30]On the territorial question and other Soviet-Japanese problems, *see* Pond, *Japan and Russia: The View from Tokyo*, 52 FOREIGN AFFAIRS 141-152 (Oct. 1973). At the Japanese-Soviet summit meeting in Moscow in October 1973, the Russians again offered the return of only the southernmost two of the islands, Habomai and Shikotan. Premier Tanaka had sought the return of all four.

[31]KEESING'S CONTEMPORARY ARCHIVES 26082 (Sept. 3-9, 1973). A month earlier an American consortium of Tenneco, Inc., Texas Eastern Transmission Corporation, and Brown & Root signed a preliminary agreement to provide up to $3 billion in loans from the U.S. Export-Import Bank and private Western banks for construction of a pipeline and liquefaction plant to make possible the shipment of 2 billion cubic feet of gas a day from the Tyumen fields in Western Siberia to American East Coast ports through the Soviet port of Murmansk, 33 FACTS ON FILE 631 (Jul. 22-28, 1973).

[32]34 FACTS ON FILE 403-04 (May 18, 1974).

[33]30 FACTS ON FILE 27 (Jan. 15-21, 1970); 32 FACTS ON FILE 173 (Mar. 5-11, 1972). The Japanese had already agreed on January 24, 1970, to a joint project to build a seaport at Nakhodka.

[34]33 FACTS ON FILE 874 (Oct. 14-20, 1973).

[35]In the communique issued at the end of the talks, the two governments agreed to increase economic cooperation, including the development of Siberian resources, and observed that Soviet-Japanese economic cooperation in Siberia "does not rule out the participation of third countries." The main points of the communique are in KEESING'S CONTEMPORARY ARCHIVES 26254 (Dec. 24-31, 1973).

[36]33 FACTS ON FILE 1022 (Dec. 2-8, 1973). The Soviets actually seem to have chosen to increase domestic production, which eases the problem of supplying Eastern Europe with the large amount (54% of total exports) it needs and also earns a substantial windfall profit, estimated by a Senate Banking subcommittee to be as much as $2 billion for 1974, 34 FACTS ON FILE 283 (Apr. 13, 1974); 34 FACTS ON FILE 696 (Aug. 24, 1974). The Soviets say that they plan no increase in oil exports before the early 1980's.

[37]34 FACTS ON FILE 696 (Aug. 24, 1974).

[38]Hudson, *supra* note 26, at 705-07. Hudson's essay is extremely interesting both for its description of the legal and political tangle that obstructs development of the reserves on the seabed in the East China Sea and for his suggestion that Japanese businessmen accorded great significance to the Tyumen oil project with the Soviets. Now that this Siberian venture has failed, China may compete in Japan on a more equal basis with the Soviet Union.

[39]M. KOSAKA, *supra* note 12, at 5.

[40]Fuji Kamiya observed that postwar Japanese nationalism "has been most successfully espoused by the parties of the left." He characterized the strong anti-U.S., anti-Chinese stance of the Japan Communist Party, for example, as nationalist. He also argued that because the Japanese feel less threatened by China and the U.S.S.R. and are more resentful of dependency on the United States, a nationalist reaction has been building in Japan during the last few years. The new Japanese nationalism—"a curious blend of dependency feelings *(amae)*, frustration, and self-confidence inspired by Japan's rapidly expanding economy"—has reduced the strength of the L.D.P. and threatens to undermine domestic support for the security treaty. *See* Kamiya, 12 ASIAN SURVEY 720-21 (Sept. 1972).

[41]*See* Taira, *Power and Trade in U.S.-Japanese Relations*, 12 ASIAN SURVEY 980-98 (Nov. 1972), *and* Saxonhouse, *supra* note 3.

[42]*See* Hsiao, *supra* note 24, at 122 and ELLINGWORTH at 23-24.

[43]*See* Eckstein, *Economic Growth and Change in China: A Twenty-Year Perspective*, 54 CHINA QUARTERLY 227-31, 241 (Apr.-June 1973); Rawski, *Recent Trends in the Chinese Economy*, 53 CHINA QUARTERLY 1-33 (Jan.-Mar. 1973).

[44]ELLINGWORTH at 24.

[45]We have relied in this seciton on Brown, *Chinese Economic Leverage in Sino-Japanese Relations*, 12 ASIAN SURVEY 753-71 (Sept. 1972).

[46]Firms in the chemical industry were among the first to endorse China's "four principles." *Id.* at 768.

[47]*Id.* at 770-71.

[48]M. KOSAKA, *supra* note 12, at 15.

[49]*Id.* at 27-40, especially at 34-40.

China, Lump Sum Settlements, and Executive Agreements

DAVID G. LUTHER, JR.*

On returning from a trip to the People's Republic of China in February, 1973, Dr. Henry Kissinger predicted negotiations in the near future which would resolve the linked issues of United States private claims against the P.R.C. and P.R.C. blocked assets in the United States.[1] It would not seem too bold to presume that such an agreement will take the form of a lump sum settlement, concluded by the State Department, by which the blocked assets would be used to release the Chinese from any further obligations arising from the U.S. private claims.[2] Thus another improvement in Sino-American relations might be realized.

However, in dollar value, the set-off would be quite lopsided. The blocked assets have been estimated to be worth $78,000,000[3] whereas the Federal Claims Settlement Commission, working pursuant to the China Claims Act of 1966,[4] has certified awards of $196,861,834 against the P.R.C.[5] The legal issue to which this settlement might give rise and to which this note addresses itself is whether (1) a lump sum agreement as a settlement device (2) can be concluded via a pure executive agreement (3) with complete assurances to the contracting nations of finality and conclusiveness.

I. THE LUMP SUM AGREEMENT AS A SETTLEMENT DEVICE

The lump sum agreement, by which international claims are settled simply and expediently through diplomatic channels without resorting to international adjudication, has become popular since World War I.[6] It was inevitable that this device would catch the attention of the United States—whose nationals have increasingly been the victims of expropriation and nationalization.[7] While the lump sum agreement is not solely a phenomenon of the 20th century—the U.S. paid Great Britain $2,664,000 in 1802 to settle certain debt claims[8]—it has become extremely useful because it arrives at speedy over-all settlements, assigns no liability, and is not mistrusted like the more traditional international arbitral commission. China, with an even greater sensitivity to intrusion on her national sovereignty than most socialist nations, would probably reject any kind of adjudicatory mechanism asserting jurisdiction over the Chinese state.

*B.A., Duke University, 1973; J.D. candidate, Stanford Law School.

The lump-sum settlement would be responsive both to this concern and to the concerns of other nations with competing claims:

> [T]he respective advantages of the devices, the national and the international claims commissions, will ultimately depend upon the standing, legal philosophy, foreign policy and financial stability of the nation with which the United States is to reach a settlement agreement. A mixed claims commission with Canada may be preferable to a lump-sum agreement, whereas a lump-sum agreement with the U.S.S.R., Bulgaria, or Egypt would probably be preferable to a commission composed of one American member, a member of that other state, and an umpire, whose every award would have to be enforced against that other state.[9]

The desire for trade with the U.S. should provide the necessary inducement, a prerequisite to claims settlements,[10] to override any ideological qualms of the P.R.C.

Beyond being attractive to international polities, the lump sum arrangement is a valid and proper tool for handling the claims of private individuals against foreign nations. By the traditional rubric, only states can be subjects of international law; so individuals, who have no standing to assert claims within this jurisdiction, must look to their government for protection. Indeed, a government is left largely to its own initiative in pursuing the claims of its nationals against other governments. The U.S. Supreme Court approved this doctrine in *United States v. Diekelman*[11] and has never retreated:

> One nation treats with the citizens of another only through their government. A sovereign cannot be sued in his own courts without his consent. His own dignity, as well as the dignity of the nation he represents, prevents his appearance to answer suit against him in the courts of another sovereignty except in performance of his obligations, by treaty or otherwise, voluntarily assumed. Hence, a citizen of one nation, wronged by the conduct of another nation, must seek redress through his own government. His sovereign must assume the responsibility of presenting his own claim, or it need not be considered. If this responsibility is assumed, the claim may be prosecuted as one nation proceeds against another, not by suits in the courts, as of right, but by diplomacy, or if need be by war.

The settlement of international claims is a type of foreign intercourse, and the U.S. Constitution has vested such responsibilities exclusively in the national government.[12] Once the national government has acted, individual claimants cannot reject the overtures made on their behalf.

Naturally, dealings between nations produce awards to a nation, rather than to individuals, to be distributed at that nation's discretion. *(United States v. Weld.*[13]*)*. The claimants have only been presented a chance to recover through the efforts of their government and must accept their awards subject to any condition, even that of partial settlement.[14] This view received judicial approval in *William v. Heard,*[15] a case involving an award by the Second Court of Commissioners for the Alabama Claims.

> The fund was, at all events, a national fund to be distributed by Congress as it saw fit. True, as citizens of the United States had suffered in person and property by reason of the acts of the Confederate cruisers, and as justice demanded that such losses should be made good by the government of Great Britain, the most natural disposition of the fund that could be made by Congress was in payment of such losses. But *no individual claimant had as a matter of strict legal or equitable right, any lien upon the fund awarded,* nor was Congress under any legal or equitable obligation to pay any claim out of the proceeds from that fund.[16]

This bypasses any difficulties posed by the difference in a straight set-off between the claims certified by the Federal Claims Settlement Commission and the $78 million of Chinese assets. The lump sum is received in full settlement of claims, and if a fund were insufficient to pay all domestically determined rewards, there would be a *pro rata* sharing among awardees.[17]

Moreover, such a partial settlement does not amount to a deprivation of constitutional rights under the fifth amendment.[18] The case precedents reason in the vein of *Williams v. Heard* that since the claimant has no legal or equitable interest in the settlement fund, there can be no deprivation. However, this logic is not entirely satisfactory because, despite the fiction that the individual's cause has become his sovereign's, the individual's relation to his property is diminished or changed by the international release of his claim.[19] *Gray v. United States,*[20] a Court of Claims opinion, goes so far as to suggest that a compensable right is involved. However, the right in *Gray* is enforceable only if, and to the extent, the United States provides a remedy.[21] Thus, even the most liberal assurance of recovery to the claimant in *Gray* contemplates partial settlement and imposes no obligations or remedies beyond the settlement fund.

II. SETTLEMENT OF PECUNIARY CLAIMS
VIA EXECUTIVE AGREEMENTS

Though the lump-sum device may be legally valid, there remains to be determined the issue of whether it may be wielded by the executive acting alone. The treaty making power specifically involves the participation of the Senate[22] ; yet, by the reference to other types of international arrangements in the prohibitions upon the states,[23] the Constitution implicity recognizes the existence of non-treaty engagements. Indeed, there are broad constitutional grants of power to both the President[24] and Congress[25] which would have no practical meaning without the concomitant control over relations with other governments. The mention of pacts other than treaties and of grants other than treaty-making add up to foreign intercourse without the Senate's advice and consent. This position was approved in *B. Altman and Co. v. United States*[26] in which the Court gave effect to an international instrument that technically was not a treaty, as the Constitution defines that term.

Admittedly, nowhere in the Constitution is the President explicitly authorized to enter upon international executive agreements; but equally absent are any prohibitions against his doing so.[27] Since Article II, Section 1 mandates that "[t]he executive power shall be vested in a President," the general doctrine is that this authority is plenary, subject only to the exceptions and qualifications of the Constitution.[28] Thus the President's commission to carry on diplomatic relations includes the wherewithal to execute international agreements.[29] In the *United States v. Curtiss-Wright Export Corp.*,[30] after deciding that a congressionally approved executive agreement was valid, Justice Sutherland refers to

> [t]he very delicate, plenary and exclusive power of the President as the sole organ of the federal government in the field of international relations—a power which does not require as a basis for its exercise an act of Congress, but which, of course, like every other governmental power, must be exercised in subordination to the applicable provisions of the Constitution.[31]

This dictum to the effect that some of the President's powers in the field of foreign affairs are not conferred expressly by the Constitution but are derived from the existence of the U.S. as a sovereign nation has been cut back somewhat since, in *Youngstown Sheet and Tube Co. v. Sawyer*[32] and *Reid v. Covert*[33]. *Youngstown* directs that exercises of presidential authority must be founded in the provisions of the Constitution and cannot intrude upon Congress's grant over foreign commerce. *Reid* questions the assertion in *Curtiss-Wright* that access to the international arena is inherent to sovereignty, but actually goes no further than the admonition that "no agreement with a foreign nation can confer power on the Congress, or any other branch of the government, which is free from the restraints of the Constitution."[34] Despite the retreat from *Curtiss-Wright*, however, *Reid* and *Youngstown* qualify rather than eliminate the power of foreign intercourse.

The real debate, then, is not over the existence of the executive agreement but over the proper scope of its employment.[35] One extreme is represented by Green Hackworth who, as legal adviser to the Department of State, told a Senate subcommittee that the same instrument could be either a treaty or an agreement if the President labeled it so.[36] As the other end is the position that the President is limited in his initiative to military and diplomatic (*e.g.*, receiving ambassadors) matters plus dealings entrusted to the Chief Executive by custom and tradition.[37] The courts have arrived at a stand somewhere in between. *B. Altman and Co. v. United States*, which recognized international compacts other than treaties, did not equate the two but only deemed them similar for the purpose under consideration.[38]

That an executive agreement settling pecuniary claims against the P.R.C. can be included within this range of arrangements similar to treaties is sustained by a long history of usage and a few judicial precedents.[39] Though several lump sum settlements have been arrived at by treaty,[40] there have been numerous instances of agreements concluded on executive authority alone in American diplomatic history.[41] This "usage argument" for executive agreements was attacked in general by former Senator Sam Ervin at hearings before a Senate Subcommittee:

> The legal basis for the use of executive agreements is unclear at best, and most frequently has been grounded on the argument of usage—a legal justification that is not entirely satisfactory. As I have often noted in various other contexts, murder and rape have been with us since the dawn human history, but that fact does not make rape legal or murder meritorious. In effect, reliance on usage in this instance grounds concepts of constitutionality on acquiescence rather than on the written document, and is, to my mind, wholly unacceptable.[42]

Despite Senator Ervin's parallels, in the Anglo-American common law tradition, long-established government practices derive persuasive authority of validity. Added to this long history are settlements in 1960 by executive action with Rumania[43] and Poland.[44] The agreement with Rumania is particularly pertinent to the present case, because there, as with the P.R.C., the U.S. claims were certified by the Federal Claims Settlement Commission before a settlement was reached.

This history of executive agreements has been supplemented by two cases arising out of the Litvinov Assignment. Under that agreement, the Soviet Union assigned to the U.S. government, through an exchange of notes with President Roosevelt, all its claims against private citizens of the U.S. These claims could provide the funds to reimburse U.S. citizens who had been victims of Russian nationalization, and this assignment, concluded on executive authority alone, was adjudged valid in both *United States v. Belmont*[45] and *United States v. Pink.*[46] The *Belmont* court was explicit:

> The recognition, establishment of diplomatic relations, the assignment, and agreements with respect thereto, were all parts of one transaction, resulting in an international compact between the two governments. That the negotiations, acceptance of the assignments and understandings in respect thereof were within the competence of the President may not be doubted. Governmental power over internal affairs is distributed between the national government and the several states. Governmental power over external affairs is not distributed, but is vested exclusively in the national government. And in respect of what was done here, the Executive had authority to speak as the sole organ of that government. The assignment and agreements in connection therewith did not, as in the case of treaties, as that term is used in the treaty making clause of the Constitution (Art. 2, § 2), require the advice and consent of the Senate.[47]

The opinion in the *Pink* case was more succinct: "A treaty is a 'Law of the Land' under the supremacy clause (Art. VI, Cl. 2) of the Constitution. Such international compacts and agreements as the Litvinov Assignment have a similar dignity."[48] As the lump sum settlement with the P.R.C. will probably come as part of a series of negotiations involving recognition, the parallel to the agreements in the Litvinov cases is striking.

III. FINALITY OF THE SETTLEMENT

The validity of the lump sum settlement as an international

instrument (when it has been executed by the President) interests a foreign nation only as it relates to the legal issue of finality. The desire is for assurances that the obligations imposed by the claims are totally discharged and, in the case with China, do not raise an obstacle to trade. With no judicial review, these assurances are easily proffered. As stated in *Cross v. Pace*,[49] "The duty of righting the wrong that may be done our citizens in foreign lands is a political one, and appertains to the executive and legislative departments of the government. The judiciary is charged with no duty and vested with no power in the premises."

Further, there may be a specific statutory proscription against judicial intrusion. The China Claims Act of 1966 adopted by reference[50] the prohibition in the International Claims Settlement Act of 1949 as amended against the review of Federal Claims Settlement Commission certifications.[51] Amendment now could equally incorporate that Act's provision for a *pro rata* sharing of the settlement fund as a final disposition.[52] Such clauses have been quite effective in previous programs; deviation from statutory authorization was the sole cause for judicial intrusion in *United States v. Weld.*[53] Therefore, the P.R.C., which would be initially absolved of its obligations by the signing of the lump sum settlement, would receive additional assurances from a domestic program that was conclusive if statutorily consistent.[54]

IV. CONCLUSION

The legal issues of a set-off of P.R.C.-blocked assets to U.S. private claims as concluded between the Secretary of State and the Chinese Foreign Minister are three. First, the lump sum settlement, which has come into its own in the 20th century, is a valid instrument of U.S. foreign intercourse. It creates no liability to the claimant in the government; the individual consequently is deprived of no rights. Second, whatever quibblings there are over the scope of executive agreements, long usage and case precedent establish the settlement of pecuniary claims squarely within the range. And third, the foreign nation which has been released of obligations to private citizens by its agreement with the U.S. government is offered further protection by a conclusive domestic distribution program.

NOTES

[1] 68 *Dep't State Bull.* 313 (1973); also quoted in L.A. Times, Feb. 23, 1973, § 1, at 20, col. 1.

[2] On December 16, 1950, the U.S. froze all Chinese assets within its jurisdiction on the grounds that China's entry into the Korean War constituted an act of belligerance. *See generally*, Lee and McCobb, 4 N.Y.U.J. INT'L L. & POL. 1 (1971). In response, the P.R.C. assumed control of all U.S. owned property in China. *Hearings on S. 3675 Before the Subcomm. on the Far East and the Pacific of the House Comm. on Foreign Affairs*, 89th Cong., 2d sess., 4 (1966).

[3] L.A. Times, Feb. 23, 1973, § 1, at 20, col. 5.

[4] 22 U.S.C. § 1643 (1970). The Act was intended merely to obtain information concerning the amount and validity of the claims and did not provide for the payment of those awards.

[5] FOREIGN CLAIMS SETTLEMENT COMM., 1972 ANN. REP., Exhibit II, at page 24-25.

[6] *See* R. LILLICH, INTERNATIONAL CLAIMS: THEIR ADJUDICATION BY NATIONAL COMMISSIONS 15 (1962).

[7] Clay, *Aspects of Settling Claims Under the Yugoslav Claims Agreement of 1948*, 43 GEO. L.J. 582, 582-83 (1952).

[8] Convention for the Payment of Indemnities and Settlement of Debts of January 8, 1802, 1 *Malloy, Treaties* 610 (1910). The U.S. also obtained lump sum settlements in the 19th century from France, Spain, Great Britain, Denmark, Peru, Belgium, Mexico, Brazil and China. *See* Christenson, *The United States-Rumanian Claims Settlement Agreement of March 30, 1960*, 55 AM. J. INT'L L. 617 (1961).

[9] Soubbotitch, Book Review, 16 RUTGERS L. REV. 634, 637 (1962).

[10] Despite the attractiveness of the lump sum settlement, no country will enter into one unless it perceives benefits to itself. *See* LILLICH, *supra* note 6, at 106-07 *and* Rubin, *Nationalization and Compensation, A Comparative Approach*, 17 U. CHI. L. REV. 458 (1950).

[11] 92 U.S. 520, 524 (1875).

[12] United States v. Pink, 315 U.S. 203, 233 (1941); United States v. Belmont, 301 U.S. 324, 331 (1936); United States v. Curtiss-Wright Export Corp., 299 U.S. 304, 316 (1936).

[13] 127 U.S. 51 (1887).

[14] *See* Williams v. Heard, 140 U.S. 529, 537-38 (1891). Kondo v. Katzenbach, 356 F. 2d 351, 358 (D.C. Cir. 1966); American and European Agencies v. Gillilland 247 F. 2d 95, 97-98 (D.C. Cir. 1957); *and* Fraenkel v. United States, 320 F. Supp. 605, 607 (D.C.N.Y. 1970).

[15] 140 U.S. 529 (1891).

[16] *Id.* at 537-38. (Emphasis added.)

[17] Recent settlements have resulted in the following recoveries on claims: Mexico (1941), 99%; Mexico (1943), 100%; Yugoslavia (1948), 90%; Panama (1950), 90%; Rumania (1960), 40%; Bulgaria (1963), 75%. *Hearings on the Foreign Assistance Act of 1965 Before the House Comm. on Foreign Affairs*, 89th Cong., 1st Sess., 1235-36 (1965).

[18] *See* 356 F. 2d at 358.

[19] *See* Oliver, *Executive Agreements and Emanations from the Fifth Amendment*, 49 AM. J. INT'L L. 362, 364 (1955).

[20] 21 Ct. Cl. 1, 340 (1886)

[21] *Id.* at 406. Subsequent cases taking this view are Cushing v. United States, 22 Ct. Cl. (1886) and The Schooner Betsy, 44 Ct. Cl. 506 (1909).

[22] U.S. CONST. art. II, § 2.

[23] *Id.* at art. I, § 10.

[24] *Id.* at art. II, § § 1, 2, 3.

[25] *Id.* at art. I, § 8.

[26] 224 U.S. 583 (1911).

[27] President Theodore Roosevelt wrote concerning the agreement he made in 1905 with the Dominican Republic for administering custom houses of that country: "The Constitution did not explicitly give me the power to bring about the necessary agreement with Santo Domingo. But the Constitution did not forbid my doing what I did. I put the agreement into effect, and I continued its execution for two years before the Senate acted; and I would have continued it until the end of my term, if necessary without any action by Congress. But it was far preferable that there should be action by Congress, so that we might be proceeding under a treaty which was the law of the land and not merely by a direction of the Chief Executive which would lapse when that particular Executive left office." *Roosevelt, An Autobiography* 551-52 (1913), quoted in Simpson, *Legal Aspects of Executive Agreements,* 24 Iowa L. REV. 67, 77 (1938).

[28] Alexander Hamilton makes this argument in the Pacificus Papers in support of the President's authority to declare neutrality. He points out, in contrast, the limited grant to the legislative branch in article I, § 1: *"All legislative powers herein granted* shall be vested in a Congress". (Emphasis added.)

[29] Though this argument is logical and it is constitutionally valid when applied to the President, it may be questionable if its rationale is extended. Simply stated, the argument is that although the President has no express power to make international agreements, the ability to make such agreements arises as an implication of those powers he does have over the control of foreign relations. By extension, this rationale might be applied to authorize Congress to conclude arrangements with foreign nations on its own. However, Congress has never been called the "sole organ of the government in foreign relations," as John Marshall termed the President. *Cf. Hearings on S. 3475 Before the Subcomm. on the Separation of Powers of the Senate Comm. on the Judiciary,* 92d Cong., 2d Sess. 322-23 (1972).

[30] 299 U.S. 304 (1936).

[31] *Id.* at 320.

[32] 343 U.S. 579 (1952).

[33] 354 U.S. 1 (1956).

[34] *Id.* at 16.

[35] "The problem surrounding the imbalance of power between the Legislature and the Executive in foreign policy decision making is not the constitutionality of executive agreements; rather, congressional concern is with the expanded scope and use of the device." Tomain, *Executive Agreements and the Bypassing of Congress,* 8 J. INT'L LAW & ECON. 129, 130 (1973).

[36] Fraser, *The Constitutional Scope of Treaties and Executive Agreements,* 31 A.B.A.J. 286 (1945). *See also* McDougal and Lans, *Treaties and Congressional Executive or Presidential Agreements: Interchangeable Instruments of National Policy,* 54 YALE L.J. 181 (1945).

[37] Fraser, *supra* note 36, at 288.

[38] 224 U.S. at 601.

[39] One commentator around the turn of the 20th century remarked that the legal literature on executive agreements was sparse because the power of the President to conclude such had seldom been challenged. Moore, *Treaties and Executive Agreements,* 20 POL. SCI. Q. 385, 403 (1905).

[40] *See* R. LILLICH, *supra* note 6, at 129-30.

[41] For some of the older instances, *see* 2 HYDE, INTERNATIONAL LAW, CHIEFLY INTERPRETED AND APPLIED BY THE UNITED STATES 27 (1922); MATHEWS, AMERICAN FOREIGN RELATIONS, CONDUCT AND POLICIES 431 (1928), Barret, *International Agreements Without the Advice*

and Consent of the Senate, 15 YALE L.J. 18, 63 (1905), Hyde, *Agreements of the United States Other Than Treaties,* 17 GREEN BAG 229 (1905), Hyde, *Constitutional Procedure for International Agreements,* 31 PROC. AM. SOC. INT'L L. 45 (1937), Moore, *supra* note 38.

[42]*Hearings on S. 3475 Before the Subcomm. on the Separation of Powers of the Senate Comm. on the Judiciary,* 92d Cong., 2d Sess. 4 (1972).

[43]Agreement With Rumania, March 30, 1960, T.I.A.S. No. 4451.

[44]Agreement with Poland, July 16, 1960, T.I.A.S. No. 4545.

[45]301 U.S. 324 (1936).

[46]315 U.S. 203 (1941).

[47]301 U.S. at 330.

[48]315 U.S. at 230. The courts have expounded only the vague, general limitation that executive agreements cannot destroy the constitutional rights of a person. An American naturalized citizen in *Seery v. United States,* 127 F. Supp. 601 (Ct.Cl. 1955), recovered for damage to her Austrian villa, which U.S. soldiers had used as an officers' club, despite an agreement whereby the U.S. had attempted to discharge all its obligations in Austria. Quite simply the Court of Claims held that the government had tried to deprive Seery of a compensable right which amounted to an impairment of her constitutional rights, 127 F. Supp. at 606. This could not even have been done by treaty. Even so, *Seery* has little pertinence to lump sum settlement with China via executive agreement, since such settlements involve no compromise of constitutional rights (notes 13-21 *supra* and accompanying text).

[49]106 F. Supp. 434, 488 (1952).

[50]22 U.S.C. § 1643 (h).

[51]22 U.S.C. § 1623 (b).

[52]22 U.S.C. § 1627 (c).

[53]127 U.S. 51, 58 (1887).

[54]The assurances to the P.R.C. are extensive. The only claims which can be adjudged valid against China are those determined under the authority of 22 U.S. § 1643 (1970), *supra* note 4. This collection of claims, to which no more may be added after July 6, 1972, precludes further action in a wide range of claims. Section 1643 charts the purpose of the subchapter as giving final definition to claims arising from nationalization, expropriation, intervention, other takings of, or special measures against the property of U.S. nationals by the Chinese Communist regime. This regime, furthermore, is taken by § 1643 (a) (5) to include any political subdivision, agency, or instrumentality of the P.R.C. Thus, the category of claims that has been defined covers all acts tinged with the approval of the Chinese government. Though it touched off an argument over when the Act of State Doctrine would be recognized to protect foreign sovereignties, *Banco Nacional de Cuba v. Sabbatino,* 376 U.S. 398 (1964) did point up that the courts will go far in characterizing the acts of instrumentalities as those of their government. Sabbatino has not been cut back in this regard. Also, *see generally,* 12 A.L.R. Fed. 707.

ABOUT THE AUTHORS

Dr. Edward Friedman is an associate professor of political science at the Madison campus of the University of Wisconsin. Asis is his primary geographic area of interest, with a special focus on China. He enjoys teaching and researching this area from the perspectives of modern political philosophy and political sociology, analyzing events in terms of the successes and failures of a variety of methodological approaches. He is an active member of both the Association for Asian Studies and the Committee of Concerned Asian Scholars.

Hans Heymann, Jr., is a member of the senior research staff of the Rand Corporation. His background includes study in international economic relations, and in recent years much of his research has focused on Southeast Asia, especially with respect to the effects of development and of American foreign policy there. In 1973, he was assigned to investigate China's approach to the acquisition of advanced technology. This article is one outgrowth of that study.

Dennis Ray is an associate professor in the department of political science at the California State University at Los Angeles. He has a continuing interest in the economic and political development of less-developed countries. In 1973, he was a faculty fellow and research associate at the Center for Chinese Studies at the University of California at Berkeley; some of the research he did there was used in this article.

Judith Banister is a doctoral candidate in demography and applied economics at the Food Research Institute, Stanford University. After graduating from Swarthmore College and doing a year of graduate work at the University of Denver, she traveled to and lived in Taiwan and Hong Kong. She was a member of the first delegation of the Committee of Concerned Asian Scholars to visit China.

Kim Woodard is a Ph.D. candidate in the political science department at Stanford University. He has contributed articles to the Far Eastern Economic Review *and book reviews to the* China Quarterly. *He studied Chinese in an intensive language program in Taipei during 1969 and 1970, and subsequently lived in Hong Kong for a year. In 1971 he was a member of the Friendship Delegation of the Committee of Concerned Asian Scholars which visited the People's Republic of China. This article was written in connection with research done for his doctoral dissertation.*

Professor Victor Li holds an endowed chair in international legal studies at Stanford Law School, and is also the director of the Center for East Asian Studies at Stanford. He has special interests in the P.R.C.'s use of law, both for internal affairs and external relations, and in the development of trade with China. Professor Li served as an intermediary in the initial visit of the P.R.C. ping-pong team to the United States, and has himself visited China on several occasions.

P. Edward Haley is an associate professor of international relations at Claremont Graduate School and Claremont Men's College in Los Angeles. His published work examines American foreign policy and greater-power involvement in the Middle East. He is currently an international affairs fellow of the Council on Foreign Relations, working on a study of the Committee on Foreign Affairs in the U.S. House of Representatives. Harold Rood is a professor of political science at Claremont, and is also a member of the staff at the Stanford Research Institute. He is the author of a number of studies on military questions, including war in the nuclear age. Both authors have followed international politics in East Asia for some years.

David Denny is an economist in the Bureau of East-West Trade at the United States Department of Commerce in Washington, D.C.

David Luther is a law student at Stanford Law School. He received his B.A. from Duke University.

Related Titles
Published by
Praeger Special Studies

*CHINA AND JAPAN—EMERGING GLOBAL POWERS
Peter G. Mueller and Douglas A. Ross

*CHINA AND SOUTHEAST ASIA
Peking's Relations with Revolutionary Movements
(expanded and updated edition)
Jay Taylor

CHINA'S AFRICAN POLICY
A Study of Tanzania
George T. Yu

CHINESE AND SOVIET AID TO AFRICA
edited by Warren Weinstein

FACTIONAL AND COALITION POLITICS IN CHINA
The Cultural Revolution and Its Aftermath
Y. C. Chang

*SINO-AMERICAN DETENTE AND ITS POLICY IMPLICATIONS
edited by Gene T. Hsiao

*SOVIET AND CHINESE INFLUENCE IN THE THIRD WORLD
edited by Alvin Z. Rubinstein

TRADE WITH CHINA
Assessments by Leading Businessmen and Scholars
Patrick M. Boarman
with the assistance of Jayson Mugar

*Also available in paperback as a **PSS** Student Edition

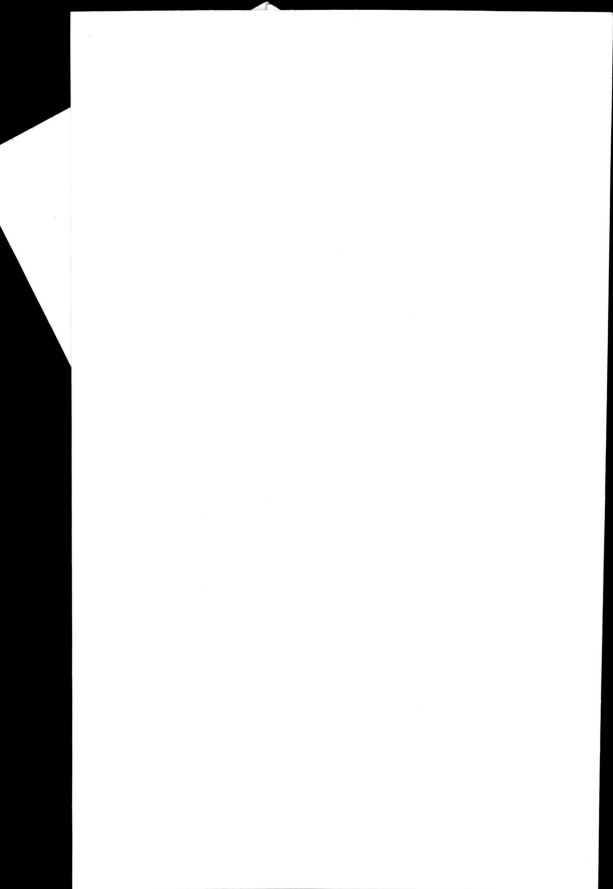